Logic and Objects

Prentice Hall International Series in Computer Science

C. A. R. Hoare, Series Editor

BACKHOUSE, R. C., *Program Construction and Verification*
DEBAKKER, J. W., *Mathematical Theory of Program Correctness*
BARR, M. and WELLS, C., *Category Theory for Computing Science*
BEN-ARI, M., *Principles of Concurrent and Distributed Programming*
BIRD, R, and WADLER, P., *Introduction to Functional Programming*
BORNAT, R., *Programming from First Principles*
BUSTARD, D., ELDER, J. and WELSH, J., *Concurrent Program Structures*
CLARK, K, and McCABE F. G., *Micro-Prolog: Programming in logic*
CROOKES, D., *Introduction to Programming in Prolog*
DAHL, O-J., *Verifiable Programming*
DROMEY, R. G., *How to Solve it by Computer*
DUNCAN, E., *Microprocessor Programming and Software Development*
ELDER, J., *Construction of Data Processing Software*
ELLIOTT, R. J. and HOARE, C. A. R. (eds.), *Scientific Applications of Multiprocessors*
GOLDSCHLAGER, L. and LISTER, A., *Computer Science: A modern introduction (2nd edn)*
GORDON, M. J. C., *Programming Language Theory and its Implementation*
GRAY, P. M. D., KULKARNI, K. G. and PATON, N. W., *Object-Oriented Databases*
HAYES, I. (ed), *Specification Case Studies*
HEHNER, E. C. R., *The Logic of Programming*
HENDERSON, P., *Functional Programming: Application and implementation*
HOARE, C. A. R., *Communicating Sequential Processes*
HOARE, C. A. R., and JONES, C. B. (eds), *Essays in Computing Science*
HOARE, C. A. R., and SHEPHERDSON, J. C. (eds), *Mathematical Logic and Programming Languages*
HUGHES, J. G., *Database Technology: a software engineering approach*
HUGHES, J. G., *Object-oriented Databases*
INMOS LTD, *Occam 2 Reference Manual*
JACKSON, M. A., *System Development*
JOHNSTON, H., *Learning to Program*
JONES, C. B., *Systematic Software Development using VDM (2nd edn)*
JONES, C. B. and SHAW, R. C. F. (eds), *Case Studies in Systematic Software Development*
JONES, G., *Programming in occam*
JONES, G. and GOLDSMITH, M., *Programming in occam 2*
JOSEPH, M., PRASAD, V. R. and NATARAJAN, N., *A Multiprocessor Operating System*
KALDEWAIJ, A., *Programming: The Derivation of Algorithms*
KING, P. J. B., *Computer and Communications Systems Performance Modelling*
LEW, A., *Computer Science: A mathematical introduction*
MARTIN, J. J., *Data Types and Data Structures*
McCABE, F. G., *High-Level Programmer's Guide to the 68000*
MEYER, B., *Introduction to the Theory of Programming Languages*
MEYER, B., *Object-oriented Software Construction*
MILNER, R., *Communication and Concurrency*
MORGAN, C., *Programming from Specifications*
PEYTON JONES, S. L., *The Implementation of Functional Programming Languages*
PEYTON JONES, S., and LESTER D., *Implementing Functional Languages*
POMBERGER, G., *Software Engineering and Modula-2*
POTTER, B., SINCLAIR, J. and TILL, D., *An introduction to Formal Specification and Z*
REYNOLDS, J. C., *The Craft of Programming*
RYDEHEARD, D. E. and BURSTALL, R. M., *Computational Category Theory*
SLOMAN, M. and KRAMER, J., *Distributed Systems and Computer Networks*
SPIVEY, J. M., *The Z Notation: A reference manual (second edition)*
TENNENT, R. D., *Principles of Programming Languages*
TENNENT, R. D., *Semantics of Programming Languages*
WATT, D. A., *Programming language Concepts and Paradigms*
WATT, D. A., WICHMANN, B. A. and FINDLAY, W., *ADA: language and methodology*
WELSH, J. and ELDER, J., *Introduction to Modula 2*
WELSH, J. and ELDER, J., *Introduction to Pascal (3rd edn)*
WELSH, J., ELDER, J. and BUSTARD, D., *Sequential Program Structures*
WELSH, J. and HAY, A., *A Model Implementation of Standard Pascal*
WELSH, J. and McKEAG, M., *Structured System Programming*
WIKSTRÖM, Å., *Functional Programming using Standard ML*

Logic and Objects

Francis G. McCabe

Prentice Hall
New York London Toronto Sydney Tokyo Singapore

First published 1992 by
Prentice Hall International (UK) Ltd
Campus 400, Maylands Avenue,
Hemel Hempstead,
Hertfordshire, HP2 7EZ
A division of
Simon & Schuster International Group

Printed and bound in Great Britain by
Dotesios Ltd, Trowbridge, Wiltshire.

Library of Congress Cataloging-in-Publication Data

McCabe, F. G. (Frank G.), 1953-
    Logic and objects/Francis G. McCabe.
        p.   cm. – (Prentice Hall international series in computer science)
    Includes index.
    ISBN 0-13-536079-X
        1. Logic programming (Computer science).   I. Title. II. Series.
QA76.63.M42 1992
005.1–dc20   92-5056
                                                                 CIP

British Library Cataloguing in Publication Data

A catalogue record for this book is available from
the British Libary

ISBN 0-13-536079-X (pbk)

---

2 3 4 5   96 95 94 93 92

For Mary Ann and Jessica

Contents

List of programs

List of Figures

List of Tables

Preface

In this book we explore a set of extensions to logic programming which increase its usefulness and applicability. It is our aim to address some of the deficiencies of logic programming languages, particularly with regard to the design and construction of large programs. While the ideas are (on the whole) presented in relation to logic programming, it is a simple matter to apply them in the more practical setting of Prolog.

At the same time as enhancing the notational power of logic programming (without modifying the declarative semantics that underpin it) we are also able to shed light on some issues in other branches of computing; in particular the object oriented programming paradigm. We aim to answer such questions as

'What is an object?'

and

'What is inheritance?'

in the context of logic programming. We would like to achieve a deeper understanding of such issues without necessarily accepting unquestioningly the definitions of these concepts from conventional procedural disciplines.

In fact we choose to redefine, to some extent, the ideas of object oriented programming in a way which is more general and powerful. So, for us an object is not simply an arbitrary collection of values and methods; instead we view an object declaratively:

'an object is what we know to be true of it'.

This is in contrast with other approaches which liken objects to types, and the inheritance of object descriptions to type hierarchies.

In our exploration of an extended notation for object oriented programming we are careful to stay within logic. In particular, we will take care to construct a system with a *first order* logical characterization. The result is a language which is a special case of standard logic programming, and yet we can also embed standard logic programming within it. In other words we have a language which is *equivalent* to normal logic programming languages but which enables us to express the large scale structure of programs more clearly.

For whom this book tolls

This book is not intended to be a tutorial introduction to logic programming nor to programming in Prolog. For such a tutorial, we refer the reader to [CM81, Bra90, O'k90, Dod90, SS86] or one of the many other excellent books on the subject. Instead, this book is aimed at programmers who have some experience with Prolog (or another language based on logic) and who would like to see how to extend the practicality of the language.

Thus we will not dwell on how to represent facts and rules, nor will we explain the use of 'cut' (neither will we use it much). However, where we use a feature which, while it is to be found in many Prolog systems, is not necessarily in use by all Prolog programmers, we do attempt to give a reasonable explanation of it. A good example of this might be the use of **functor**, which is used on page 186. This primitive is not normally needed by a Prolog application programmer, and therefore the average application programmer may not be familiar with it. We need it, however, in order to explain the semantics of the language feature *overriding inheritance*. So we give **functor** a logical explanation in order to complete the explanation of overriding inheritance. In fact, we have minimized our dependence on Prolog primitives, preferring to concentrate on the features offered by logic rather than those offered by Prolog.

On the other hand, it is often the case that a programmer who has had some experience with programming in Prolog, can become rather frustrated by the lack of scope (sic) of the basic language. Thus, the first deficiencies which are often felt by programmers are the lack of program structuring which arises from the 'flat' layout of a Prolog program and the lack of functions and expressions.

This book aims to address these deficiencies, and to offer possible insights in how logic programming can be integrated with object oriented programming as well as functional programming. We believe that the result is pleasing: that there is a smooth extension to standard logic programming which naturally captures much of the flavour of these other programming paradigms.

Structure of the book

In Chapter 1 we give an introduction to the problems that many Prolog (and logic) programmers face when attempting to construct large programs. We examine the nature of programming, and whether the flat style of 'pure' logic programs adequately reflects the style of large programs. We also look at how some workers have attempted to combine logic programming with object oriented programming.

In Chapter 2, we cover the basic elements of the *L&O* language. This is an object oriented extension which is a super-set of the normal logic (and Prolog) programming languages.

The programming power of $L\&O$ is explored in Chapter 3. In this chapter, we look at some of the techniques which arise directly from the $L\&O$ notation. We look at how modules can be built, how we represent knowledge as collections of classes and how inheritance is used.

The 'larger' aspects of programming are addressed in Chapter 4. Here we explore how an $L\&O$ application might be built. In fact, we see in this chapter how the classification techniques developed in Chapter 3 can be used to classify applications, and how this gives rise to program support tools and libraries in a natural way.

Chapter 5 explores the utility of the $L\&O$ language as a vehicle for describing pictures and and graphical applications. In this chapter we see how pictures can be modelled using terms, and how the syntactic process of answering queries and evaluating sub-goals and expressions can be interpreted as operations over pictures. We also see how a graphically-based application might be constructed.

In Chapter 6 we explore a small but complete $L\&O$ application, from its conception to realization. The application revolves around the demonstration of an algorithm to solve the travelling salesman problem. Using this demonstration, a user can select towns to visit and see how the algorithm 'goes about' solving the problem.

In Chapter 7 we explore a larger scale application domain – namely how we can pack boxes in an efficient manner. This chapter, which is contributed by Tony Solomonides, examines some of the theory behind packing and it also shows how a packing algorithm can be formed into a *generic* application which can be used to schedule timetables and plan projects as well as pack boxes together.

The fundamental semantics of $L\&O$ programming is examined in Chapter 8. This semantics is established by constructing a mapping from $L\&O$ programs to standard logic programs and proving the soundness and completeness of this mapping. We also look at the semantics of equations and functions in the context of logic programming and show how there is a simple semantic basis for incorporating them into our language.

Finally, in Chapter 9, we see how we can implement $L\&O$ as an efficient programming language. We do this by constructing a preprocessor – written in Prolog – which generates Prolog programs from $L\&O$ programs. The preprocessor is capable of generating Prolog programs which are nearly as efficient as standard Prolog programs – i.e., a Prolog program which has been embedded as an $L\&O$ program can be preprocessed into another Prolog program which is nearly as efficient as the original. This gives us the confidence to use $L\&O$ as our programming language with the knowledge that we do not have to lose performance.

In the various appendices we give listings of the major components of the preprocessor as well as the complete travelling salesman program and parts of the packing program. A complete set of the $L\&O$ software is available via 'anonymous'

FTP from 'doc.ic.ac.uk'.

Acknowledgments

The early work which underpins this book was supported by the S.E.R.C. and later work has been supported by the Esprit Basic Research programme.

Many people have commented on and contributed to earlier drafts of this book; they have helped me enormously. Whilst not wishing to single any one out, nor to slight by way of omission, I would like to acknowledge C.A.R. Hoare, K.L. Clark, R.A. Kowalski, D.H.D. Warren, D. Chu, T. Duncan, I.T. Foster, L. Monteiro, A. Porto, M. Sergot and A. Solomonides for their invaluable and individual contributions.

I would also like to acknowledge the support of Mary Ann, my wife, for putting up with all the late nights and hard work which kept me away from her.

CHAPTER ONE

Introduction and background

Logic as a paradigm for programming has been applied successfully to a large number of domains. In particular, as represented by the programming language Prolog, logic programming has been shown to be a practical vehicle for building applications ranging from natural language understanding, programming language compilers, intelligent databases and expert systems.

The mature perspective which arises from this experience allows us to identify a number of deficiencies in the support that logic programming gives to building applications. In this chapter we intend to look at some of these – namely the lack of adequate structuring techniques for large programs and the primitive nature of expressions in programs. This serves as a background and context for the introduction of our own language – *L&O* – with which we aim to address some of these problems.

1.1 What is logic programming?

An interesting and difficult and relevant question is

'when do we know that we are doing logic programming?'

More particularly, suppose that we have an arbitrary language together with a mapping function from it to a set of first order Horn clauses (or just pure Prolog clauses); can we then conclude that our language is a logic programming language? This question is highly relevant to us since we want to 'fix' the standard logic programming language to make it more productive as a programming language. The answer in general is – of course – no. Consider, for example, a BASIC compiler which compiles BASIC programs into a set of first order clauses. Such a compiler might, for example, translate the BASIC Program 1.1 into the set of Prolog clauses about the binary predicate **stmt** shown in Program 1.2.

```
10 A = 3
20 B = 7
30 IF A<B THEN B = B DIV A
40 IF A>B THEN A = A DIV B
50 IF A≠B THEN GOTO 30
60 END
```

Program 1.1 A BASIC program

```
stmt(10,E):- assign(1,3,E,E1),stmt(20,E1).    % A is 1st variable
stmt(20,E):- assign(2,7,E,E1),stmt(30,E1).    % B is 2nd variable
stmt(30,E):- val(1,E,V1),val(2,E,V2),         % compare A & B
    (V1<V2 -> assign(2,V2/V1,E,E1);E1=E),     % divide B by A
    stmt(40,E1).
stmt(40,E):- val(1,E,V1),val(2,E,V2),
    (V2<V1 -> assign(1,V1/V2,E,E1);E1=E),
    stmt(50,E1).
stmt(50,E):- val(1,E,V1),val(2,E,V2),
    (V1=V2 -> stmt(60,E);stmt(30,E)).         % if A ≠ B goto 30
stmt(60,E).
```

Program 1.2 A translated BASIC program

(Before we can use Program 1.2 we need to augment it with suitable definitions for **assign** and **val** which respectively simulate assignment and returning values of variables in a given state E.) To execute the translated BASIC program we pose the query:

```
stmt(10,nil)?
```

over Program 1.2. The proof of this query will follow a path which is analogous to an execution of the original BASIC program; which means that the answers generated by the **stmt** program are directly equivalent to the answers generated by the original BASIC program – the two are isomorphic 'up to renaming of programs'.

What we have done with our BASIC compiler is to describe, albeit in terms of logic, the semantics of BASIC programs. This, in turn, may allow us to analyse BASIC programs and to prove certain properties of these programs. However, the fact that we can compile from BASIC into logic clauses does not mean that we have shown that BASIC is a logic programming language; indeed it would be surprising if we could.

While our mythical BASIC compiler is an extreme example, there are others which are more subtle. For example the definite clause grammar (DCG) formalism

[CM81] is an extremely simple modification of logic programming in which each grammar rule maps on to a simple clause with a few extra parameters. Yet the DCG notation is arguably not equivalent to logic programming either! The reason for this is that DCGs have a particular intended domain of discourse which is not sufficiently general to be a logic programming language.

To see this let us look at a simple example. If DCGs were a logic programming language then we should be able to represent *any* clause in the DCG notation, in particular we should be able to represent the fact

        `likes(john, mary).`

as a DCG rule. As a first approximation we might map this sentence into the DCG rule:

        `likes(john, mary)--> {}.`

However, these formulae are not equivalent to each other. The grammar rule reads

    'A non-terminal symbol of the form `likes(john,mary)` can be reduced
    to the empty string'

which is not at all the same as

    'john likes mary'

The divergence from logic programming shows up in other places within the DCG formalism. For example the sequencing connective ',' in a DCG rule is non-commutative, so the rules

        `nt1-->a,b.`   (I.i)

and

        `nt2-->b,a.`   (I.ii)

are not logically equivalent. This shows that ',' cannot be a name for standard conjunction in DCG form. In fact there is no equivalent to conjunction in DCGs. We should add a small caveat to this conclusion – in the degenerate case, where either a or b reduces to the empty string then (I.i) and (I.ii) are equivalent; however, this is not the case for arbitrary non-terminals a and b.

On the other hand it is possible to *encode* sentences such as

        `likes(john,mary)`

in DCGs in such a way that we *simulate* logic programming within the DCG notation, i.e., we can construct a compiler which translates clauses into DCGs. However, as was the case with our BASIC compiler, this is not sufficient to show that DCG is a logic programming language.

   Another class of logic programming languages is represented by the assortment
of concurrent logic languages such as Parlog [Gre87], Strand [FT90], Concurrent
Prolog [Sha83] and Guarded Horn Clauses [Ued85]. The logical status of these
languages is even more difficult to determine than DCGs. A concurrent logic
clause *does* have a declarative semantics, and in this sense a concurrent logic
program consists of sentences of logic. However, many of the logical consequences
of these logical sentences are eliminated by the 'committed choice' proof procedure
and are not solutions in the *intended* interpretation. For example, the declarative
reading of a Parlog program such as Program 1.3, which is about triples of lists

```
mode merge(?,?,^ ).
merge([E|L1],L2,[E|L3]):-
    merge(L1,L2,L3) .
merge(L1,[E|L2],[E|L3]):-
    merge(L1,L2,L3) .
```

Program 1.3 A Parlog merge program

in a **merge** relation, is a long way from the procedural reading given by the Parlog
model of cooperating processes:

   'A **merge** process can be non-deterministically reduced into a simpler
   merge process in one of two ways depending on which of the first two
   arguments are known.'

This reading is markedly different to a Prolog reading where the procedural interpretation of the **merge** clauses can be expressed in problem solving terms:

   'A **merge** goal can be reduced to a simpler **merge** sub-goal in one of
   two ways (corresponding to the two clauses for **merge**).'

This distinction is important. As we shall see later in Section 1.3.2, the use of a
modified proof procedure is one of the more popular techniques used to achieve the
effect of assignment in a logic programming-style system. The fact that the proof
procedure in concurrent logic languages is technically incomplete in a particular
way is essential to understand the semantics of programs in these languages.

   Prolog's procedural interpretation is actually stricter (and therefore less general) than we have said because, viewed as a theorem prover, a Prolog system is
not *complete*. There are goals which have solutions which cannot be discovered
by Prolog's simple left-right-depth-first execution strategy. However, for many
practical applications Prolog's strategy is adequate for it to be viewed as a programming language even if it cannot be viewed realistically as a general problem
solver.

The problem with languages like Parlog is that they are not completely honest in their intentions: Parlog is a language of communicating processes executing in parallel yet its syntax – which uses the language of clauses and of true facts – fails to convey this intention. If Parlog's notation reflected this intended domain of discourse more accurately then perhaps it would be easier to decide if concurrent logic languages are logic programming languages. In this respect DCGs and BASIC are more obvious formalisms.

While BASIC and DCGs may not be logic programming languages, we do not wish to imply that they are not valid programming languages. In fact we feel that a programming (or any) notation should reflect as far as is possible the intended domain of discourse and DCGs in particular are a good example. DCGs are an extremely useful tool for describing grammars (whether formal grammars for programming languages or the less formal natural grammars). Furthermore, a language sub-system like DCGs is intended to augment logic programming rather than to replace it, and therefore it might be considered unfair to ask even if the DCG notation on its own amounted to a logic programming language.

The soundness of programming languages

One might ask whether it is important that a programming language be seen to be a logic programming language. A major characteristic that we would like to have in any programming language is *soundness*. If we can borrow the rigour that has been developed in the field of mathematics in general and predicate calculus in particular and apply it to the design of a programming language then it too may be sound.

The primary reason for having a sound foundation for our languages is that we do not like to have unpleasant surprises, especially in programming languages. There are a number of features in Prolog – as opposed to standard logic programming – which the careful Prolog programmer stays well clear of because such features can *apparently* be benign but can lead into a tricky morass of special cases and correspondingly hard to detect bugs.

A good example of such a feature is the repeat-cut-fail combination, which can be seen in the classic Prolog technique for processing a file by reading a data item from it, processing the data and then *failing* in order to read the next term, as shown in Program 1.4.   The repeat-cut-fail loop is difficult as a direct result of the fact that it always fails, but the *interpretation* of this failure varies: sometimes failure represents a successfully terminated loop; at other times the loop has failed through some error or unexpected failure within the loop. The difference is often difficult to determine. Furthermore, if the `transform` program fails to handle a particular term which has been read in, then the reading loop will still terminate normally, and the only evidence of the program's failure would be a gap in the output. (If there is a lot of output that gap might be missed.)

On the other hand, if the program is written as a tail-recursive loop, as in Program 1.5, then the program will only fail if something has gone wrong, i.e.,

```
read_write:-
    repeat,
        read(X),                        % read next term from file
        (X=end_of_file,!,fail;          % exit loop?
        transform(X,Y),                 % process item
        write(Y),
        fail).                          % causes a new iteration
read_write.
```

Program 1.4 A `repeat-cut-fail` loop

```
read_write:-
    read(X),                            % read next data term
    r_w(X).                             % handle it
r_w(end_of_file).
r_w(X):-                                % end of data stream?
    X ¬= end_of_file,
    transform(X,Y),                     % process item
    write(Y),
    read_write.                         % loop using tail-recursion
```

Program 1.5 A tail recursive loop

if **transform** fails to handle a particular input item, and the program succeeds only if all the input is successfully handled. Because there is confusion between 'successful' failure and 'unsuccessful' failure when using the repeat-cut-fail combination, programs which use this technique can be extremely obscure and difficult to debug. It is not for nothing that it has been likened to the Prolog equivalent of GOTO.

(It should be pointed out at this moment that neither of these programs can be considered to be 'pure' logic programs due to the use of input/output primitives; however, that is not the point – while it is certainly legitimate to write Prolog programs which perform input/output, it is much less satisfactory to do so in an unsafe manner.)

There are many features of Prolog which must be used carefully if unpleasant surprises are to be avoided. It is precisely those features of Prolog which are not well-founded that can lead to problems in practice. However, it is also true that much of Prolog's power as a practical programming language comes from these same features.

A second major benefit of a soundly based language is that we can more easily integrate other well founded paradigms into it. So, for example, we might hope to combine a soundly based object oriented programming system – or a functional system – with logic programming in the confidence that we will not get any nasty surprises.

1.2   Extensions to logic programming

One of the key features of a logic programming language is that it has a dual semantics: a declarative or model theoretic semantics and an operational or proof theoretic semantics. The relationship between the declarative and procedural semantics is formalised by the notion of *logical consequence*.

We can say that a formula is a logical consequence of a program if it is true whenever the program is true. What is crucial to the power of logic (and logic programming) is that we can *guarantee* that if certain rules (i.e., the rules of inference) are obeyed when constructing a new formula then that formula is true whenever the original formulae are true. This guarantee allows us to construct and develop formulae without needing to verify whether they are true.

So, we could be rather strict and declare that any logic programming language must at least include the following features:

- there must be a *language* in which to construct formulae,

- a *domain of discourse* consisting of sets of relations which may be said to satisfy (or not, as the case may be) those formulae, and

- *inference rules* for deriving new formulae from old ones. The inference rules guarantee that any new formulae which are generated from a set of formulae (i.e., a program) are logical consequences of that set.

- The inference rules must be such that they can be implemented on a computer in such a way that sets of axioms can be viewed as programs to be executed.

The constraint that the system be computerizable (sic) includes the fact that it should be possible to express algorithms in the language with the correct complexity. For example, a program which expresses a linear algorithm (in time or space) should not be converted into an algorithm which is quadratic (say), by virtue of the procedural semantics of the language system. It would not be reasonable to describe a system which manages to execute linear algorithms in quadratic time as a programming language.

This constraint is harder to obey than one might imagine: it is not possible to express, in Prolog, an algorithm which will update an array in constant time – the fastest array update that is possible in Prolog is $O(\log n)$ in complexity; which in turn means that Prolog is inherently not suitable for expressing algorithms which require constant time array access.

Strictly speaking then, any language which does not satisfy these criteria is not a logic programming language. However, we can talk of extended logic programming languages which go beyond the strict definition in some way. We identify two types of extension: conservative and radical. We would classify a conservative extension of logic programming to be one which maintains the dual semantics of declarative and procedural semantics and a radical extension is one which does not.

Under this definition the negation-by-failure inference rule is radical unless one is careful about the declarative semantics of sets of axioms. We can see why this is so with the simple program in Program 1.6.

```
a.
b :- ¬q.
```

Program 1.6 A simple program with several models

Amongst the models of this set of axioms are $\{a,q\}$ and $\{a,b,\neg q\}$. This is because we have no information either way about q; so it can be assumed to be true or false: i.e., either q or $\neg q$ may be true. Using the negation-by-failure inference rule b would be shown to be a logical consequence of the set of clauses even though b is not true in all models of the program.

Much work in recent years has been expended in the effort to find an alternative declarative semantics for logic programs which smoothly incorporates negation-by-failure. In particular, the work on *stable models* by Gelfond and Lifshitz [GL88], represents an interesting avenue for establishing a sound semantics for negation-by-failure.

There are a number of ways in which we *can* extend logic programming to enrich logic programming practice without compromising its integrity. Some of these extensions address deficiencies in logic programming as a general purpose practical programming language and others can be used to tailor logic programming language to specific application domains.

1.2.1   Functions and relations

It can be argued that in any professional programming language, we should be able to define functions and to write appropriate expressions in the text of a program. Such an ability is important because functions are often an integral part of the programs we write. Nevertheless it remains the case that Prolog is a relational language and most Prolog compilers do not allow the programmer to define functions or to have expressions appearing in arbitrary places within a program; this results in a gap in the expressive power of logic programming. One possible way to close this gap would be to integrate the logic programming and functional programming paradigms into a single formalism. However, before we explore such a combination in detail, we should examine more carefully why a functional extension is needed for logic programming.

Intended interpretations are not always neutral

A relation is a set of tuples; a predicate identifies that set. In the notion of a predicate there is no implied ordering between the arguments of the tuples – no argument is more important than the others. From a mathematical point of view the ordering of the arguments of a relation can be said to be *neutral*. Often this is reflected in the way that we interpret a predicate; for example, in the '<' inequality relation neither the first argument nor the second can be said to be more important.

In practice there are many Prolog programs where the programmer's intentions are not so neutral, and the arguments of predicates are ordered in some way. Such programs have a non-neutral intended interpretation. Perhaps a classic example of this in practice is the famous **append** program in Program 1.7. The

```
append([],X,X).
append([E|X],Y,[E|Z]):-append(X,Y,Z).
```

Program 1.7 The **append** program in Prolog

append clauses describe a logical relationship between triples of lists, with no implied emphasis on the individual arguments. However, this does not reflect many programmers' intentions; if asked to explain this two line program most Prolog programmers would say:

'This program appends the lists in the first two arguments to form the result in the third argument...'.

Of course, the **append** program does describe a relation and therefore has other uses, so our typical Prolog programmer would carry on:

'but **append** can also be used for other things like splitting lists and even searching a list'.

Indeed, **append** is a favourite example which is often used to show how one program can be used for many different purposes. Even though a neutral interpretation of the clauses for **append** is possible, the intended interpretation is far from neutral. The three arguments have a definite input/output relationship which is not adequately expressed by the relational syntax. We even describe the use of **append** for splitting lists as 'using the program backwards'.

Our **append** example is not an isolated case: in practice many – if not most – Prolog programs have an intended reading which is not adequately expressed by the neutral relational notation. This gap between the intentions of the programmer and the written formulae leads programmers to make errors and to write unreadable programs.

Prolog programs may not be invertible

Many Prolog programs are not invertible, i.e., they cannot be safely invoked with more than one pattern of known and unknown arguments. This can be for many reasons, ranging from the fact that most built-in primitives in most Prolog systems are not invertible, to the more basic problem arising from the order of evaluation used by Prolog.

In nearly all commercial Prolog language systems the standard **is** built-in predicate, which is used to evaluate arithmetic expressions, has a fixed usage. The first argument must hold the expression to evaluate and it must be known at the time of the call (sometimes the expression must be known earlier at compile-time) and the second argument must be an unbound variable. We cannot use **is** backwards; for example, to guess the possible expressions that can lead to a given value. In this way can we say that **is** is not invertible, and in consequence any program which uses **is** is not likely to be invertible either.

(Not all logic programming systems are as limited as Prolog in their arithmetic. IC-PROLOG [CF80] implemented a fully relational view of arithmetic where the system would guess at answers to a SUM or TIMES goal if not enough arguments were known to make it deterministic. Subsequent backtracking would find alternative solutions. Unfortunately the price of this generality was the restriction of numbers to the positive integers. Micro-Prolog [CM84] was more modest – it implemented any input/output usage of arithmetic so long as it was deterministic.)

A simple example of a non-invertible program is shown in Program 1.8 for computing the length of a list. This program really only works for two patterns

```
length([], 0).
length([E|L], N):-
    length(L, N1),
    N is N1+1.
```

Program 1.8 The **length** of a list

of use: we can use it to compute the length of a list, or to check that a list has a given length; but if we use it to *generate* a list of a given length then much useless computation is performed, and furthermore it will go into an infinite loop on backtracking to find subsequent solutions.

The problem with `length` in reverse is not simply that Prolog arithmetic is not invertible, but that, in order to generate a list of a given length, the conditions in the body of the recursive clause need to be re-ordered. Program 1.9 shows the inverted from of `length`; note that we had to adjust the `is` condition to perform an explicit subtraction. Also, in order to ensure proper termination, we need to add the strictly redundant condition `N>0` to the recursive clause.

```
length([], 0).
length([E|L],N):-            % inverted length
    N>0,
    N1 is N-1,
    length(L,N1).
```

Program 1.9 <code>length</code> in inverse

The syntax of Prolog gives no hint of the complexity of the behaviour of the `length` program. In practice, few Prolog programs are truly invertible; and almost no programs with more than one condition in the body of a defining clause are invertible. In terms of programming language design, this non-invertibility represents an inconsistency between the syntax of clauses (with the corresponding semantics of relations) and the available power in the Prolog language which is somewhat less than relational.

The proliferation of intermediate variables.

Prolog is one of the few modern programming languages that does not have a fully integrated system of expressions. Instead, any expressions within a program must be encapsulated into conditions involving `is`. Goal sequences such as:

$$\ldots,\texttt{X1 is X+1, foo(}\ldots\texttt{,X1,}\ldots\texttt{),}\ldots \tag{I.iii}$$

are fairly frequent in large Prolog programs. Even in conventional procedural programming languages one would not have to write this, the natural way is surely:

$$\ldots,\texttt{foo(}\ldots\texttt{,X+1,}\ldots\texttt{),}\ldots$$

The variable `X1` that we had to introduce in (I.iii) in order to 'carry' the value of the expression is of no other interest to us. With complex expressions there can be additional variables which are also not of interest except within the expression. An expression notation can be used to hide these variables; with the result that the programmer has less typing and more obvious programs. Furthermore, a compiler for a functional language can more easily optimise the implementation of expressions (using a stack for example to hold intermediate values) than can a standard Prolog compiler. While in principle it may be possible for a Prolog compiler to detect such intermediate variables in a clause, the recovery of this information is a difficult and error-prone process.

Incompleteness of functional programming

Functional notation, on the other hand, is not complete either; there are a number of situations where functional notation is inadequate. For example, the set of equations for `wife` in Program 1.10 is intended to capture a database of people who are married to each other.

```
wife(philip)=liz.
wife(charles)=diana.
wife(tom)=mary.
```

Program 1.10 The `wife` function

The `wife` function is perfectly suited to the problem of determining the wife of a man, however an equally valid use of essentially the same information would be to determine the husband of a wife. This use amounts to using the *inverse* of the `wife` function which of course is not in general a function and is prohibited by most functional programming systems.

In this case, the intended use of the underlying relation is genuinely neutral with respect to the arguments and the functional notation is overly constraining. In general, when representing databases a relational notation is often more natural compared to functional notation.

Another limitation of a purely functional style of programming is illustrated when we attempt to describe programs which exhibit don't care non-determinism, such as the non-deterministic `merge` program we saw in Program 1.3 on page 4. The problem here is to describe a function whose value depends at least partly on *when* it is called. Such non-deterministic programs are important in real-time systems and operating systems where the output of a program depends on the run-time behaviour of the input.

Some functional systems represent this type of program by employing the concept of multi-valued functions; i.e., functions which can have more than one value for a given input value. This is a contradiction – such 'functions' are actually relations – and allowing them within a programming language leads to confusion as well as degrading the mathematical basis of the language. Clearly, we need to be able to combine the use of a functional notation to describe functions and a relational notation to describe relations.

1.2.2 Programming on a larger scale

We have argued the case that the notation used to write programs should be able to reflect the intention of the programmer and so we would use a functional style to denote functions and a relational style to denote relations. The same principle applies to programming at a larger scale: any notation for 'programming in the large' should reflect the nature and problems that arise when constructing large programs. However, here we do not have a well-defined formalism ready to hand which we can integrate into logic programming. Rather we must search for and possibly invent such a system. Generally, it is assumed that some notion of *module* is required to describe the larger scale structure of programs.

Prolog programs and modules

There are a number of schemes for modules in Prolog, but with many of them it is not immediately obvious what a module is. Some of the existing possibilities include name-based modules, predicate-based modules and higher-order functions.

Name-based modules   The simplest module system in Prolog, and one of the earliest, is the *name-based module* approach such as that used in micro-Prolog [CM84]. This module system is based on structuring the Prolog compiler's symbol table into separate sub-dictionaries – each corresponding to a module.

There are two classes of symbols in a name-based module system: private symbols and published (exported or imported) symbols. This distinction applies as much to atoms as predicate symbols and function symbols. Private symbols are local to an individual dictionary. If a private symbol occurs in more than one dictionary then the different occurrences represent different symbols. A symbol is published either by exporting it or by importing it; in either case it is potentially available to be be imported by other dictionaries. Typically, a published symbol will be exported from one owning module and imported by all the other modules which refer to the symbol.

There are a number of problems with the pure name-based style of module. In particular it is necessary to declare all those atoms which are to be referred across module boundaries. When a program is called between modules, the atoms which may be present in the *data* that is transferred by the call must also be accessible by the called program. In order to ensure this, it is necessary to publish all the atoms which might occur in the data; which we can do by exporting or importing them. In practice, it turns out to be easier to require both the modules involved to import these 'data' atoms – it is not required for one of them to own the shared symbols. This publishing process is often somewhat tedious as there may be many

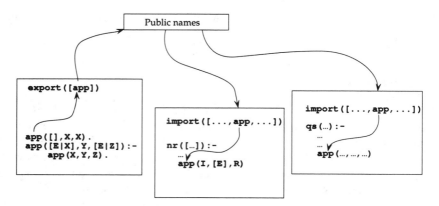

Figure 1.1 *A name-based module system*

atoms involved when data is communicated across modules, especially compared to the number of predicate symbols which need to be published.

In fact we could argue that the default intention regarding the classification of a symbol is different for atoms and predicate symbols: generally, a programmer is more likely to want an atom to be globally available across all modules, whereas a predicate symbol is more likely to be private.

It is also hard to implement a name-based module system in which symbols can be dynamically published and/or made private. This is particularly important in interactive programming environments when programs are under development.

If a symbol is to be *published* (i.e., exported or imported) when it used to be *private*, then all the previously private occurrences of the symbol must be located and made equal to the other occurrences of the symbol which are already public. On the other hand, if a previously public symbol is to be made private then all the existing references must be separated out and made private. Implementing this kind of module edit is a difficult problem similar in complexity to the problem of implementing a garbage collector.

Finally, it is not easy to allow for generic or parameterized modules where one may wish to *tailor* a module for different applications. This again is due to the view of a module as being a structuring of the symbol table and a generic module would require us to be able to have 'holes' in it where the module parameters are referred to.

Experience with micro-Prolog's modules suggests that name-based module schemes are well suited to the provision of libraries of programs or application front-ends. Such modules are often used to extend the underlying system. A library which is packaged up as a module provides new primitives while the module structure can be used to hide the implementation details of the library or front-end from the user. Name-based module systems are less well suited to the dynamic process of developing large programs from smaller components.

Predicate-based modules   A variation on name-based modules partitions only the predicate symbol name space rather than the whole symbol space. In this scheme, we automatically publish all the atoms to all modules. As a result we can eliminate the tedious publishing of atoms that is present in micro-Prolog's module scheme. A typical example of this approach to modules is in the module system in Quintus 2.0 Prolog [Cor87].

However, this liberalization introduces some extra problems due to the fact that the status of a symbol in a Prolog program can change depending on its context. As a result, we have to modify certain basic operations such as the meta-call, **assert** and **=..** to include the module name.

The predicate naming problem   Consider the rather contorted program in Program 1.11; this program has three modules, and the program c in $module_3$ ultimately depends on all three modules for its definition.

```
module₁:
    a(P):- P=foo.

    foo:-      ...            % module₁'s definition of foo

module₂:
    b(X):- module₁:a(P),      % invoke 'a' from module₁
        X=..[P,a,b].

    foo:-      ...            % module₂'s definition of foo

module₃:
    c(C):- module₂:b(C),      % invoke 'b' from module₁
        call(C).

    foo:-      ...            % module₃'s definition of foo
```

Program 1.11 Which **foo** is the right one?

A call to c of the form:

```
...,module₃:c(X),...
```

results in the execution of the following sequence of goals:

```
...,P=foo,...                                        (I.iv)
...,X=..[P,a,b],...                                  (I.v)
```

        ```
        ...,call(X),...
        ```
                                                                        (I.vi)

At the moment when the Prolog system attempts to evaluate the `call(X)` goal, the variable `X` is bound to the term `foo(a,b)`. The intention of the goal

        ```
        ...,call(foo(a,b)),...
        ```

is to invoke a program called `foo` with arguments `a` and `b`. Our problem is to determine which modules to search for the definition of the `foo` program.

    Notice that the symbol `foo` changes in status from being a simple constant atom – as in (I.iv) – to a function symbol – as a result of (I.v) – through to a predicate symbol – in the context of (I.vi). As a result, there are many places that one might look for the definition of `foo`:

- the module in which the call `c(X)` is located,

- $module_3$ in which the text of the `call(X)` condition is located,

- $module_2$ in which the call `X=..[P,a,b]` is evaluated (or located), or

- $module_1$ where the symbol `foo` originally appeared in the condition `P=foo`.

- We might even have a notion of a current or default module in which case we might search there for `foo`'s definition.

None of these choices will always lead to the intuitively correct program to invoke, yet it is also possible to give examples which will justify each choice.

    The ambiguity arises because in the context in which `foo` first appears it is as a constant symbol not a predicate symbol; but, in order to call it, we have to re-interpret the `foo` constant as a predicate symbol. It is not easy to recover the correct context for `foo` as a predicate symbol from the occurrence of `foo` as an atom.

    There is no perfect solution to this problem: we can only propose a heuristic which will pick the right program some of the time. Typically, a Prolog system resolves the issue by searching some predetermined list of modules (starting with the default module for example) for `foo`'s definition and using the first one it finds. As with the name-based scheme, this module scheme does not immediately allow generic modules either. Incidentally, the name-based module system focusses on the module where the `foo` symbol which is used to make up the call first appears. This choice seems to be 'right' nearly all the time.

    Problems such as these arise from the lack of an adequate logical formulation. Perhaps it would be more fruitful to recognize that large programs are naturally *composed* of many smaller ones rather than being *decomposed* into modules from an amorphous collection of clauses. This perspective might allow us to consider more carefully the logical status of modules and of module composition. One field in which program structure has been given great prominence is object oriented programming. An explicit aim of object oriented programming is to make it easy to construct big programs from small ones.

1.3 Object oriented and logic programming

In a 'normal' programming language – such as Pascal – the programmer designs a program by separately specifying data types and a control portion of the program which operates on values. The control portion of the program is structured around a central control structure in which data values are seen to flow through various procedures defined in the program.

In contrast, when using an object oriented programming language, the programmer designs his programs in the context of the kinds of objects to be modelled in the system. There is often no overall control flow visible in such a program; instead there may be many smaller control flows which are embedded in descriptions of individual objects and which correspond to the local activities and operations which are allowable on the objects.

The complete collection of programs is often *event driven*. All the events that might occur in an application – such as a window being uncovered, a key stroke occurring, or a telephone call is being received, are collected into a queue of events. Based on the type of each event, an appropriate response is evoked from one of the collection of objects in the system.

Each fragment of an object oriented program corresponds to the description of an individual object or class of objects. The program associated with a given object mainly consists of a set of 'message handlers' or 'methods' which respond to the various kinds of events that can occur to an object. Specialized programming techniques such as inheritance and message passing combine to make it easy to program these fragments.

Object oriented programming is a powerful programming paradigm which significantly affects (and, we hope, improves) the way that programmers build applications. While it is beyond the scope of this book to explore object oriented programming in general we do aim to look at it in relation to logic programming. Before examining our own work, it is worth taking the time to see how others have approached the problems of combining logic and object oriented programming.

What is object oriented programming?

We can interpret the object oriented concept in one of two ways: as a collection of interesting features as captured by a language such as Smalltalk [GD83], or in a more philosophical vein as a way of building programs. The distinction is important because if we take the former view then if we want to add object oriented features to logic programming our task reduces to lifting the salient features of Smalltalk (say) and transplanting them into Prolog (say). If we allow ourselves to take the more philosophical view then we must *interpret* the various features of common object oriented languages in the context of logic programming, if possible without compromising the logical basis of logic programming.

The investigation of object oriented programming and its relationship to logic programming has been quite an active field in recent years. The published work falls into two distinct categories: the work of people such as Hayes [Hay79] and others in which the main effort is to fit some of the concepts of object oriented programming into logic without compromising logic and other work which mainly concentrates on incorporating object oriented language features – in particular local state and assignment – into Prolog.

1.3.1   Logic programming and static objects

Some attempts at combining logical objects have explicitly attempted to maintain the logical nature of programs while using object oriented ideas. They tend, as a result, to be able to include some idea of program structure but do not – on the whole – include any notion of state or behaviour in the resulting systems; this is due more to the declarative (i.e., fixed) nature of logic programming rather than a deficiency in these approaches.

Hayes' logic of frames

An early attempt to formalize the *frame-based notation* (frames themselves are an early precursor to modern object oriented programming languages) was described by Hayes [Hay79]. The frame concept is sufficiently close to that of an object for us to able to appreciate Hayes' approach. Hayes characterizes a frame as a conjunction of properties. For example, if we determine that a house should include a kitchen and a garage etc. then this would be written as the λ-expression:

$$\lambda x.house(x) \supset \exists y_1, y_2.kitchen(x, y_1) \wedge garage(x, y_2)$$

In other words if an object is a house then it must also have a kitchen and a garage (and whatever else is required of a house). In his paper Hayes convincingly casts in logical terms the kinds of inferences which seem common in frame-based formalisms. This includes the *criteriality assumption* – for instance, if an object has a kitchen and a garage then it must be a house. The criteriality assumption for houses (say) would be expressed in Hayes' formalism as:

$$\forall x.house(x) \equiv (\exists y_1, y_2.kitchen(x, y_1) \wedge garage(x, y_2))$$

which states, formally, the concept of a house being equivalent to a conjunction of a kitchen and a garage: something is a house iff it is associated with a kitchen and a garage. While criteriality is certainly an interesting concept – particularly when we need to represent world knowledge – it is not especially relevant to the problem of writing large programs. We are more concerned with structuring programs than defining what a program is.

One apparently trivial problem with Hayes' formalism is that the same predicate symbol cannot be used to denote different relations for different frames. This implies that all slot names in all frames must be distinct. The issue is more important than Hayes suggests, especially in a system which includes inheritance.

This is because we use inheritance to describe the relationships between relations in different objects. In this context we may sometimes wish to identify two occurrences of a predicate symbol as being the same but in other circumstances they may represent different relations. It is not enough to relegate the problem to 'nothing more than syntactic sugar'.

The 'isa' interpretation

Another way in which logic programmers have described objects (and in particular inheritance) is through 'isa' axioms [Kow79]. In this formulation we would express the fact that birds can fly (for example) with the rule:

$$\text{can\_fly(X) :- X isa bird.} \tag{I.vii}$$

This rule states that any thing X which **isa** bird is also in the **can_fly** relation. Similarly, we could also express that animals can walk:

$$\text{can\_walk(X) :- X isa animal.} \tag{I.viii}$$

We can describe the relationship between classes of objects – i.e., describe the inheritance links between them – by means of rules about the **isa** predicate such as

$$\text{X isa animal :- X isa bird.} \tag{I.ix}$$

which expresses the assertion that all birds are animals. If we want to find out if birds can walk we postulate the existence of a bird **tweety** (say):

$$\text{tweety isa bird.} \tag{I.x}$$

and pose the query

```
can_walk(tweety)?
```

If we follow a proof of this query we can see how the rules for **can_walk** and **isa** are used to solve the goal:

```
can_walk(tweety)?
tweety isa animal?                          by (I.viii)
tweety isa bird?                            by (I.ix)
□                                           by (I.x)
```

This approach suffers from two defects. The first stems from the fact that in the rules for **can_fly** and **can_walk** etc. we mention terms such as (**bird** and **animal**) which denote the set of all birds and animals. Although we manage to avoid being explicit about the members of the sets of birds and animals, by using a constant to denote this set we are nevertheless using a set theoretic formulation of objects: we are forced to name explicitly the sets of objects that we are interested in.

   One consequence of this approach is that when we wish to ask a general question such as

'Can birds walk?'

we have to postulate the existence of at least one representative bird (i.e., `tweety`) before we can even ask the question. In fact this aspect of the 'isa' formalism is shared with some conventional object oriented systems: often it is only instances of classes which can respond to messages rather than classes as a whole.

We shall see that in our $L\&O$ programs it is not necessary to identify explicitly the set of all birds (or animals). We do not have to have a term which denotes the set of all birds (or animals) but instead we identify simply what is true of birds (and animals). This allows us to ask general questions about birds even if there is no tweety (or any other birds).

Finally, it is difficult to see how the 'isa' notation can be used to describe a module system, since there is no notation or methodology for structuring of programs.

Zaniolo's objects

In [Zan84] Zaniolo shows how a limited form of object oriented programming can be implemented in Prolog. He uses a translation between his object oriented programming notation and Prolog to give a layer of objects above Prolog. Like Hayes and others, Zaniolo's system does not support objects with state; however he does have some of the other features of object oriented programming.

Suppose that we wanted to describe a person as being an object with an associated age and a rule that tells us that a person likes anyone who likes logic. In Zaniolo's framework we do this by embedding the rules in a `with` declaration shown in Program 1.12. Syntactically, this `with` declaration is a Prolog clause

```
person(Age) with [
    age(Age),
    (likes(X) :- X:likes(logic))].
```

Program 1.12 The **person** class

about the binary predicate `with`. The left argument of the `with` statement is a term which denotes the class of objects being described and the right argument is a list of the methods for that class. Each method is syntactically a clause which can have embedded in it calls to other objects – as in this case. The condition:

```
...,X:likes(logic),...
```

represents an invocation of the object identified by the value of the variable X for a proof of the goal `likes(logic)`.

The notation for sending a message to an object in Zaniolo's system consists of a call to the ':' predicate – written as infix with the object name on the left and the method or query on the right. (The notation *Object:method* seems to be a *de facto* standard for indicating the invocation of a method within an object in many object oriented extensions to logic programming.) A method call is evaluated by searching the **with** definitions for one which matches the object and then invoking the appropriate clauses contained in the **with** list to solve the query part of the call.

There is a simple scheme for inheritance hierarchies. To declare that **tom** (say) is a particular kind of **person** we would write:

```
tom isa person(33).
```

or that people are examples of life-forms:

```
person(A) isa life_form.
```

It is possible to have several **isa** declarations in a class; however only one method definition can be used from a given object (or *class*) definition to solve a query. If more than one class has a definition of a method only one of them will be used.

We can use some of the search power of Prolog to go beyond the capabilities of normal object oriented programming languages. For example, we can search for objects which satisfy a given criteria. This possibility arises from the fact that the **with** declarations of a class are also Prolog statements. So, a program can be constructed which uses the database of **with** statements to search for objects which have some required attributes. For example, if we wanted to find a **person** object whose age was less than 15 we could do so by using the goal

```
P isa person(_),P:age(X),X<15?
```

This query makes use of the Prolog structure of the **isa** declarations to locate an object that might satisfy the message. Clearly, if there are many objects in the system then this search could become very expensive.

Zaniolo's work has inspired many variations, including our own. However we extend his work and put it on a firmer logical basis. In addition, we also identify and support a separate type of information structuring which is useful for many applications: the 'part-of' structure.

The POL system

A similar approach to Zaniolo's to incorporating features of object oriented programming is taken in the POL system [Gal86]. This system incorporates some aspects of the 'isa' style of objects with some new features; in particular a more sophisticated form of object search which is accompanied by a set of higher-order operators which make it easier to specify the search.

A POL program consists of regular Prolog clauses mixed – at the same syntactic level – with special declarations relating to objects and classes. An individual object is declared via an assertion of the **instance** relation. As with the 'isa' formulation, objects and classes are identified by constant symbols which denote the elements and sets concerned. Again, as with the 'isa' approach, before we can discuss the properties of individual objects, it is necessary to define one:

```
tweety instance penguin.
```

Here **tweety** is the object name and **penguin** is the *class* identifier. As we shall see, declarations such as these are useful when an object retrieval search is requested. Associated with an object are a set of instance variables. The value of instance variables is represented by assertions where the slot name – i.e., the name of the instance variable – is the predicate symbol and the object and value of the instance variable form its arguments. Program 1.13 shows how we might describe **tweety** in this way.

```
age(tweety,3).
colour(tweety,blue).
no_of_legs(tweety,2).
```

Program 1.13 A description of **tweety**

This representation makes it easy to access an object's instance variables; however, as with Hayes's frames, slot names must be unique: two classes of objects should not use the same name for different slots.

Defining and invoking methods is more complicated than defining and accessing instance variables. A method of a class is declared with a **with** statement:

```
penguin with X:mode(swim).
```

The 'X' variable is mandatory and is used to keep track of which object invoked a method especially during the execution of that method. Since the name of the original object that invokes a method is always maintained, it is possible to construct programs which involve restarting the inheritance mechanism. For example, suppose that we wanted to describe a rule which expressed the fact that

'two legged animals run, while four legged animals gallop'.

This rule – which is true of all animals and therefore belongs to the **animal** class rather than to subsidiary types of animals – relies on knowing how many legs an animal has; this information is not held in the **animal** class but in the various special cases of animal. Program 1.14 shows how we can define this rule in the class for **animal**.

When such a method rule is invoked, the variable 'X' is bound to the name of the original object used in the original call. For example, in order to determine **tweety**'s fast mode of travel, the sub-goal

```
animal with X:mode(run)    :- X:no_of_legs(2).
animal with X:mode(gallop) :- X:no_of_legs(4).
```

Program 1.14 animals that run and gallop

```
...,tweety:no_of_legs(2),...
```

must be evaluated. This allows us to determine how many legs **tweety** has from within a program in the **animal** class.

Notice that we could not construct such a rule in Zaniolo's scheme because the context of a method call is lost once the method is entered; so, once we have 'entered' the animal class it is not possible to go back and determine other properties of **tweety**.

POL has no concept of a syntactic scope for a method declaration; as a result there is no way of indicating the objects referred to by the conditions in the body of a method declaration, except by using an explicit variable to hold the object. This variable is used to dynamically maintain the scope of a call which in Zaniolo's work can be maintained statically.

The POL system provides many of the features found in object oriented programming but does not really provide a coherent philosophy of objects; certainly not with respect to logic programming and objects. Gallaire [Gal86] does not attempt to construct a declarative semantics for POL objects; so in that sense the POL system is an operational system rather than a descriptive one.

LOGIN – Logic with inheritance

The LOGIN language [AKN86] represents a rather different approach to incorporating objects into logic. In fact, LOGIN might not be viewed as an object oriented programming system at first glance: there is no identified notion of objects, methods and classes for example. Nor is there any attempt to organise programs 'in the large'. However two features unique to LOGIN allow us to describe inheritance 'in the small'.

LOGIN is a typed language; all terms have a type associated with them. Unification between terms involves unifying the associated types of each term as well as unifying the terms themselves. When unifying two terms the types of both must be coercible to the same type; this is only possible if the terms have the same type or if one of them is a sub-type of the other. Type declarations allow the programmer to state that a set of terms of a given type are a sub-type of another type. This allows us to describe a kind of inheritance:

```
penguin < bird.
bird < animal.
```

These two sentences state that terms of type **penguin** are of type **bird**, and terms of type **bird** are of type **animal**; and in consequence penguins are also animals.

In fact the symbols **penguin**, **bird** and **animal** here refer to the *function symbols* of terms. Thus, for example, we know from these two sentences that terms whose function symbol is **bird** are a sub-type of terms whose function symbol is **animal**. A second innovation in LOGIN is to use so-called ψ-terms instead of conventional terms. Arguments in a complex ψ-term (corresponding to a normal compound term) are indicated by attribute/value pairs rather than by position. So, if we wanted to describe a conventional term such as:

```
tr(tr(nil,able,nil),lab,tr(nil,mab,nil))
```

as a ψ-term then we could write:

```
tr(right=>tr(left=>nil;right=>nil;label=>mab);
    left=>tr(label=>able;right=>nil;left=>nil);
    label=>lab)
```

The order that we write the sub-terms within a ψ-term is not important since its arguments are identified by selector functions rather than by their position.

It should be obvious that there is a one-to-one correspondence between equivalent ψ-terms and conventional Herbrand terms. Furthermore, ψ-terms are an extension to terms of the standard database formulation of atomic formulae where arguments can be represented by attribute/value pairs rather than being indicated by their positions within the formula.

Apart from the extra documentation inherent in ψ-terms there is also the syntactic convenience of omitting unreferenced arguments and of not having to follow a fixed ordering of arguments. This syntactic convenience is balanced by a slightly more difficult representation of shared variables (where the expected type of the variable must be given) and the fact that circular terms can be described.

Using the type declarations, we can describe a kind of inheritance over terms (and hence objects). However this inheritance is somewhat weaker than the inheritance that we have discussed so far. There is no possibility of overriding or default inheritance. Nor can we express notions which involve the use of self. Therefore we cannot express – in the type language – our rules for fast moving animal for example.

1.3.2   Dynamic objects

While many workers have concentrated on combining the more declarative aspects of object oriented programming and logic programming, others have attempted to model *assignment* in a logic programming context. An interesting example of this is the work by Conery on 'logical objects' which we examine below. Others have used the committed choice logic programming languages such as Parlog and Concurrent Prolog to model assignment.

Logical objects

Almost in strict contrast to LOGIN, the problem addressed by Conery in [Con88a]
is that of representing objects with a mutable internal state. The contrast is
enhanced by the fact that Conery does not even attempt to address issues such as
program structure and inheritance. (However, a later work – described in [Con88b]
– extends these ideas into a complete object oriented system.) In Conery's scheme,
classes are represented by specially paired clauses called object clauses.

person(A,ID) ∧ `age(ID,A)` ← *person(A,ID).*   (I.xi)

person(A,ID) ∧ `likes(ID,X)` ←*person(A,ID)* ∧
    `age(X,Y)` ∧ `Y<A`.   (I.xii)

Program 1.15 The object clauses for person

So, for example, Program 1.15 contains a definition for a *person* class which has
methods in it for `age` and `likes`; where *person(A,ID)* is an object literal and
`age(ID,A)` and `likes(ID,X)` are procedure literals. (We use a different font to
distinguish *object literals* from `procedure literals`.)

A query to this program is really a pair of queries which are linked through
shared variables. One part of the query involves only procedure literals; the other
part of the query consists of object literals which represent the objects in the
system. A complete proof involves both proving the existence of the objects and
proving that those objects satisfy a given set of constraints. The two sub-proofs
are linked and are performed simultaneously.

If we wanted to find out if a particular person `jack` (say) liked another person
`jill` (say) then we would use the query:

    ←new_person(jack,20) ∧ new_person(jill,18) ∧
        likes(jack,jill).

The `new_person` program has a special role in the description of a class. Each
class must include such a program. Its primary function is to introduce a new
object literal into the system. Our `new_person` program may be defined as:

    new_person(Name,Age) ←*person(Age,Name)*   (I.xiii)

Given a query such as the one above we can construct a proof which will show if
the jack object likes the jill object:

    ←new_person(jack,20) ∧ new_person(jill,18) ∧
        likes(jack,jill).
    ←*person(20,jack)* ∧ new_person(jill,18) ∧
        likes(jack,jill).   by (I.xiii)

←*person(20,jack)* ∧ *person(18,jill)*∧
        `likes(jack,jill)`   by (I.xiii)
←*person(20,jack)* ∧ *person(18,jill)*∧
        `age(Y,jill)` ∧ `Y<20`   by (I.xii)
←*person(20,jack)* ∧ *person(18,jill)*∧ `18<20`   by (I.xi)

After the main proof is completed (which in this case is with the proof that `18<20`) we get a residual query consisting only of object literals:

    ←*person(20,jack)*∧ *person(18,jill)*

The proof continues as an object-only proof to verify that *person(20,jack)* and *person(18,jill)* are indeed valid objects. This object proof involves using clauses supplied by the programmer which define what the valid objects are, as in Program 1.16.

    person(A,ID) ←`integer(A)` ∧ `atom(ID)`.

        Program 1.16 The definition of a valid *person*

It is possible to model state in this system because during the course of the proof the object literals change; thus representing the changing state of the objects. An object clause such as

    person(A,ID) ∧ `new_age(ID,B)` ←*person(B,ID)*

which is used when a person's age is to be updated, consumes a *person* object of age **A** from the current query and replaces it in the new query with a *person* object of age **B**. The effect is as though the person identified by **ID** has undergone a state change – subsequent accesses to **ID**'s age will reflect this. Furthermore, this has been achieved without informing all the objects which refer to **ID** about the new age.

    The objects themselves – and their states – are modelled by recursion over object clauses. Each time a method is invoked a new copy of the object literal is introduced to replace the one consumed by the method. The arguments of the new object literal reflect the new state of the object. Thus, in the case of changing a person's age, the old person literal is replaced in the object query by a new one with a different age (although the name is the same).

The logical nature of logical objects   It is worth examining the exact logical status of these object clauses a little more deeply. In general a query, consisting of a mixture of object literals and procedure literals, represents a request for a proof of the existence of a set of objects and for the truth of a number of conditions. Since object clauses have a declarative semantics we should be able to compare an object proof with a more conventional one. Suppose that we have a query of the form:

$$\leftarrow O_1, \ldots, O_l, P_1, \ldots, P_k$$

where the O_i are object literals and the P_j are procedure literals. Suppose that we also have an object clause

$$O \wedge P \leftarrow B$$

or more strictly

$$\forall \vec{X} \quad O \wedge P \leftarrow B$$

where O is an object literal, P is a procedure literal, B is a conjunction possibly involving both types of literal and $\vec{X}$ is the vector of the variables occurring in the clause. Since we know that an object clause is logically equivalent to two clauses we write them so:

$$\forall \vec{X} \quad P \leftarrow B \tag{I.xiv}$$
$$\forall \vec{X} \quad O \leftarrow B \tag{I.xv}$$

Now suppose that O and some object literal O_i in the query unify, and also that P and a procedure literal P_j unify also. Then we can successively resolve O_i and P_j from the query with these two clauses:

$$\leftarrow (O_1, \ldots, O_l, P_1, \ldots, P_{j-1}, B', P_{j+1}, \ldots, P_k)\theta_1 \qquad \text{by (I.xiv)}$$
$$\leftarrow (O_1, \ldots, O_{i-1}, B'', O_{i+1}, \ldots, O_l,$$
$$P_1, \ldots, P_{j-1}, B', P_{j+1}, \ldots, P_k)\theta_1\theta_2 \qquad \text{by (I.xv)}$$

where θ_1 is the substitution induced by using the procedure part of the object clause and θ_2 is the substitution induced by the object part of the object clause.

The object clause inference rule involves replacing both parts of the head of the object clause simultaneously: there must be both a procedure literal and an object literal in the query which unifies with the procedure head and object head of the object clause. The condition that O_i and P_j are replaced simultaneously amounts to a further constraint that B' and B'' are unifiable (with m.g.u. θ_3 say). If we apply this substitution to the new query we obtain two sets of literals identified as $B'\theta_1\theta_2\theta_3$ and $B''\theta_1\theta_2\theta_3$ which are identical: and therefore we can factor one set out to get the new query:

$$\leftarrow (O_1, \ldots, O_{i-1}, O_{i+1}, \ldots, O_l, P_1, \ldots, P_{j-1}, B, P_{j+1}, \ldots, P_k)\theta_1\theta_2\theta_3$$

This new query is the one which is derived from our original query using the object clause inference rule employed by Conery. The effect of it has been to replace two literals in the query at the same time. Compared with standard resolution this inference is somewhat specialized – it enables literals which are not necessarily logically related to be made identical. (If similar inferences were to be applied within the so-called procedure literals then many recursions would become impossible.) As a result of relying on this specialized form of inference the system loses the fundamental relationship between the declarative semantics and the proof theoretic or procedural semantics. For example, the steps within an object proof cannot be re-ordered without changing the validity of the proof (which is what gives us the *effect* of assignment).

Logical objects gives a semantics to assignment within object oriented systems in terms of a modified proof procedure. This allows Conery to state that executions of object programs correspond to logical consequences of theories. However, there is no attempt to give systems of evolving objects a declarative semantics as well as a proof theoretic one. The lack of such a declarative reading for objects weakens the argument that logical objects are logical. However, the logical object system does represent an interesting way of representing objects with state. By modifying the proof procedure to allow the modelling of assignment we obtain a system which allows us to simulate state change rather than a purely descriptive formulation. The key issue remains of whether state-change systems are logical at all, and how one can incorporate changing state with declarative semantics.

Although we have concentrated on Conery's approach to logical objects, several other workers have arrived at essentially the same solution. This includes the work on linear objects [AP90, AP91a, AP91b] and Degano and Diomidi [DD83] who were probably the first to consider the semantics of such types of logic.

Concurrent logic programming and objects

Shapiro and Takeuchi [ST83], Kahn [KMB86], Davison [Dav88] and others have looked at the implementation of object oriented programming languages in concurrent logic programming languages such as Concurrent Prolog and Parlog. The focus of Shapiro's work was the implementation of the operational semantics of object oriented programming languages in Concurrent Prolog although this has since been sugared up into a class notation by Kahn and Davison.

This work is interesting for two reasons: it represents one of the few truly concurrent approaches to object oriented programming systems, and simultaneously, the object oriented programming notation is a useful paradigm for using these languages.

An object in concurrent object oriented logic programming consists of a continuously executing tail-recursive process. The object process consumes and responds to messages which are represented by an incrementally communicated list. Object processes may optionally have output streams of messages which are connected to other object processes. For example, Program 1.17 is a simple Parlog program which implements the notion of a bird.

```
mode bird(?,^).          % the first arg is input
                         % the second is output

bird([mode(X)|L],E):-                                        (I.xvi)
    X = fly,
    bird(L,E).
bird([covering(X)|L],E):-                                    (I.xvii)
    X = feathers,
    bird(L,E);
bird([M|L],E):-                                              (I.xviii)
                  % go here if all else fails

    E=[M|X],
    bird(L,X).
```

Program 1.17 A Parlog program for the `bird` class

The first two clauses implement methods for **mode** of travel and covering respectively. A bird object is modelled by a sub-goal of the form:

```
...,bird(M,E),...
```

where M is the stream of messages to be consumed by the bird process. As this stream becomes successively instantiated, the methods in bird are invoked. For example, if the first instantiation binds M to [mode(U)|M1], then the first bird clause is activated and the goal reduces to:

```
...,U=fly,...,bird(M1,E),...                           by (I.xvi)
```

The execution of the sub-goal U=fly has the effect of returning an answer to the original sender of the mode message.

The role of the third clause in Program 1.17 is to handle those messages which cannot be answered by the first two. When this clause is triggered (it can respond to any message but will only do so if the other two fail to respond) the effect is to pass on the message that could not be 'understood' by the first two clauses to the output stream E; this, in turn, may mean that any process which is linked to E will handle the message. So if the second instantiation of bird's message stream was to bind M1 to [breathes(W)|M2], then the bird process reduces to:

```
...,E=[breathes(W)|X2],...,bird(M2,X2),...             by (I.xviii)
```

If **E** is connected to another object process then that object process will receive the message **breathes(W)** which could not be handled by **bird**.

We can use this technique to implement inheritance – when we create a new **bird** process we also create a new **animal** process. This **animal** process is connected to the **bird** process via the latter's Exception stream. As a result we would always have two processes representing a bird object:

    `...,bird(M,E),...,animal(E),...`

Any messages that are not handled by the **bird** clauses directly are passed to the **animal** process. So, when the **bird** process failed to handle the **breathes** message it is placed on the animal's message stream:

    `...,bird(M2,E2),...,E=[breathes(W)|E2],animal(E),...`

The construction of all these interconnecting streams can make the creation of a new object quite expensive. Furthermore, implementing multiple inheritance adds considerable complexity to the scheme. However, implementing inheritance by interconnecting streams allows for inheritance links to be dynamic as they can be in Smalltalk.

As with Conery's objects, local state is modelled within an object process by the use of recursion. State variables are held as non-stream arguments to the object process. As an object changes state then the process recurses with new values in these variables. Overall, the same remarks apply as for Conery's logical objects: by relying on particular properties of the proof procedure – in this case Parlog's execution strategy – the crucial link between the declarative semantics of an object and the procedural semantics of its behaviour is lost. Thus we are left with an interesting machine which we can manipulate – i.e., program – to obtain the effect of object oriented programming and state change, but which no longer has any obvious connection to logic.

1.4   Summary

In this chapter we have identified a number of problem areas with logic programming as a programming language. In particular these concern the fact that there are no adequate methods for structuring programs at a larger scale than clauses, and the simple clausal syntax does not properly reflect the intended uses of practical programs.

We have also looked at the relationship of object oriented programming and logic programming as some of the workers in the field have seen it. There have been two main areas of interest: the use of object oriented techniques to statically structure programs and knowledge, and the simulation of dynamically changing systems within logic programming.

In the rest of this book we are concerned with our own approach to these issues, and we will introduce and develop our own language extension which addresses some of these deficiencies.

CHAPTER TWO

Elements of *L&O*

In this chapter we introduce a particular logic programming language which we call '*L&O*' (for Logic and Objects). This language, which is based on logic programming (i.e., in practice Prolog), incorporates two extensions which are intended to simplify and ease the task of programming large applications. The granularity of logic programming is increased by incorporating concepts of classes as found in object oriented programming languages. Expressions and functions are introduced where they are appropriate; they can enhance the convenience of programming in many situations. As well as introducing new language features, we also explore some of the programming power that these new features give – in particular the object oriented aspects. The programming power of the *L&O* language is explored further in Chapter 3 where we discuss modules and inheritance. In Chapter 4 we look at issues relating to programming methodology.

In this chapter we are content with a relatively informal understanding of the concepts and semantics of our extensions. Later, in Chapter 8, we examine the semantics of functions and objects more carefully and show how the relevant constructs can be properly incorporated into the logic programming formalism.

2.1 Class templates

The primary intuition which underlies any object oriented language concerns the nature of an object. Our object oriented notation depends on a particular way of looking at the world. As people, we experience objects that occur in the world through our senses. We see them, feel them, hear them and smell them. For example, if we see a ball bouncing on the street, we perceive that it has a certain shape, and that it makes a certain kind of noise as it bounces. Other than through our senses there is no independent way of appreciating our bouncing ball – there is no way we can 'know' the ball other than by interpreting what our senses tell us. In practice, this does not unduly concern us even though we know

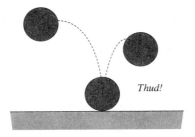

Figure 2.1 *A bouncing ball*

that those senses can be misled. Our senses are good enough and reliable enough for us to be able to perform effectively. (Sometimes we deliberately mislead our senses; for example, in the flight simulation machines that are often used to help train pilots to fly. The quality of the illusion in a simulator can be so high that the pilot experiences the simulation as reality. As a result, the training received in a simulator is almost equivalent to actual flying practice.)

A logic system can also be said to 'perceive' the world; it does so by means of the assertions held in the system. For example, if a logic program contains the fact

```
likes(john,mary).
```

then the logic programming system can be said to 'know' this fact. We might say that the logic system perceives (in a rather passive sense) the fact that John likes Mary. However, just as we cannot verify the information we receive with our senses, so it is not possible to verify within a logical system that John does indeed like Mary. Any connection between the logical statement and reality is completely outside logic itself; indeed it would be outside any symbolic system. The best that a logical system can do is to make deductions based on the assumption that John likes Mary. On the other hand, if we wish to use the logical description, we might choose to assume that John likes Mary, and thus establish the connection. This assumption is worth making if it enables useful conclusions to be drawn.

Extrapolating from this, we can see that it may be enough to describe an object in terms of the assertions that we can make about it. These assertions would allow us to make further deductions and computations; just as being able to see a bouncing ball may be enough to allow us to pick it up. As a result we choose, as our fundamental intuition, to view an object as being simply the collection of things that we know to be true of it. Traditionally, in the language of logic, such a collection of facts is called a *theory*. Thus, an object is a theory and our object oriented extension to logic programming centres around our wish to be able to describe more than one theory within a single system.

One consequence of this view of an object is that two objects are differentiable if and only if there is some fact which is different for the two objects. If there is no query whose answer is different when asked of two sets of descriptions, then those descriptions refer to the same object; even if the descriptions are themselves different. This is not a totally new concept: two logic programs may define the same relation even if the programs are different.

2.1.1 Syntax of *L&O* programs

Predicate logic allows us to describe large (even infinitely large) collections of facts by means of formulae: a clause containing universally quantified variables stands for the infinitely many possible ways of replacing those variables with actual data terms. We use the same concept to describe collections of theories: we have formulae – which also may contain universally quantified variables – to describe theories. The *L&O* notation allows us to describe several theories within one overall program, and to describe relationships between these theories. The clauses which relate to an individual theory are grouped together and enclosed by a pair of braces and associated with an identifying term or label:

```
label:{
    axiom₁.
    axiom₂.
    ...}
```

Theory labels play an analogous role to that of predicate symbols. A predicate symbol is not part of a relation, rather it merely serves to identify and distinguish a relation. Similarly, a label is not part of any theory, rather it serves to identify a theory.

It is not necessary to restrict ourselves to simple facts inside class bodies. We can have rules with conditions as well, as in the program about the Flying Scotsman in Program 2.1. Such rules inside class templates fulfil a similar role to *methods* in conventional object oriented programming languages.

```
scotsman:{...
    colour(green).
    country(britain).
    speed(120).
    journey_time(Distance,T):-
        speed(S),
        T is Distance/S
}
```

Program 2.1 The Flying Scotsman program

In general, a class template may have two components: a *class body* – such as in Program 2.1 – and a set of *class rules* (not to be confused with normal rules occurring inside class bodies). Class rules are used to relate different class templates to each other through inheritance. A class rule of the form:

```
label<=mabel
```

where `label` and `mabel` are terms, states that any fact in the theory identified by the label `mabel` is also in the `label` theory. We can say that the theory denoted by `label` inherits the facts associated with the `mabel` theory. There can be any number of class rules for any given label. As we shall see, each of the class rules will be tried in turn when solving a goal within a Prolog-style *L&O* system.

Messages and deduction

In object oriented programming languages, computation is expressed in terms of messages passed between objects. A message sent to an object is interpreted as a request to perform one of its methods; and the result of a computation can be viewed as the response that an object makes to a message.

In a logic programming system, computation is identified with deduction. Normally any axiom in a program can potentially be used in any deduction step, however, since we are dealing with potentially more than one set of axioms, we must be more specific as to which axioms can be used in each deduction step. We do this by associating a label with every sub-goal.

A query to an *L&O* program is written by prefixing the query condition with the label associated with the theory that we want to invoke. So, for example, we can use the query (II.i) to determine how long it will take to the Flying Scotsman to travel a 1000 miles:

```
scotsman:journey_time(1000,X)?
```
(II.i)

This query is to be interpreted as:

'Display values for X for which the condition

```
journey_time(1000,X)
```

is true with respect to the `scotsman` theory.'

The question mark in the query (II.i) distinguishes it as a *relational query*. We will see that we can also have an expression query where we wish the system to evaluate an expression rather than prove a goal. An *expression query* consists of an expression suffixed by an '=?'. Since we have prefixed the `journey_time` condition with the `scotsman` label, only those axioms which are in the `scotsman` template will be used to solve it, although in order to solve the `journey_time` condition it might become necessary to invoke predicates defined in other theories.

In general, *all* sub-goals (and expressions) have associated with them a *label* and a *predication* (or *expression*). The predication part of a sub-goal corresponds to the normal sub-goal in standard logic programming terms, and the label identifies the context of the sub-goal (or expression). In cases where the label is not given explicitly it is determined implicitly by the context of the sub-goal or expression.

Our query can also be interpreted as sending the `journey_time` message to the **scotsman** object. The **scotsman** object/theory responds to this message by attempting the relevant `journey_time` proof. A successful completion of that proof corresponds to the successful handling of the message by the **scotsman** object/theory. We might like to call this the '*message passing interpretation of logic*'. In this interpretation we identify the rules and equations which are embedded in a class as corresponding to methods in conventional object oriented programming languages.

Complex labels

In the examples that we have seen so far, the label associated with a theory has been constant. We can also use terms with variables as labels; in effect, we can *parameterize* theories. The fact that labels may be parameterised leads to great expressive power. For example, we can express what we know of trains in general, rather than an individual train, as with the axioms in Program 2.2.

```
train(S,Cl,Co):{
    colour(Cl).
    speed(S).
    country(Co).
    journey_time(Distance,T):-
        T = Distance/S.
}
```

Program 2.2 The <code>train</code> class template

The variables in the label term `train(S,Cl,Co)` are universally quantified over all the axioms in the class. If we explicitly expressed the quantifiers in the train class template we would get:

$$\forall S, Co, Cl . \texttt{train}(S, \; Cl, \; Co) : ($$
$$\texttt{colour}(Cl) \wedge$$
$$\texttt{speed}(S) \wedge$$
$$\texttt{country}(Co) \wedge$$
$$\forall Distance, T . (\texttt{journey\_time}(Distance, T) \leftarrow$$
$$T = Distance/S) \;)$$

```
train(120,green,britain):{
    colour(green).
    country(britain).
    speed(120).
    journey_time(Distance,Time) :-
        Time = Distance/120.
}
```

Program 2.3 A specific instance of `train`

In a conventional logic program, a clause with variables in it stands for all the possible ground instantiations of that clause. The fact that normally there are infinitely many such ground versions of the clause is what differentiates first order predicate logic from propositional logic where there may only be finitely many ground formulae.

We can extend this idea to *L&O* programs by viewing the set of axioms which describes a particular train as being an instance of a more general set of axioms relating to trains in general. The parameters in this more general theory stand for the particular forms of the theory in much the same way that the variables in a clause stand for the particular forms of the ground propositions.

To obtain the specific set of axioms which correspond to the `scotsman` from the general `train` theory we can substitute for the variables in the `train` label. Local clause variables occuring in clauses within the theory are left uninstantiated. So, if we instantiate S (which is the speed of the train) to 120, and we instantiate Cl to `green` and we instantiate Co to `britain`, we will get the set of axioms in Program 2.3.

This program contains the same axioms that we had for the class template in Program 2.1; therefore what follows from one set of axioms also follows from the other. From this point of view the two theories are identical. Of course, the label

```
train(120,green,britain)
```

is not identical to the label `scotsman` but this is, in principle, no different to having the same relation identified by several different predicate symbols. The set of possible derivable consequences, and therefore the associated theory, is the same. However, as when two relations are defined with different predicates, the task of *proving* that one class template is equivalent to another is not even expressible in a first order language.

Variable labels
In nearly all Prolog systems we can have a variable in place of a call; in some Prologs we can also have variables in place of predicate symbols or function symbols. This feature, which for historical reasons is called the meta-variable feature,

allows Prolog programmers to build powerful generic programs; a typical example being the standard definition of negation-by-failure in Program 2.4.

```
not(X):- X, !, fail.          % call negated goal
not(X).                       % succeed if goal failed
```

Program 2.4 The negation-by-failure program

In *L&O* we can, in addition to this kind of meta-variable, allow the label of a labelled condition to be represented by a variable. Such a variable should normally be bound to a term corresponding to a label when the call that it labels is executed; the call then proceeds as though the variable were replaced in the text of the program by its value; i.e., by the label that it denotes.

Variable labels allow us to define relations (and functions) which are about objects and theories. For example, to express the conditions under which a given train is compatible with a given country, we might write:

```
compatible(Train,Country):-
      Country:terrain(T),Train:suitable(T).
```

This rule states that a train is compatible with a country if the country's terrain is suitable for the train. We organize our database of trains and countries so that each country is associated with a class template which contains some data about its terrain; as in Program 2.5.

```
egypt:{...
      terrain(flat).
      ...}
```

Program 2.5 The terrain of `egypt`

Each **train** class template contains a predicate which identifies a range of suitable terrains (see Program 2.6).   In order to determine if the **scotsman** train would be suitable for **egypt** we would pose the query:

```
compatible(scotsman,egypt)?
```

In solving this query we will get the following sub-goals:

```
...,Country:terrain(T),Train:suitable(T),...
```

```
scotsman:{...
    suitable(T) :-
        not too_hilly(T).
    ...}
```

Program 2.6 The suitability of the Flying Scotsman

Where **Country** and **Train** are bound to **egypt** and **scotsman** respectively. These sub-goals are therefore equivalent to the sub-goals:

    ...,egypt:terrain(T),scotsman:suitable(T),...

which are solved in the normal manner.

The problem of determining the exact location for the **compatible** rule raises an interesting programming methodology issue. We could put it with the **train** class template or with the **country** class template or even both; alternatively we could put the rule in a different class altogether. From the point of the *L&O* programming language it makes no difference where the rule is located. We simply note that we do not force any particular solution: the programmer may put the rule where it is most appropriate and useful.

Variable labels and object search

It is possible, in principle, to interpret conditions with variable labels which are still uninstantiated at the time of the call. It is instructive to see what might happen in these circumstances. So, if we are given a condition of the form:

    ...,Variable:predication,...

where the label **Variable** is unknown at the time that it is invoked, one suitable behaviour of the system would be to search each of the *L&O* programs in turn (through backtracking in a Prolog style system) to see if it can satisfy the **predication** sub-goal.

A successful search results in the **Variable** label being instantiated to the appropriate value – a term corresponding to the label of an existing class template in the system. We can use this value to guide subsequent evaluations. This represents a form of *object search*. For example, if we had a condition such as

    ...,X:colour(red),...

where **X** is unbound at the time of the call, then we might express the meaning of this as

   'find an object which is coloured red'

Although object search can be a powerful technique, we would not recommend it lightly since the computations involved may be very expensive.

If we have a condition in which the *predication* is not known – i.e., it is an unbound variable at the time that the system attempts to execute it – then we would have to guess that too. Such a query might be taken to mean 'is there anything true about this object?'. Although potentially valid (since we could attempt all the known predicates in the same way that we attempt all the known labels) we prefer to regard the case where the predication in unknown as an error and report it as such to the programmer.

2.1.2   Computing with class rules

Class rules are used to solve sub-goals by transferring their proofs from one class template to another (as determined by the class rule itself). If the proof of a sub-goal is successful in the new class then it is also successful in the old one. So, if we have a condition of the form:

```
...,bird:breathes(X),...
```

and if we had a class rule which states that birds are animals:

```
bird<=animal.
```
(II.ii)

then, we can use this class rule to start to solve the **breathes** condition by replacing the **bird** label with an **animal** label:

```
...,animal:breathes(X),...
```

The proof proceeds as though the label were actually **animal**; the whole condition succeeds if **breathes(X)** is true in **animal**. Usually, there will be axioms in the **animal** class which define the meaning of **breathes**, however there could be another class rule for **animal** which transfers the **breathes** condition to yet another class. In general, whenever we have a condition of the form:

```
...,label:predication,...
```

a deduction step can consist either of the use of a rule from within the class body to reduce the predication to a conjunction keeping the label the same, or the application of a class rule to replace the label with a new one. This represents a simple and obvious extension to the normal rule of inference used in logic programming.

A normal class rule *augments* the definitions in a class template – both the inherited and the local clauses can be used to help solve queries. The deduction system uses the local clauses for a predicate (or local equations for a function) before any class rules for the class template are attempted.

In addition to the normal class rule, there is also a second kind of class rule – the overriding class rule. This form of class rule is similar to the normal class rule except that only predicates which are not defined locally may be inherited. So, for example, we might have used the class rule:

```
bird<<animal
```

instead of the normal rule in (II.ii). In this case, we only use the class rule in answering questions of the form:

```
bird:breathes(X)?
```

if there are no local clauses for **breathes** in the class body for **bird**. In Chapter 3 we will also see that we can further modify the normal class rule with a differential inheritance filter which is more selective about what can and cannot be inherited.

The keywords self and super

Two special keywords arise in the context of using class rules: the **self** keyword and the **super** label. The **self** keyword is a special term which has a value which is dependent on the context: it denotes the original or first label that is in force at the point of its use. Often this simply means the label which is associated with the class body in which the **self** reference occurs; however, if one or more class rules have been used to get to this class body then **self** refers to the original label. We shall explore more fully the role of **self** in Chapter 3.

The **super** label is used when we want to by-pass any local definitions of a predicate (or function). A **super** labelled call uses only those definitions which are available through the use of class rules. Thus **super** is often used when we want to redefine or modify an inherited predicate (or function) in terms of other inherited programs. For example, suppose that we had a system of classes which relate to windows, in a multiple window display system. In such a system, we would have classes for windows and for labelled or titled windows:

```
titled_win(Title,Pos,Size) <= window(Pos,Size).
```

When a titled window is moved, it is desirable to move the label at the same time that we move the window itself. We can implement this by defining a local version of move in the **titled_win** class template which performs the required adjustment. A first approximation to this version of **move** is shown in Program 2.7.

```
titled_win(Title,Pos,Size):{...
    move(A):-
        window(Pos,Size):move(A),
        move_title(A).
    ...}
```

Program 2.7 A titled window class template

With this program, as it stands, we are required to know that a `titled_win` is a special case of `window`. Since titled windows might also be special cases of other *L&O* programs, for example a titled window could be a graphic region or a process, it may not be clear which of `titled_win`'s **super**-classes to invoke to complete the move.

```
move(A):-
      super:move(A),
      move_title(A).
```

Program 2.8 A super-labelled move

We can use the **super** keyword, as in Program 2.8, to 'get around' the problem. The use of a **super** label on the **move** sub-goal means that only the inherited definitions of **move** are to be used to solve it; in particular we do not use any local definitions for this sub-goal. Whichever **super**-class has the definition of **move** will be used to move the window. Notice that we do not need to know which of those **super** classes has the correct definition. **super** references make it easy to construct systems where relations are defined as a modification of, as opposed to strict additions to, relations defined in ancestors, as in the case of moving labelled windows.

2.2 Functions and conditional equalities

As we discussed in Chapter 1, in our opinion a programming language – especially a declarative one – should allow the programmer to write expressions in programs. The standard Prolog way of writing expressions involves the **is** predicate which can be rather clumsy to use:

```
...,X1 is X+1,foo(...,X1,...),...
```

However, we can write an expression wherever it is most appropriate:

```
...,foo(...,X+1,...),...
```

Apart from being able to use such expressions, we can also define functions over terms. This effectively combines the functional and relational programming paradigms into a single framework based on logic programming.

We define functions within a class body by means of conditional equalities. A conditional equality is a statement of the form:

```
f(t₁,...,tₙ)=G  :-  C₁,...,Cₘ
```

This states that the terms $f(t_1, \ldots, t_n)$ and G are equal whenever all of the conditions C_i hold. A conditional equality is a syntactic variant of a normal clause: it can be viewed as a clause about the binary predicate '='. The intention of an equation is to describe a function; the function being described is represented by the principal function symbol of the term on the left-hand side of the equality (i.e., f). In the equation below the principal function symbol on the left-hand side of the equation is `double`; thus this equation forms the definition of the `double` function:

```
double(X)=X+X.
```

A complete definition of a function may consist of several equations, each corresponding to a different case of the function's input. Furthermore, an equation can be recursive, as the definition of the `fibonacci` function in Program 2.9 shows.

```
fib(0)=1.
fib(1)=1.
fib(N)=fib(N-1)+fib(N-2).
```

Program 2.9 The `fibonacci` function

Apart from arithmetic functions, we can also have functions over structures, lists and trees. For example, the `length` function in Program 2.10 computes the length of a list.

```
length([])=0.
length([E|L])=length(L)+1.
```

Program 2.10 The `length` function

The most famous logic program is probably **append**. We can define an analogous function using equations. Program 2.11 combines the use of operators and equations to define an infix symbol '<>' for appending lists. The conditional part of the equation can be used to describe constraints on the application of the equation. For example, in the equations for **merge** in Program 2.12, which equation applies depends on the relative order of the elements at the heads of the two input lists. The conditional part of an equation can also be used as a kind of **where** or **let** clause to introduce auxiliary variables. This allows us, for example, to write the equations for quick-sort in Program 2.13. One English reading of the main equation for **sort** in Program 2.13 could be

```
:-op(700,xfy,<>).          % append function is also an infix operator

[]<>X=X.
[E|X]<>Y=[E|X<>Y].
```

Program 2.11 An append function

```
merge([D|L1],[E|L2])=[D|merge(L1,[E|L2])]:-D<E.
merge([D|L1],[E|L2])=[E|merge([D|L1],L2)]:-D>=E.
```

Program 2.12 The merge function

'The **sort** of the non-empty list [E|L] is equal to the **sort** of the list
L1 appended to [E] and to the **sort** of the list L2 where L1 and L2 are
obtained by partitioning L about the element E.'

This combined application of conditions in equations to describe 'let' clauses as
well as conditional expressions means that our syntax can be simpler than that
found in other functional languages such as Hope [BMS80].

Equations and functions

The syntax of equations is not itself sufficient to guarantee that they describe
functions. For example, in Program 2.14, the left-hand sides of the equations
overlap; that is, more than one equation may be used to reduce an expression. In
consequence a **split** expression might have more than one value. For example,
some possible values of the expression **split([1,2,3])** are: [], [1], [2], [3],
[1,2], [1,3], [2,3] and [1,2,3]. Therefore, one could not say that **split** was
a function. In fact it is not – a better description of the meaning of **split** is that
it is a relation.

On the other hand, not all equations with overlapping left-hand sides describe

```
sort([]) = [].
sort([E|L]) = sort(L1)<>[E]<>sort(L2):-
     part(E,L,L1,L2).
part(E,[],[],[]).
part(E,[D|L],[D|L1],L2):-
     D<E,part(E,L,L1,L2).
part(E,[D|L],L1,[D|L2]):-
     D<E,part(E,L,L1,L2).
```

Program 2.13 The quick-sort function

```
split(X) = [].
split([E|L]) = [E|split(L)].
```

Program 2.14 The `split` 'function'

relations. In our clauses for **merge** the inequality conditions

      `D<E`

and

      `D>=E`

constrain the equations sufficiently to make them exclusive.   If equations are genuinely overlapping – i.e., if the left-hand sides unify and the conditions are insufficient to prevent overlap – then they describe a multi-valued function (a contradiction in terms); in other words they describe a relation.

Many equational programming languages impose a constraint that the left-hand sides of equations should not overlap syntactically (i.e., the left-hand sides of different equations should not be unifiable); this constraint tends to make programs less readable since overlapping equations must then be folded into a single equation using conditional expressions to differentiate the subcases.

For example, if we are required to rewrite the **merge** function in Program 2.12 so that the equations do not overlap then we have to collapse the two equations into a single one and use an if-then-else expression to express the alternative right-hand sides as shown in Program 2.15.

```
merge([D|X],[E|Y]) = if D<E
             then [D|merge(X,[E|Y])]
             else [E|merge([D|X],Y)].
```

Program 2.15 The **merge** function without overlapping equations

Since the programmer's intention when using equations is clearly to describe a function, it is feasible for us to insist (and for the compiler to rely on the fact) that the equations do describe a function. However, rather than insist on the left-hand sides of equations being exclusive we allow overlapping left-hand sides; but we insist that the equations are *semantically* exclusive – the left-hand side of an equation together with its condition part must be sufficient to ensure that the equation is exclusive and no other equations will apply. In any given situation only one equation can ultimately apply. Since this is not a syntactic property of an equation – we cannot type check the equation to ensure that this condition is met – we must trust the programmer.

2.2.1 Expressions in programs

We can use functional expressions in clauses as well as within equations. This permits an integrated language with equations used to describe functions and clauses used to describe relations. Probably the most common use of expressions in regular Prolog clauses would be to replace conditions of the form:

```
...,I1 is I+1,...
```

For example, in Program 2.16, the **index** program searches a list for an element, and if the element is there it returns the position in the list at which the element was found. This is a relation because an element might occur in a list more than

```
index(E,L,I):-
    index(E,L,1,I).
index(E,[E|_],I,I).
index(E,[D|L],I,J):-
    index(E,L,I+1,J).
```

Program 2.16 The **index** relation

once – so **index** succeeds once for each such occurrence. The use of the expression I+1 is so natural in this context that it almost passes without comment. In fact one of the most frequent errors novice programmers make when using Prolog is to write these types of expressions instead of using calls to the **is** built-in predicate.

Another common situation where we use expressions is in the description of constraints. This is used in Program 2.17 where we declare that two trees have the same leaf-profile if their leaf profiles are the same.

```
same_leaves(L1,L2):- leaves(L1)=leaves(L2).

leaves(nil)=[].
leaves(t(L,Lb,R))=leaves(L)<>[Lb]<>leaves(R).
```

Program 2.17 The **same_leaves** program

Expressions can appear anywhere in clauses, including in the head of a clause. This allows a simple definition for the increment relation, where the pair (X,Y) is in the `inc` relation if Y is equal to X+1:

        inc(X,X+1).   % expression in head

Expressions as top-level queries

We can ask the *L&O* system to evaluate an expression at the top-level using an '=?' query. For example, to append the three lists [1], [a] and [2] together, we would use the query:

        [1]<>[a]<>[2]=?

to which the system responds with:

        [1,a,2]

Expressions that cross class boundaries

As with relations, there may be functions which are not defined completely (or even partially) within the class body where they are used. In order to invoke a function which we know is defined in another class template we use an extended form of expression syntax where the label is mentioned explicitly. Thus an expression of the form

        label:Expression

indicates that the `Expression` is to be evaluated using the equations defined in the program identified by `label`. Alternatively, class rules can be used to inherit function definitions as well as relation definitions. In the case where a function is partially defined locally and partially inherited, then no special mechanism is required: the local portion of the definition will be used where appropriate and the non-local definition will be used otherwise.

If there are no defining equations for a function then we must use some extra syntax in order to differentiate the function expression from a regular term. In this case we prefix the expression with a colon:

        :Expression

Such an expression will be automatically evaluated in the context of the inherited classes. Actually, this syntax is shorthand for

        super:Expression

which states more obviously the context in which the given expression is to be evaluated.

Quoted expressions

Applications which involve some degree of metalogical programming are very common in Prolog. In such circumstances we would often wish to quote terms which syntactically resemble expressions. For example, any compiler program for our equations would be required to manipulate the names of expressions rather than their values. In order to handle these terms we have to be able to quote terms and expressions. Quoting a term has the effect of suppressing any interpretation of the term (or any of its sub-terms) as an expression – its value is simply itself. Our syntax for quoted terms is:

    'E

where E is any expression, for example

    '(N+1)

Quoted terms are not interpreted as being evaluable even if they would be so otherwise. So, the value of this expression is the term:

    N+1

even though + is a (predefined) function.

A classic example of the use of quote is in **assert**ing an equation, particularly if the equation involves functions which are already partially defined. Suppose that the first equation for **foo** made

    foo(X)=f(X).

Then, if we wanted to assert another equation for the **foo** function (say), we need to use:

    ...,assert(' (foo(X)=bar(X))),...

Using quote here prevents both the left-hand side of the equation (which is syntactically another expression involving the **foo** symbol) and the right-hand side of the equation (which is also syntactically an expression involving **bar**) being interpreted as expressions. Without the quote, the equation that is actually asserted might have looked like:

    ...,assert(f(X)=bar(X)),...

which is probably not what the programmer has in mind.

A related operator to ' is unquote or '#'. '#' is a standard built-in function from terms which denote expressions to the values of those expressions. Thus we have the equivalence

    #('E)≡E

With a combination of ' and # the programmer can explicitly control the evaluation of expressions.

A quoted expression can be selectively unquoted within its structure also; by means of the '#' operator. This is similar to the Common LISP comma operator ',' [Sea82] which also unquotes its argument. Such unquoted expressions are evaluated in the same context as the expression which contains the back-quoted term. The effect is of providing a template or program fragment which has holes in it; the value of the whole expression is the quoted structure with the holes filled in by their values. For example, if we wanted to have a term in which the main function symbol was '<>' (which we have already defined to be the **append** function) but which had arguments which were values rather than terms, then we could write the term:

    '(#(2+4)<> #(X*Y))

If X and Y were bound to 7 and 5 respectively, this term would have the value:

    6<>35

A variation of back-quote and hash is the quote-hash which quotes only the function symbol of a term unquoting all the arguments:

    '#(2+4<>X*Y)

which has the same value as the previous example.

2.3   Mutable theories

In many applications it is necessary to perform real or destructive assignments of variables (destructive because the old value of the variable is not available after re-assignment). Primitives which can implement destructive assignment are necessary because not all applications are actually declarative in nature. One example of this would be a ticket reservation system such as a theatre ticket booking system or an airline seat reservation system. A customer would be justifiably angry if a theatre seat or airline ticket was sold to another customer as well. Once a seat has been booked it is simply no longer available – the availability of the seat has been retracted from the database – and any computerized ticket reservation system must respect this seat assignment.

In a language such as Smalltalk state is expressed as the current values of an object's local variables (the instance variables). In particular, since Smalltalk variables have other objects as their values, the latest state of those objects are always available to the Smalltalk variable. This situation does not arise naturally in a declarative language such as Prolog. A logic programming language is referentially transparent: the value of a variable is independent of the description of the value. Thus we can guarantee that the value of X is 5 if we know that

```
X=2+3
```

In a procedural language (such as Pascal) the value of a variable depends on its prior history. Thus we can have the two sets of Pascal statements:

```
X:=2; X:=X+3;
```

and

```
X:=X+3; X:=2;
```

which are identical except for their order, but which result in completely different values for X (5 and 2 respectively). Similarly, the value of a Smalltalk object also depends on its prior history. These are so-called mutable objects as opposed to immutable objects which do not change over time. At first sight it may seem that we are not able to represent mutable objects in our *L&O* notation since logic programming does not itself include the concept of mutable variables. However, since labels are just terms we can get some of the effect of mutable objects by allowing programs to return new labels.

```
train(Speed,Cl,Cn):{
    ...
    change_sp(Newspeed)=train(Newspeed,Cl,Cn).
    ...
}
```

Program 2.18 A function that returns trains at new speeds

So, for example, we can change the speed of a train by defining a special function that returns a new label, as in Program 2.18, that reflects the train's new speed. An expression of the form:

```
train(90,green,britain):change_sp(200)=?
```

results in the value

```
train(200,green,britain)
```

which can be used in a subsequent call to find out the length of time a 1000 mile journey will take at 200 mph:

```
...,(train(90,green,britain):change_sp(200)):
              journey_time(1000,Time),...
```

This ability to return new labels as a result of some computations is not exactly the same as having mutable objects since we are not actually changing an existing object, merely creating a new one. This means that all the relevant consumers of the train at its new speed must be given the new label explicitly, otherwise there could be an inconsistency in the interpretation of the train's speed.

2.3.1   `assert`, `retract` and *L&O* programs

In a conventional Prolog system we would use primitives such as **assert** and **retract** to achieve the effect of destructive assignment. In our *L&O* language the basic Prolog primitives of **assert**, **retract** and clause are naturally extended to allow clauses and equations to be added to (or subtracted from) class bodies and to allow class rules to be added and subtracted also. Of course any such programs which actually use **assert** and **retract** may be hard to justify logically but we do not concern ourselves with this aspect in this discussion. By asserting class rules we can create new instances of a class. For example, if we want to be able to create a new person `jim` (say) then we can do so using a call such as:

```
...,assert((jim<=person(male,30))),...
```

Thereafter, to access `jim`'s attributes we use the normal querying techniques:

```
jim:age(X)?
```

If we need to be able to **assert** into a class body then we use a small fragment of a class template as the argument to **assert**:

```
...,assert(jim:{age(31)}),...
```

This condition would have the effect of adding the clause:

```
age(31).
```

to `jim`'s class body. We can add any number of clauses to a class body in a call to **assert** by having a mini-class body in the call. Notice that since we defined `jim` originally using an overriding class rule the above call to **assert** has the effect of overriding the default value of `jim`'s age. The **retract** primitive is extended in a similar way to **assert**: we can **retract** class rules and clauses (and equations) from within class bodies. So, for example, to retract `jim`'s age we would use the condition:

```
...,retract(jim:{age(X):-B}),...
```

This removes the **age** clause from `jim`'s class body and to bind the variable `X` to **31** and the variable `B` would be bound to **true**. This is directly analogous to Prolog's normal **retract** primitive. Using **retract** in this way has an interesting property – since `jim` has been asserted to be a 30 year old person, when `jim`'s age is explicitly retracted the old default value becomes valid again. If we were to ask `jim`'s **age** after the **retract** we would get this old value of 30 again. Thus we can use **assert** and **retract** to implement 'default' values in an object oriented database.

In some implementations of *L&O*, **assert** and **retract** may be constrained so that only clauses which have been dynamically asserted can be subsequently retracted. This allows the *L&O* language processor to generate better code in the normal case where the *L&O* program has been written by the programmer and where it is unlikely that either **assert** or **retract** will be performed.

Since it is possible that a normal Prolog program can be encapsulated within a class template, and since such a program may also invoke primitives such as **assert** and **retract** we must also deal with the situation where an **assert** or **retract** call does not mention a label explicitly. In this case we will assume that the intended label is the **self** label. This has the advantage that different **assert**s occurring in different class templates will not interfere with each other; unless of course, the programmer wanted them to.

2.3.2 Dynamic variables in *L&O* programs

As we have already seen, a classical Prolog system has primitives which can add and remove clauses from the program. With these primitives it is possible to implement dynamic global variables.

For example, if we wanted to have a dynamic global variable u which was accessible from anywhere in the program then we might use an assertion such as:

u(Value).

to hold its value. To access the variable's value, we insert a condition of the form:

...,u(X),...

into the program; and to modify it we **retract** its old value and **assert** a new one:

...,retract(u(X)),assert(u(X+1)),...

Whilst very powerful, there can be massive performance penalties associated with using **assert** and **retract** to implement dynamic variables. This is because the **assert** primitive must, in general, invoke a Prolog compiler in order to add the **asserted** clause. The **retract** primitive is similarly expensive since it must retrieve the clause being deleted; which may involve searching and backtracking. Furthermore, this technique is clumsy to use and liable to errors on the part of the programmer.

In *L&O* we have a special kind of variable, called a *dynamic variable*, which is intended to be used in this kind of context. These variables can be assigned to and their value accessed in much the same way as variables in conventional programming languages. The difference between *L&O* dynamic variables and variables in 'C' (say) is that our variables can take on any term as their value.

Unlike assertions which have been generated using **assert**, when a dynamic variable is re-assigned then its old value is lost. This restriction can allow a more efficient implementation of dynamic variables; especially since many Prolog systems already have some support for re-assignable variables (albeit often in different guises). The *L&O* language processor will make use of these facilities where possible, otherwise the implementation of dynamic variables may be through `assert` and `retract`.

A dynamic variable is declared using an *initialisation statement* in a class body. This simultaneously declares the dynamic variable for that class and defines its initial or default value. For example, the variable `balance` may declared in the `account` class as in Program 2.19.

```
account:{
    ...
    balance:=0.
    ...
    }.
```

Program 2.19 The `account` class template

The use of the `:=` operator distinguishes the `balance` declaration from a zero-ary function. In general, an initialization statement is similar to an equation, except that there may be only one such statement for each variable:

```
label:{
    ...
    variable:=value:-Cond₁,...,Condₙ.
    ...
    }.
```

The programmer should ensure that the conditions $Cond_i$ do not fail, otherwise the results are not defined.

A dynamic variable's value can be accessed in an expression exactly as if it were a zero-ary function. Within its defining class body its name suffices, and outside it either the form:

```
label:variable
```

or just

```
:variable
```

can be used, again as for zero-ary functions. Dynamic variables can be re-assigned using the `:=` operator as a goal. Thus the `credit` program in Program 2.20 can be used to increase an account's balance.

```
account:{
    balance:=0.      % declare the balance var
    ...
    credit(X):-
        balance:=balance+X.
    ...
}.
```

Program 2.20 A method for credit-ting an account

Any sub-class of a class which contains dynamic variables also has copies of them. So, if we had a special purchase account (say), which was defined through inheritance:

    purchase<<account

then any purchase 'object' also has a balance. If we were to ask a purchase account to be credited then the normal credit method defined in the account class will correctly alter the purchase account's balance. So the query

    purchase:credit(10)?

will increment the balance variable in the purchase class rather than in the account class. Variables which are associated with other classes can also be re-assigned using the := operator. The name of the variable must simply be prefixed by the appropriate label, as in:

    ...,account:balance:=30,...

Finally, we would emphasise that dynamic variables do not have an adequate logical characterization. When we look at the relationship between *L&O* and logic programming we shall ignore them. Furthermore, as a matter of programming style, we recommend that only restricted and essential use is made of them. On the other hand, they are none-the-less important in being able to construct practical large-scale applications. Furthermore, using them, we can also differentiate the use of primitives such as **assert** and **retract** for maintaining programs compared to simply recording values of variables.

2.4 Summary

In this chapter we have introduced the basic elements of an *L&O* program. We have seen how programs are grouped together into *classes*, and that class rules can be used to establish inheritance relationships between programs.

Within each class, we can use clauses to describe relations, and equations to describe functions; as may be appropriate to the task. The equational notation and the clausal notation are combined into a whole, allowing clauses to reference functions (using expressions in arguments) and also allowing functions to reference relations (via the conditional part of equations).

In the following chapters we explore the potential of *L&O* as a programming language – we see how the language gives rise to a new class of programming techniques and how large-scale applications can be built.

CHAPTER THREE

Programming techniques

In this chapter we look at some of the programming techniques used to build *L&O* programs. Initially, we shall see how class templates can be used to structure large programs into collections of modules. As a module language, the *L&O* notation permits powerful variants of modules including parameterized or generic modules.

Another programming style which is natural to the *L&O* language is the data driven programming technique. This is an extension of standard object oriented programming style, where the object which is sent a message is generalized to include expressions. Data driven programming is particularly suitable in those situations where we can talk of a 'sub-language' within the application. For example, a graphics sub-language might contain expressions which correspond to graphical objects; the manipulation of these graphical expressions is simplified by using the data driven programming technique.

We also explore in more depth the issues which are involved in using class templates for knowledge representation. Of particular interest to us is the dual structure of knowledge: the traditional 'isa' structure – which is described using the inheritance relation between objects – and the 'part-of' or 'consists-of' structure – which relates how objects can be composed of component objects. In this latter context we introduce the notion of *broadcasting* a message to multiple objects (for example, broadcasting a message to all the carriages that make up a train to find out if the guard is present on the train).

3.1 Class templates and modules

The programming language Prolog inherits from standard logic a very flat structure: a Prolog program consists of a set of clauses, each of which is typically both small and simple. There is no notion of a hierarchical decomposition of a Prolog program such as may be found in conventional block structured languages like Pascal or 'C'.

The flat structure of large Prolog programs (such as those written by more than one person) can be difficult to understand. A large program may include several thousand clauses and define hundreds of different predicates. It is simply not the case that all predicates are equally central to a given application; yet the language of clauses does not allow the programmer to reflect the natural structure of the predicates within the program. For example, an application might include a group of clauses or equations to define a list sorting program as in Program 3.1.

```
sort([])=[].
sort([El|List])=insert(El,sort(List)).

insert(El,[])=[El].
insert(El,[E|List])=[El,E|List]:- El<E.
insert(El,[E|L1])=[E|insert(El,L1)]):- not El<E.
```

Program 3.1 A sort function

A cursory glance at the text of any application program which includes Program 3.1 as a component may not immediately reveal that the **insert** function, which is an auxiliary program used to implement the **sort** program, is not useful to other parts of the application.

We can wrap up the **sort** function into a class template; as a result, we can more readily identify the natural structure of both the **sort** program itself and the complete application program. The **simple** class template in Program 3.2 identifies those functions needed to implement the **sort** function itself. Furthermore the grouping implied by the syntax can be taken advantage of by a compiler: it can optimize the programs defined in the class template together rather than trying to optimize each relation and function independently.

3.1.1 Generic modules

We can imagine that it could be necessary for **sort** to be able to sort more than one kind of list, equally it may be necessary to sort lists in reverse order. Traditionally, in Prolog, we make a program like this more powerful and flexible by parameterising it; in particular, we can parameterise Program 3.1 by means of the ordering relation used by **sort** and **insert** to compare elements.

The name of the actual ordering relation to use must be passed to the **sort** program when it is invoked:

```
...,sort([3,1,2],'<'),...
```

```
simple:{
    sort([])=[].
    sort([El|List])=insert(El,sort(List)).

    insert(El,[])=[El].
    insert(El,[E|List])=[El,E|List] :-
        El<E.
    insert(El,[E|L1])=[E|insert(El,L1)]) :-
        not El<E
}.
```

Program 3.2 The sort module as a class template

In order to modify Program 3.1, we must add the new ordering parameter to the sort equations and to the insert equations wherever the new parameter is needed to compare elements (see Program 3.3).

```
sort([],Ord)=[].
sort([El|List],Ord)=insert(El,sort(List,Ord),Ord).

insert(El,[],Ord)=[El].
insert(El,[E|List],Ord)=[El,E|List] :-
    Ord(El,E).
insert(El,[E|L1],Ord)=[E|insert(El,L1,Ord)]) :-
    not Ord(El,E).
```

Program 3.3 A parameterized sort function

Readers who are unfamiliar with certain Prolog systems (in particular MacProlog) may notice that we have used a rather strange construction in Program 3.3. When we actually call the 'order' parameter, we use a variable predicate symbol:

```
Ord(El,E)
```

In many Prolog systems this would not be possible so directly, instead we would have to write:

```
...,call(Ord,El,E),...
```

whose meaning is much the same. This call goal is true whenever the goal

```
...,Ord(El,E),...
```

is true for any given instantiation of `Ord`. If the *n*-argument form of `call` is not available, it might be necessary to use the term constructor primitive '`=..`' to dynamically construct the call:

```
...,C=..[Ord,El,E],call(C),...
```

This form requires the underlying Prolog system to construct the call from a list of the arguments and then execute it. This is clearly a rather expensive way of comparing two elements.

Notice that, in addition to being used where it is needed, the `Order` parameter must be 'passed around' the `sort` program in order to ensure that it can be applied when it is needed. This style of parameterization can lead to many occurrences of the new parameter(s). From the point of program design, this style of parameterising programs is rather inelegant since it requires that we pass the control parameter around the program so that we can apply it where needed even though it is never inspected. Thus we must mention the variable `Ord` in *every* `sort` equation as well as in every `insert` equation in order for us to be able to use it where it is actually needed.

This proliferation of parameters can be avoided when we use *L&O* programs; especially where the labels have parameters. We can parameterise a module to construct *generic modules*. A generic module is one which is parameterised in the label – we have already seen a simple generic module, in Program 2.2 on page 37, where we had a single program which described a class of trains rather than a single one. The module parameter that generalizes the `sort` function in Program 3.4 references an ordering theory; this method of adding parameters leads to a much more obvious program for generalized sorting.

In Program 3.4, we only need to mention the `Order` parameter where it is declared – i.e., in the `simple` label – and where it is needed to determine if one element is `less` than another.

```
simple(Order):{
    sort([])=[].
    sort([El|List])=insert(El,sort(List)).

    insert(El,[])=[El].
    insert(El,[E|List])=[El,E|List] :-
        Order:less(El,E).
    insert(El,[E|L1])=[E|insert(El,L1)]) :-
        not Order:less(El,E)
}.
```

Program 3.4 The `simple` sorting class template

When we want to invoke a **sort** using this style of program we will specify in the call which ordering to use. One suitable element ordering which we might use is that of numbers in their natural ordering as shown in Program 3.5. In our implementation of such an ordering we define a set of axioms which characterizes what we know to be true of natural numbers; although it must at least include a definition for the **less** predicate.

```
natural:{
    less(I1,I2):- I1<I2
    }.
```

Program 3.5 The **natural** theory of numbers

Given such a definition, the expression which indicates a sort of a list of natural numbers in their natural ordering is:

```
simple(natural):sort([3,1,2])=?
```

which reduces to the answer:

```
[1,2,3]
```

In order to sort lists in descending order we construct another theory which knows about numbers in descending order.

```
descending:{
    less(I1,I2):- I1>I2
    }.
```

Program 3.6 The **descend** theory of numbers

Such a class template is shown in Program 3.6, and we can use the same **simple sort** program to sort lists in descending order:

```
simple(descending):sort([3,1,2])=?
```

This expression reduces to:

```
[3,2,1]
```

In Program 3.4, we chose to parameterize the **simple** module with a whole *theory* of element ordering, as opposed to simply the ordering *predicate*. When we use a condition such as:

```
...,Order:less(E1,E),...
```

we are, in effect, querying the parameter theory – **Order** – for an instance of the **less** relation in that theory. This style of parameterization allows the implementer of the **sort** module to decide which predicates/functions are needed: in the **simple** program we only need the **less** relation, whereas a slightly different implementation of sorting may have required other relations. Furthermore, this style of parameterisation also leads to a powerful extension of the notion of generic modules; one which allows us to *compose* theories into more complex structures.

More complex orderings

We are not limited to simple orderings such as **natural** and **descending** when sorting lists; we can construct more complex orderings such as one based on a *cartesian product* of two domains. Each point in such a cartesian product consists of a coordinate pair represented by a term such as (x,y) where the first coordinate x comes from the first domain or dimension and the second coordinate y comes from the second dimension. To compare two points – such as (2,5) and (2,4) – where the first coordinate consists of ascending numbers and the second consists of descending numbers we would use the query:

```
cart(natural,descending):less((2,5),(2,4))?
```

Program 3.7 describes some of what we know of cartesian products as a generic module which has as parameters the theories corresponding to the two dimensions. As with the natural and descending class templates, the **cart** class template must at least contain a definition for the **less** predicate.

In our cartesian product of two dimensions, we define one pair to be **less** than another if the first elements of the pairs are **less** according to the first component dimension; and if the first elements of the two pairs are equal then the one pair is **less** than another if the second elements or the pairs are **less** according to the second dimension. Thus, in the example above, the pair (2,5) is less than (2,4) since the first arguments are the same and **less(5,4)** is true in **descending**. Combining the Program 3.4 with the **cart** theory in Program 3.7, we can sort a list of pairs:

```
cart(O1,O2):{
    less((X,Y),(U,V)):-
        O1:less(X,U).
    less((X,Y),(X,V)):-
        O2:less(Y,V).
    ...}
```

Program 3.7 The **cart** class template for cartesian products

```
simple(cart(natural,descending)):
    sort([(3,4),(1,6),(3,2),(10,5)])=?
```

```
= [(1,6), (3,4), (3,2), (10,5)]
```

This ability to express different forms of ordering, effectively by composing ordering relations in a cartesian product, is absent in the module systems of most programming languages.

3.2   Data driven programming

In many *L&O* programs we can easily identify an 'external' object that is being described. For example, if we have a class template about trains then the object in question is a train. We can measure the correctness of a *L&O* description of a train by looking at a real train. We have also seen that theories (i.e., class templates) in *L&O* programs can be viewed and used as modules. With such programs it is slightly less obvious what concrete object a module such as simple in Program 3.4 might refer to. However, we can still claim that a module class template has a logical structure – a sort module contains a set of definitions about a related set of functions and relations which are about sorting.

The *data driven programming* technique allows us to consider another style of programming where the program structure reflects the expressions that are to be manipulated and processed rather than some external notion of a physical object. This technique is particularly suited to the implementation of sub-languages within the host Prolog (or *L&O*) language, where some set of terms is to be given an extra interpretation.

For example, Prolog systems normally have a class of terms which represent arithmetic expressions – such as $2 + 3$ – and a set of predicates which are defined over terms of this kind – such as is and '<'. The standard is built-in predicate is true of two terms when their arithmetic interpretation is the same and the '<' predicate is true when the first expression is less than the second.

The set of terms which denote arithmetic expressions and the set of predicates which are defined over those terms form a *sub-language* within the standard logic programming framework. There are often many such sub-languages in a typical commercial Prolog system, each relating to a specific domain – such as file handling, string processing and graphics. Here we are interested in the programming techniques that we might use to implement such sub-languages.

To explore this we look at a version of arithmetic expressions which parallel the standard arithmetic expression sub-language. In our version of arithmetic expressions, we would use a term of the form:

```
plus(i(3),times(i(5),minus(i(2),i(4))))
```

to represent the expression $3 + 5 * (2 - 4)$. We want to construct an evaluator – called **was** – for such expressions. In regular Prolog we can easily construct such a program. The clauses in Program 3.8 analyse separately each type of expression that the **was** evaluator might encounter.

So, we have one **was** clause for addition (i.e., implementing **plus** expressions) another clause for **times** and so on. (This is much the same technique as was actually used in early Prolog implementations of arithmetic.)

```
was(plus(X,Y),Z):-
    was(X,X1), was(Y,Y1),   % evaluate the arguments
    Z is X1+Y1.             % actual addition
was(times(X,Y),Z):-
    was(X,X1),
    was(Y,Y1),
    Z is X1*Y1.
    ...
was(i(X),X).
```

Program 3.8 An evaluator for **was** expressions

If our **was** evaluator forms part of a published library of predicates, we might well want to allow users of **was** to extend the system themselves. Allowing for such expandability is a good insurance policy. In any successful application or language system there are usually many more users than programmers; allowing users to extend the system themselves potentially removes a bottle-neck which can result from the inability of the programmers to keep up with users' demands.

For various reasons, including a desire to protect the rights of the author of the **was** program, we may not want to provide users with access to the source of our **was** program. So, it would be useful to be able to extend programs like **was** without access to the original source. It is quite possible to do this in Prolog by making use of the meta-variable facility.

Program 3.9 shows a generic **was** program which knows about unary and binary expressions. Written in an extended Prolog – with function and predicate variables (see Section 3.1.1), this generic **was** evaluator 'knows' about unary and binary expressions in general; but none in particular. It needs to be augmented by a collection of programs, each of which implements a specific type of expression. Program 3.10 shows how we might write the implementation parts of the **plus**, **times** and **i** expressions.

Using this framework to implement **was**, we can add a new **user** expression type without having to modify the **was** program itself simply by providing a definition

```
was(F(X,Y),Z):-              % binary operators
    was(X,X1), was(Y,Y1),
    F(X1,Y1,Z).
was(F(X),Z):-                % unary operators
    was(X,X1),
    F(X1,Z).
```

Program 3.9 The generic **was** program

for the new expression:

```
user(X,Y,Z):-...
```

The new definition is completely separate from the **was** evaluator, and therefore there is no need for a user to be able to modify or even access the source of **was**. A call to **was** may contain an arbitrary mix of predetermined and user defined expressions:

```
...,was(plus(user(i(2),i(3),i(5))), X),...
```

In the evaluation of a **was** condition the various operators show a dual role: that of a data expression and that of a predicate symbol (i.e., a program name). This duality is the essence of data driven programming.

A practical sub-language will often define more than one predicate and function over the terms in the sub-language. These predicates (and functions) may involve different uses for the language terms. For example, in our version of the arithmetic expression sub-language, we might want to be able to do more than simply evaluate expressions; we might want to differentiate them also. In order to differentiate expresions, we must extend our notation to include *symbolic variables* (we can only differentiate an expression with respect to a symbolic variable which may appear in the expression).

Program 3.11 shows how, along the lines of our first definition of **was** in Program 3.8, we could define **diff** using a separate clause for each type of expression. As with the **was** evaluator, we are equally keen to allow our users to extend the **diff** evaluator to differentiate the user defined expressions. Again, we would very

```
plus(X,Y,Z):- Z is X+Y.
times(X,Y,Z):- Z is X*Y.
i(X,X).
```

Program 3.10 An implementation of specific **was** expressions

```
diff(plus(F,G),DX,plus(DF,DG)):-
    diff(F,DX,DF),
    diff(G,DX,DG).
```

```
diff(i(X),DX,0).              % the differential of a constant is zero
diff(v(DX),DX,1).             % the differential of a variable is 1
diff(v(DX),DY,0)  :- DX!=DY.
```

Program 3.11 The differentiation of was expressions

much prefer it if those same users did not have to modify the diff program itself in order to implement their extensions.

In this case, our technique of using function and predicate variables to implement the individual evaluation/differentiation functions is no longer adequate. This is because we are now required to define a collection of programs for each of the operators that may occur in a diff expression as well as a was expression. Unfortunately, we have already defined the individual programs for plus, times etc. (and user of course) to evaluate their arguments as opposed to differentiating them. Whilst we could change them so that instead of evaluating expressions they differentiate them, this would be at the cost of not being able to evaluate expressions. What was an elegant technique for programming begins to look more complicated and less easy to use. What we need is a general technique for manipulating sub-languages.

L&O allows us to generalise the Prolog technique by making use of the labels in queries to represent expressions. In this approach a separate class template is constructed for each type of expression in the sub-language that we may encounter. These templates provide methods for both evaluating and differentiating expressions. Program 3.12 shows the class templates for some of the expressions that we are likely to encounter in our sub-language.

Program 3.13 shows the structure of the *L&O* program for a user type of expression; and it also contains methods for was and diff.

We evaluate an expression by putting the expression to be evaluated as the label of a was query:

```
plus(i(3),times(i(5),minus(i(2),i(4)))):was(X)?
```

we differentiate an expression with a similar query:

```
times(v(x),plus(i(2),v(y))):diff(x,X)?
```

We call this technique *data driven programming* because the data (i.e., the expression to be evaluated) is placed where we would normally expect to see a program name! Data driven programming is quite a powerful – if somewhat underused – programming technique for logic programming. In Chapter 5 we look in some

```
plus(X,Y):{
     was(Z):-                        % evaluate plus expression
          X:was(X1),
          Y:was(Y1),
          Z is X1+Y1.

     diff(DX,plus(X1,Y1)):- % differentiate plus
          X:diff(DX,X1),
          Y:diff(DX,Y1).
     }
i(X):{
     was(X).
     diff(DX,0).
     }
v(X):{                              % v(X) represents a variable
     diff(X,1).
     diff(Y,0):-X!=Y.
     }
```

Program 3.12 An *L&O* implementation of expression evaluation

detail at another major example of this style of programming – graphics. As we shall see in this case the data referred to are the various graphic objects and the programming involved refers to the various calculations and operations we wish to perform on our pictures.

3.3   The structure of objects

A prime objective of any programming language, particularly a logic programming language, must be to permit programmers to construct succinct models of the real world. Constructing a model involves observation and abstraction: observing

```
user(X,Y):{                         % A user defined type of expression
     was(Z):- ...                   % How to evaluate it
     diff(DX,Z):- ...               % How to differentiate it
     }
```

Program 3.13 The **user** expression template

phenomena and abstracting the relevant features. An important part of this process is identifying the apparent structure of objects. It is worth seeing how features of the *L&O* language can aid in this process.

We identify two ways that objects can be structured: by *inclusion* and by *specialization.* By inclusion, we mean that an object can often be thought to be composed of sub-objects; for example, a train may have an engine and some carriages each of which are objects themselves. On the other hand, however an object is composed, we might see it as a special case or type of another object. A steam train is a train whose engine uses steam. Such a train is a train like any other, but we know more about it: a steam train is a special case of a train. Similarly, to describe logic theories we can use analogous ways of relating them to each other: a theory might be constructed by including references to other theories, and/or a theory may be a specialization of one or more other theories.

3.3.1   Inclusion and broadcasting

Inclusion refers to the 'part-of' or 'consists-of' structure of an object. We use arguments of the label which are themselves labels, to denote the fact that the incorporated labels are included in the object; the exact interpretation of the included labels depends on the definitions of the programs within the body of the class. For example we might say that a train consists of an engine and a set of carriages. The label which identifies such a train might look like:

```
train(steam_engine,
     [first_cl1,first_cl2,buffet_car,
     second_cl1,second_cl2,guards_van])
```

In Program 3.14, we see how we might compute the maximum speed of a given train from the power of its engine and the load of its carriages by using data from a label parameter.

```
train(E,C):{...
     speed(P/W):- E:power(P),      % find engine's power rating
          C:load(W).               % note – not the final version
}
```

Program 3.14 To compute the speed of a **train**

Each type of carriage which can be part of a train will have a description as a class template, and will contain definitions – such as **load** – which characterize

```
guards_van:{...
    load(20).
    guard_present.
}
first_cl_i:{...
    load(35).
...}           .
steam_engine:{...
    power(10000).
}
```

Program 3.15 The parts of a train

the individual types of carriage. For example, Program 3.15 expresses the fact that a guard's van is moderately heavy and has a guard on it.

In Program 3.15 we also declare that a First Class carriage is heavier than the guard's van, and that the power of a steam engine is 10,000 horsepower.

The query to find out such a train's maximum speed would be:

```
train(steam_engine,
     [first_cl_1,first_cl_2,buffet_car,
     second_cl_1,second_cl_2,
     guards_van]):speed(S)?
```

In order to evaluate this query, the list of carriages will be 'asked' to compute their total weight by adding up the individual weights of each carriage. To do this properly we need to be able to *broadcast* a message to more than one object at a time.

Broadcast messages

A broadcast message is one which is sent to more than one object at a time. In fact, there are several different types of broadcasting depending on the nature of the query. We might, for example, wish to make sure that the carriages in the train are all in good repair. We can express this using the broadcast query:

```
..., [first_cl_1,...,guards_van]&:good_repair,...
```

In this example, the whole train is in good repair only if all its carriages are. Such a condition is satisfied if all the objects in the list

```
[first_cl_1,...,guards_van]
```

agree on the message **good_repair**, i.e., if **good_repair** is true in every theory identified in the list.

In general we identify several types of broadcast message to a list of objects including 'and-casting', 'or-casting' and 'map-casting'.

and-casting   In and-casting the broadcast message has to succeed for each element of the collection. An and-cast condition (written with &:)

$$\dots, [\text{E}_1, \text{E}_2, \dots, \text{E}_n] \&: \text{Q}, \dots$$

to a collection of objects is equivalent to a conjunction of queries:

$$\dots, \text{E}_1 : \text{Q}, \text{E}_2 : \text{Q}, \dots, \text{E}_n : \text{Q}, \dots$$

Program 3.16 gives a straightforward method for implementing and-casting.

```
[]&:M.                          % and-cast of an empty set is always true
[E|L]&:M :- E:M,                % send the query to first element
    L&:M.                       % do the rest
```

Program 3.16 The implementation of 'and-casting'

or-casting   In or-casting (written using '\:') the message has to succeed for at least one element of the collection. An or-cast of a message

$$\dots, [\text{E}_1, \text{E}_2, \dots, \text{E}_n] \backslash : \text{Q}, \dots$$

to a list of objects is equivalent to a disjunction:

$$\dots, (\text{E}_1 : \text{Q}; \text{E}_2 : \text{Q}; \dots; \text{E}_n : \text{Q}), \dots$$

For example, for the safety of the travelling public, it is necessary that every train has a guard on it. It is necessary to prove this condition at various times when we are running a train service (for example, prior to a train leaving the platform). To show this we have to search the carriages to make sure that there is a guard on the train, which we can do with the condition:

$$\dots, [\text{car}_1, \dots, \text{car}_n] \backslash : \text{guard\_present}, \dots$$

This broadcast condition succeeds if there is a guard on at least one of the carriages. As with and-casting, we can implement or-casting via a set of clauses, as in Program 3.17.

```
[E|L]\:M  :- E:M.          % does msg work?
[E|L]\:M  :- L\:M.         % try the rest
```

Program 3.17 The implementation of 'or-casting'

map-casting   The third type of broadcasting can be called *map-casting*, since it is closely related to the high level **map** operator. Just as the **map** operator specifies the use of a predicate or function over a list of elements, so we use map-casting to send a message to a list of objects and we collect the result, either as a list or as an accumulated value.

Program 3.18 shows how to implement the **map_cast** function which 'returns' a list of the results of sending a message to a list. The **acc_cast** function is similar to **map_cast**, except that it accumulates the returned values into a single value. It has two extra arguments which represent the 'accumulator' function and the 'zero' for that function.

Notice that the construction **#F(...)** which is used in Program 3.18 in the definition of **acc_cast**, is required to force the interpretation of the variable function symbol as an 'evaluable' function.

Given this discussion on the nature of broadcasting, we can perhaps see that our earlier attempt to define speed was a little over-simplified. This is primarily because the condition

$$\ldots, [\texttt{first\_cl}_1, \ldots, \texttt{guards\_van}]:\texttt{load(W)}, \ldots$$

which we had in Program 3.14 would be better described as a broadcast condition – in particular an **acc_cast**. Program 3.19 shows the correct form of the rule which reflects our intentions about how the speed of the train is calculated. Notice that the 'zero' for the '+' function is 0.

There are many possible variations of broadcasting; one – *filter-casting* – combines certain aspects of the map-cast and and-cast. In this form of broadcast expression we send a message to a list of objects (as in map-casting) and the value of the filter-cast is the sub-list of those objects which agree on the message. We can use filter-casting to filter out those objects from a list which *fail* to re-

```
map_cast([],M)=[].
map_cast([E|L],M)=[X|map_cast(L,M)]  :- E:M(X).

acc_cast([],M,Z,F)=Z.
acc_cast([E|L],M,Z,F) =
     acc_cast(L,M,#F(X,Z),F)  :- E:M(X).  % Note use of #
```

Program 3.18 The implementation of 'map-casting'

```
train(E,C):{
    speed(P/W):-E:power(P),
        W=acc_cast(C,load,0,+)
        }
```

Program 3.19 The speed of a train using broadcasting

spond to messages. So, we might want to build a list of those carriages that have spare capacity in them, for example. The query expression:

$$[car_1,\ldots,car_n]\&^{\hat{}}\ spare\_capacity=?$$

expresses this neatly. The list of carriages

$$[car_1,\ldots,car_n]$$

is filtered, removing all carriages which do not have any spare capacity. As with the other forms of broadcast, filter-casting can be easily described in the standard version of the *L&O* language, as we show in Program 3.20.

```
[] &^ M = [].
[O|L] &^ M = [O|L &^ M]:- O:M.   % M true in O?
[_|L] &^ M = L &^ M.             % Note: repeat of test is not needed
```

Program 3.20 The implementation of filter-casting

Although we can easily describe these various forms of broadcasting in terms of simpler, more primitive, types of constructs, we include them in the *L&O* system.

3.3.2   Specialization and inheritance

Recall that we identified *specialization* as a second way of structuring our knowledge into classes. A common application of the use of specialization is in the construction of classifications: for example if we wanted to describe a classification of the animal kingdom then we would almost certainly need to be able to express knowledge of the form:

> 'A bird is a two legged animal with feathers that flies'

and

> 'A penguin is a flightless bird'

It would be very convenient if we could directly express such knowledge in a simple way; especially in the case that we want to represent exceptions as well as general rules.

We are not limited to animals for the need to specialize. Another example from conventional computing is multiple window environments (an edit window is a special case of text window which is in turn a type of window and so on). We will also see how specialization is important in the description of pictures and of applications in general.

Class rules and inheritance

The logical equivalent of specialization is *inheritance*. When we say that a bird is a special case of animal we are stating that whatever is true of animals is also true of birds: the bird theory inherits a set of consequences from the animal theory. We can express this kind of relationship between theories by means of class rules such as:

```
bird <= animal.
```

Informally this could be read as 'animal implies bird': if something is true of animals then it is also true of birds. Of course there may be other facts which are true of birds other than what is true of animals.

```
bird:{...
    no_of_legs(2).
    mode(fly).
    covering(feathers)
}.
bird <= animal.
```

Program 3.21 *A* bird *is an* animal *which flies...*

Class rules can be combined with class bodies to complete the description of the nature of birds (see Program 3.21). This combination of class bodies and class rules is reminiscent of a common Prolog programming style. The class body is analogous to the collection of assertions which define the base cases of some predicate, whereas the class rule is analogous to a rule which defines the general cases in the predicate. The difference is primarily one of scope: a normal clause declares which individual tuples belong to a given relation; while class bodies and class rules declare which relations are in a given theory. Another difference is that class rules are not usually recursive, although recursive class rules are not prohibited in *L&O*.

Class rules can be used to give names to particular instances of objects. For example, to say that 'tom is a male person of age 33' we could use a class rule:

```
tom<=person(male,33)
```

Using class rules in this way allows us to establish the links between special names and general sets of rules. For example, the class rules

```
scotsman <= train(120,green,britain).
transpacific <= train(75,silver,'USA').
```

define the theories associated with scotsman and transpacific in terms of a general train theory. In terms of what is true about the **scotsman** (or the **transpacific**), there is no difference between using a class rule and a general class body about trains, or having a specific class body about each type of train.

Multiple inheritance

The **bird** example in Program 3.21 contains a definition for **mode** of travel in the class body which states that birds can fly. In general animals may have many modes of travel (e.g. walking, hopping, running etc.). We can express this multiplicity of modes of travel by including statements in the class body for **animal** which define these other modes; as we can see in Program 3.22.

```
animal:{...
    mode(walk).
    mode(hop).                % etc.
    ...}
```

Program 3.22 Animals can hop as well as walk

The question arises, given Program 3.22, what might we expect from a query such as:

```
bird:mode(X)?
```

Given the program as defined we are due three answers:

```
X=fly          % from class body for bird
X=walk         % from animal
X=hop          % from animal
```

The first answer **mode(fly)** follows directly from the class body for **bird** and **mode(walk)** and **mode(hop)** are true by virtue of the class rule and the fact that they are true in **animal**. This situation represents a degenerate example of *multiple*

`bird <= aeroplane.`

inheritance. In general, we can obtain multiple inheritance by having several class rules. In addition to a bird being an animal, it may also be interpreted as being an aeroplane.

In which case our query is likely to generate the further answer:

`X=taxi`

Multiple inheritance introduces the problem of deciding which method to use when there are two or more independent definitions for a method. In conventional object oriented languages, a method corresponds to a sequence of actions to be performed. In any given situation only one such sequence can be invoked – there is no possibility of trying out more than one method.

If multiple inheritance leads to a choice of methods which are accessible from more than one source then there is the dilemma of selecting which one to execute. This problem is often resolved in conventional object oriented programming languages, by imposing a standard search order: the ancestors of a class are searched in some predetermined order and the first one which contains an implementation of the method is used. The search order is often based on the order of declaration of ancestors in a class.

Unfortunately, such strategies are never quite sufficient, and can introduce extra problems. In some cases it is difficult to arrange the set of inheritance declarations so that the right method implementation is invoked, and where more than one method is involved this may not be possible. (A given search order may be correct for one method but wrong – i.e., lead to the wrong sequence of actions being selected – for another.)

In the context of logic programming, it is not such a great matter to allow multiple inheritance since we are not restricted to a single definition for a relation or function. Nor is it required that a relational method be deterministic. Thus in a logic based programming language the obvious course is to inherit *all* the possible definitions of a method from all the ancestors of a theory. The alternative routes to the definition of a relation can be searched – in a Prolog style implementation – using backtracking just as we use backtracking to find alternative solutions within a single definition.

Of course while it may be convenient for an object to have multiple inheritance from different sources, we may sometimes wish to restrict inheritance to only one source. Or perhaps we will wish to *override* a definition which is derived through inheritance with an explicit definition in a class body. Both of these strategies are possible in *L&O*.

Overriding inheritance

Suppose that we want to describe a theory of penguins; these are birds that cannot fly. The simple class rule:

```
penguin<=bird
```

is insufficient since this would allow us to conclude that penguins could fly. This would follow even if the class body for `penguin` included a local definition of `mode` which does not mention flying. We need to be able to express that penguins are birds, but they cannot fly. In other words whatever is true of birds is true of penguins except anything about a penguin's mode of travel.

We can express this by using a second form of class rule called the *overriding class rule*. This is written in the same way as a regular class rule except that we use the '`<<`' connective instead of '`<=`'. The meaning of a class rule such as

```
penguin<<bird.
```

is

> 'Any relations and functions which are defined in the `bird` theory are also part of `penguin` theory, except those relations or functions which have a local definition inside the class body for `penguin`, these latter definitions overriding those inherited from `bird`.'

On its own, an overriding class rule is not sufficient to eliminate the penguin's ability to fly. We must also include a local definition for `mode` in the class body for `penguin`. This local definition has the effect of completely redefining the `mode` predicate in `penguin` so that we now have the opportunity to omit flying. This new definition may still be augmented in the normal way by other class rules if these are of the normal type.

Clearly the overriding form of class rule also introduces an element of non-monotonic reasoning to our language: by adding true statements to the penguin definition we may remove consequences from the penguin theory which were previously true. As we shall see in Chapter 8 this non-monotonicity is equivalent to that introduced by negation-as-failure.

Differential inheritance

In our specification of a penguin, we stated that it 'was a bird which could not fly'. Suppose that we wanted the other modes of travel which are available to birds (such as hopping) still to be available for penguins? Because the overriding class rule *replaces* the definition of **mode** we must somehow recreate all these other **modes** that are already available in **bird** in the **penguin** program.

One way might be to repeat the complete definition of **mode** (less the flying bit of course) in the **penguin** program; however, this could become awkward if the original definition was inherited from a large number of class templates – if **bird** had a large number of class rules for example. This reconstruction is likely to be tedious and error prone.

What we would like to be able to express is that penguins are birds, except that they cannot fly – all other facts which are true of the **bird** theory, including the rest of the **mode** relation, should continue to be true of **penguin**. We can express this with a sensitive instrument called the *differential inheritance filter*. A differential inheritance filter acts as a constraint on normal class rules.

```
penguin<=bird-[mode(fly)].
```

Logically, we can say that a class rule with a differential filter subtracts part of the theory before transmitting it: the **penguin** theory includes the **bird** theory, except for any ground facts which unify with **mode(fly)**. In general, there may be several filters to apply. The general form of a class rule with a differential filter is:

```
lb(l₁,..,lᵢ)<=mb(m₁,..,mⱼ)-[p(p₁,..,pₖ),..,s(s₁,..,sₗ)].
```

where

```
p(p₁,...,pₖ),..,s(s₁,..,sₗ)
```

are patterns denoting the atoms which are not to be inherited. If we wanted to eliminate all consequences relating to mode of travel we would use:

```
penguin<=bird-[mode(_)].
```

or just:

```
penguin<=bird-[mode/1].
```

This latter form is reminiscent of the overriding class rule: if we were to mention all the locally defined predicates in the differential filter then we would get the same effect as the overriding class rule.

Self-reference

Our class body for **animal** in Program 3.22 includes a definition for **mode** which states that animals can walk:

```
mode(walk).
```

Which is true for most animals. Other modes of travel which are common to many animals include running and galloping, however, not all animals run *and* gallop. By observing the natural world one might conclude that only two-legged animals can run and only four-legged animals can gallop. How can we express this fact? We could have extra rules in each sub-class of animal of the form

```
mode(run).
```

for a two-legged animal, and

```
mode(gallop).
```

for a four-legged animal. However, our observations of the world of animals suggest a general rule for running and galloping which we prefer to express explicitly. So how can we express this? The 'natural' rules for **mode** which are consistent with our knowledge are:

```
mode(run) :-
      no_of_legs(2).
mode(gallop) :-
      no_of_legs(4).
```

These rules, as stated, are not adequate however, as the **no_of_legs** property is neither the same for all animals nor is it derivable from a parameter of the **animal** label. We have to be able to find out, in each individual case, how many legs an animal has before we can know whether it runs or gallops.

We could resolve the problem by adding an extra parameter to the **animal** label to encode the number of legs an animal has. The **no_of_legs** property can be derived from this label parameter. However, this would mean that we would have to change all our class rules which reference keywanimal in order to add the extra parameter. Furthermore, the number of legs that an animal has might not be a simple constant: it might require computation. (We might ask for instance, whether a monkey uses two, four or five legs – its tail – when swinging through trees?)

```
animal:{...
    mode(run):-
        self:no_of_legs(2).
    mode(gallop):-
        self:no_of_legs(4)
}
```

Program 3.23 The faster modes of travel in animals

Adding an extra parameter to the **animal** label is a somewhat error prone process which is similar to the process of adding an extra parameter to a Prolog predicate. We would prefer to find a way of stating the new rule without such a global change to our system.

Our rule for mode of travel is valid for all types of animals and therefore is properly part of the **animal** class; on the other hand the rule as defined depends on sub-relations which are specific to each class of animal and which cannot themselves be encapsulated inside the **animal** class.

To resolve this conflict we use **self** reference. **self** is a keyword which at all times identifies the original label – i.e., whenever an explicitly labelled condition appears in a rule or query (including the variable label case), then within that sub-computation the **self** keyword has that label as its value. In particular **self** is invariant under the use of class rules. We can use **self** to 'root' (sic) us back into the original class template no matter where the **self** keyword occurs textually.

Program 3.23 shows how we can use **self** to state properly the rules for mode of travel. To find out if birds run or gallop, we can use a condition of the form:

```
...,bird:mode(X),...
```

which can be reduced thus:

```
...,bird:mode(X),...              % self=bird
...,animal:mode(X),...            % self=bird
...,self:no_of_legs(2),...        % X=run
...,bird:no_of_legs(2),...        % self=bird
...,true,...
```

If we were to ask a similar question of **horse** (say) then the trace would show that **self** was bound to **horse** which has four legs, and which therefore gallops.

self in unification   We can also use the **self** keyword as a normal term. Consider the program about **tom** and **jane** shown in Program 3.24. These class rules state that **tom** and **jane** are examples of **person**, i.e., that

> 'anything which is true of 33 years old male person is also true of **tom** and anything which is true of 2 years old females is true of **jane**.'

```
tom<=person(male,33).                                              (III.i)
jane<=person(female,2).                                            (III.ii)
```

Program 3.24 A program about `tom` and `jane`

As Program 3.25 shows, the class body for **person** indicate that people like children, and that people like those who like them. The second rule involves the **self** keyword.

```
person(Sex,Age):{...
     age=Age.                                                      (III.iii)
     like(P):-
          P:age<10.                                                (III.iv)
     like(P):-                                                     (III.v)
          P:like(self)
     }.
```

Program 3.25 The **person** class template

We ignore in this example the fact that a Prolog style system could easily loop with a symmetric definition such as this. To see if Jane likes Tom we get the trace:

```
jane:like(tom)?
person(female,2):like(tom)?                             by (III.ii)
tom:like(jane)?                    % self≡jane           by (III.v)
person(male,33):like(jane)?                              by (III.i)
jane:age<10?                                             by (III.iv)
person(female,2):age<10?                                 by (III.ii)
2<10?                                                    by (III.iii)
□
```

Self reference has interesting implications when it comes to understanding the semantics of an *L&O* program. If a program refers to **self** then it can only have a 'complete' meaning in terms of its various specializations: in the case of animals one would never expect to get a condition of the form:

```
...,animal:no_of_legs(X),...
```

other than by inheritance! A reference to the **no_of_legs** predicate directly in **animal** has no obvious meaning.

Error trapping and self reference

In many Prolog systems it is possible to define a special program which is invoked in the case of an error. This is used, for example, if a predicate is called when there is no definition for it. Instead of simply failing (or stopping), the user-defined error handler may be invoked. This error handler program may then be able to repair the damaged call by loading in library definitions or editing the call. Error handlers were first introduced in MProlog [BoS80] and micro-Prolog [CM84]. They are not present in every Prolog system but they are undoubtedly useful for implementing bullet-proof applications.

The basic concept of an error handler is very simple; if a call such as:

$$\ldots,\mathtt{foo(t_1,\ldots,t_n)},\ldots$$

raises an error, then the system (dynamically) replaces it by the call:

$$\ldots,\mathtt{error(error\_code,foo(t_1,\ldots,t_n))},\ldots$$

where the *error_code* is some simple constant or integer which identifies what went wrong with the call. The meaning of the original error goal is replaced by the meaning of **error** of that goal: if the error handler fails then it is as though the foo call failed, if it succeeds then the foo call succeeds also.

Error handlers (i.e., programs for the **error** predicate) can range from the very simple – report the error and stop – to programs that apply sophisticated recovery strategies. A simple example of error recovery would be to resolve an undefined predicate error by searching some predetermined set of files for the missing definition. Once such a missing definition is loaded the error handler executes the offending goal.

In a large Prolog program we may have many different situations where errors can arise; also the desired response to a given error may be different in different circumstances (e.g. sometimes it may be desirable that the system produces no visible output to avoid disrupting an on-going graphic display). Error recovery is further complicated when there are many modules in the system. Unfortunately, of those systems that allow error handlers, most only allow for a single global definition of the error handler (this is due to the complexities of trying to decide which error handler to call should there be more than one).

In *L&O* notation it is perfectly possible to allow each class template to have its own error handler. When an error occurs the error handler associated with the class template of the offending condition is invoked. To allow for inheritance we employ the **self** concept to help decide which error handler program to use. So, if a call

$$\ldots,\mathtt{foo(t_1,\ldots,t_n)},\ldots$$

raises an error, then the system (dynamically) replaces it by the call:

$$\ldots,\mathtt{self:error(error\_code,foo(t_1,\ldots,t_n))},\ldots$$

This use of the `self` keyword allows the system to ensure that whichever error handler is available (often either the handler provided in the current class template or the default system handler) is invoked correctly.

3.4   Summary

In this chapter we have outlined some of the major programming techniques that are available to the *L&O* programmer. Some of these, such as data-driven programming, are available to the conventional Prolog programmer; but others, such as the generic module facility and program structuring using inheritance are specific to *L&O*. Overall, the *L&O* notation itself seems to suggest many powerful extensions to the standard Prolog programmers' collection of techniques.

In Chapter 4 we explore some of the larger scale aspects of programming with *L&O*; in particular, we look at programming methodology as it applies to *L&O* programs.

CHAPTER FOUR

$L\&O$ programming methodology

In this chapter, we look at some of the larger aspects of programming with the $L\&O$ language; in particular we are interested in programming methodology. Building large applications is not easy in any programming language; whilst logic programming languages are often easier to program in than low-level procedural languages, it is still important to see how to build an $L\&O$ application.

We take a somewhat different approach to programming methodology which extends standard techniques such as stepwise refinement. Instead of presenting a general method that can be applied to any application, we rely on a classification of applications. By classifying applications into different types we can simplify the problem of building a particular application. Often, by identifying which classification an application would belong to, we can virtually solve the application immediately.

How to go about constructing an application is a classic problem in programming, including logic programming and Prolog programming. Although logic programming languages are higher level than languages like Pascal or COBOL, it can be just as hard to design a large Prolog program as it is to design a large program in any other language. Furthermore, this problem does not disappear simply because we are using an object oriented philosophy. It is especially in the initial phases of a project that we would like further assistance in the construction of an application, before we really know what the application is going to do.

4.1 Logic programming methodologies

There is a programming methodology which has been associated with logic programming, and other programming paradigms, namely 'divide and conquer' which is otherwise known as 'top-down stepwise refinement'. On the other hand, the classic object oriented design methodology consists of browsing a database of existing classes; and if a class meets or nearly meets the specification it is modified until it does.

The concepts which accompany the the object oriented programming paradigm raise additional methodological questions: the most obvious being how to identify the 'natural' objects in a given application. It is not clear what a systematic method for answering questions such as these would look like.

4.1.1   The 'divide and conquer' programming methodology

The divide and conquer method is a classic top-down goal oriented approach to problem solving. In this method, we start from a known goal (such as building a compiler) and progressively break up the goal into simpler and simpler sub-goals until it becomes obvious how to complete the design. This can be either because we can identify a library procedure which achieves the goal or because we can identify a recursive folding step involving a goal that has already been encountered or because the problem is sufficiently small that some intuitive programming process can be used. For example, a compiler consists of a parser and a code generator; and so if we were building one we could write down the top-level of the compiler as a single Prolog clause:

```
compile(Source,Code) :-
    parse(Source,Tree),
    generate(Tree,Code).
```

In a conventional Prolog system we would continue this process by refining what is meant by a parser and code generator and so on. We would stop the refinement process when we know that we can invoke library procedures such as I/O or arithmetic functions to complete the task. In the context of building *L&O* programs, we can also approach building a compiler in a similar top-down way. However, it may be more appropriate to construct a module structure rather than individual clauses for individual relations. So, the top-level of a compiler written in the *L&O* language might well look like Program 4.1.

The divide and conquer methodology is well suited to developing programs in a logic programming language since logic programs are naturally read in a top-down manner. Furthermore, Prolog programming environments can support this methodology well by allowing programs to be executed whilst only partially complete. Most Prolog programming environments allow partially complete programs to be executed up to the point where they are undefined; at which point some Prolog systems will allow the programmer to construct the undefined portions on the spot and continue with execution.

A major problem with the top-down design methodology is that there is a risk of duplicating effort. There may be modules in different parts of the refinement tree which have identical or very similar requirements but are not recognised as

```
compiler:{
    compile(Source,Code) :-
        parser:parse(Source,Tree),
        generator:generate(Tree,Code).
    ...
    }.
parser:{
    parse(Source,Tree):-......
    }
```

Program 4.1 Top-level of a compiler

such. The risk is that this redundancy is not detected and the same work is done more than once. This is much more likely to happen in projects which are sufficiently large to require more than one programmer since the only well-defined communication mechanism in the methodology is top-down. In order to recognise shared modules, it requires efficient 'side-ways' communication between different parts of a project. Whilst this may occur informally, the top-down methodology itself does not directly provide for such communication.

Similarly, it is quite possible to duplicate work already performed by library functions. This is particularly true if the built-in library is large (as is increasingly likely to be the case) and not well indexed. It can in fact be easier to rebuild a library function than to locate it using its specification amongst tens of thousands of others. Again, the top-down methodology does not itself suggest easy techniques for avoiding duplicating built-in library procedures.

A further problem with the divide and conquer methodology is that it does not adequately address the thorny question of identifying suitable objects for an

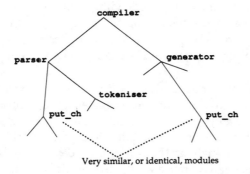

Figure 4.1 *Shared modules in a large application*

application. This is quite relevant to us since we would like to be able to develop object oriented style applications. The divide-and-conquer methodology focuses on the functional specifications of an application: it is quite clear about how such specifications can be refined to develop the application. What is less obvious, within the methodology, is how to identify the suitable groupings of data in an application. So, when we examined how to build a compiler, there was little room for investigating what the suitable data abstractions were.

The divide and conquer technique is well adapted to the discovery of algorithms, rather less so to the discovery of data structures.

4.1.2   The 'browse and modify' programming methodology

In traditional object oriented languages – such as Smalltalk – the classic programming methodology is based on an *exploration* of what is already there. So, in order to build a new application the programmer browses the collection of pre-existing classes, looking for a class (or a collection of classes) which meets or nearly meets the new requirements. Once found the pre-existing code is transformed to fulfil the new requirements.

This is an essentially 'bottom-up' approach to program design; which in turn is based on the principle that 'there is nothing new under the sun' in programming and therefore a major part of any programming task can be simplified by seeing how it was done before. There is good evidence for this: in any given organization the tasks and data abstractions that are required to support the organization are quite likely to come up again and again. In a lending library for example, techniques for locating references by author or by title are likely to be used in many of the library's applications. Therefore when a new application is required, many of the building blocks needed to implement the application are likely to be already in place in one form or another. A programmer building a new application, such as a report of all the books by a particular author which have been lent in a given period, might want to see how other reports are generated (by looking at the program which reports on the lending habits of readers for example) and how authors are located (by inspecting the program which is used by lenders to locate particular books say). Building a new application using this methodology is a matter of collecting the appropriate examples and resources and putting them together (somehow).

A rich environment increases the chances that what you need exists already: building up from pre-existing examples becomes more natural the more examples there are. A good example of this is English and speaking sentences in English. Whilst new English words are continually being coined (through creating jargon words for example) throughout the world, on a day to day basis we don't invent many new words. Instead we reuse words that we already know. Thus, for example in this chapter, there are approximately 12,000 words, yet of the more than 50,000 words in an average English dictionary, we have used only approximately 1600 different words together with just a few new words (such as filter-casting). If English had fewer words the temptation to coin new words would be much greater. Clearly, the ability to re-use existing concepts makes programming (sic) English sentences much easier.

We can support the 'browse and modify' style of programming by building a classification of all the classes in a system and using a browser/editor tool to inspect and modify them. The browser/editor tool is used by programmers to inspect what classes have previously been built with a view to (re-)using them; and possibly to modify any classes which nearly meet the specification. All programming activity should be in the context of this tool: so that any new programs which are written are automatically required to be slotted into the pre-existing classification. This directly encourages the re-use of new programs and classes, easing further development within the organization.

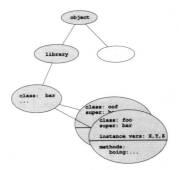

Figure 4.2 *A class hierarchy*

If more than one programmer is working on a common project, then they all share the same library. (In fact, the library may be shared by all the programmers in an organization.) Thus if one programmer implements a function, the other programmer will automatically 'see' it and use it when they come across similar requirements.

The 'browse and modify' methodology, particularly when enhanced by tools such as the browser/editor, encourages an 'exploratory' style of programming. As part of the process of building new applications we explore the database of existing applications (and fragments of applications) and new ones are often grown in an organic way out of existing sets of applications.

There are a number of dangers with using the 'browse and modify' methodology. One of the main disadvantages of this 'bottom-up' approach is that the programmer needs to have good knowledge of what is in the system (often there may be many 1000s of objects in the library). Furthermore, the effectiveness of the exploratory technique relies on an effective classification of objects. If a programmer adds a class to the library in an inappropriate place, for example by incorporating a class that can parse Pascal statements in the section of the library which handles communications, then subsequent searches of the library are unlikely to find the new class. Thus, some discipline and style is called for on the part of programmers in order to maintain the usefulness of the library.

Another danger is that there is no guidance as to the style of the application's code itself. It is easy for a program which has been 'grown' in a bottom-up fashion to be difficult to maintain and modify. Finally, there is little guidance available for genuinely new types of application. If an algorithm has to be built for which there is no precedent, then almost by definition browsing through an existing collection of applications is unlikely to be of much help. In this situation, some general purpose methodology such as divide and conquer is more likely to be effective.

In summary, it seems that the standard programming methodologies either do not adequately address the issues or do not lend enough structure and discipline to the programming process. What is needed perhaps, is some suitable blend.

4.2   Application classification

Having noted that the 'browse and modify' methodology has limitations when it comes to developing programs, it must also be said that the methodology has a sound basis in human affairs. Programmers, like any one else, learn most effectively by example; and this applies to building applications especially. 'Seeing how it is done' and developing skills 'by example' is the basis of a very honourable tradition: namely training through apprenticeship. We propose to address this directly and see how we can best aid the programmer to build on previous experience.

One way that we can support programmers developing *L&O* programs is to provide a well-founded class library classification scheme. We might measure the usefulness of a classification scheme by the ease with which programmers can locate similar applications and functions within it. So, if a reporting program was to be developed, for example, then a well-classified library will naturally guide the programmer to the appropriate places where similar applications can be found. A further measure of the utility of a classification scheme is the extent to which support tools and library functions are suggested by the structure of the library itself. We intend to explore a scheme, using the *L&O* language itself, which both classifies applications as a whole and also individual parts of applications. Thus a programmer using our classification may inspect complete applications as well as individual modules and objects.

There are several ways that we might introduce a classification scheme for applications. One 'dimension' of classification could be based on the functionality of the application (e.g. whether an application is a banking database or a chemical reaction modelling system), whereas another dimension could be based on the *style* of the application (such as whether the application has a complex graphical user interface or is intended to be used across a wide area network).

In this section we concentrate on the styles of application, without suggesting that the 'type' aspect of applications is unimportant. We identify three styles: single function applications, multi-function applications and distributed applications; in this section we shall not look at the issues relating to distributed applications.

4.2.1 Single-function applications

A classic single-function application is a language compiler. Such a program has primarily only one role: to compile programs from a given source language into a sequence of instructions for some target computer. Compilers are generally not concerned with the other aspects of developing application programs such as editing and debugging them or even actually running the compiled programs. This focussing on one role greatly helps to ease the design of the compiler.

Once we know that an application fits into this category, we can use any programming methodology that we wish to develop further the application. For example, we can continue to decompose our compiler into smaller and smaller modules until such time as we can actually implement a function. The simple sort module that we saw above in Program 3.4 on page 60 is a typical example of an end module. Again, the possibility of using generic modules means that some modules may be used several times.

4.2.2 Multi-function applications

In practice, most applications are better thought of as being multi-functional. A hallmark of a multi-functional application is that there is more than one operation which can be applied to a set of data. A multi-function application is usually centred around a single domain (such as airline reservations or computer aided designs) but in the context of that domain the application may be required to perform many different functions.

There are several distinct types of multi-function application, we shall look at two: the *abstract database* and the *abstract pipeline*. A concrete database application consists of a store of data – often in a highly specific format – and a retrieval/update mechanism for examining the data. Usually the data in a database consists of a set of records – for example, account transaction records in an accounts package or references in a library say.

If we abstract from concrete database examples we are left essentially with a collection of objects and a set of operations over those objects. This model encompasses many more applications than would normally be recognized as database applications. For example, a diagram editor consists of a database of pictures (or more accurately parts of pictures) that is queried by viewing the pictures on the screen. The database is maintained by commands that add new circles or stretch existing pictures and so on. Even a word processor can be seen as an abstract database: the words in the document being edited forms the database and the various print and editing tools form the means to maintain the database.

An abstract database has essentially three components: a collection of objects, a vocabulary of available commands and a shell program that links the data and tools in such a way that a user can interact with the application. For us to be able to distinguish abstract databases from other styles of application we insist that the tools in the vocabulary can operate on any object in the database (although the exact operation may be specialised to the actual data item).

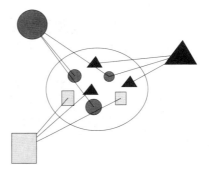

Figure 4.3 *An abstract database*

This structure can also be reflected in the structure of class templates that make up the application. Each of the data objects in the application is represented by a class template and the tool vocabulary may be represented as methods which are defined over these objects or as a library of modules which contain the command definitions.

Data objects

Once an application is analysed with respect to its functionality the remaining problem of actually identifying the objects in the system is often greatly simplified. Typically, in any application, there are two types of object: those which arise from and represent the user's database and those which are needed to implement the various tools which operate over that database.

In an abstract database style *L&O* application each dynamic class template encapsulates the predicates, functions and variables which are valid for a particular data object. For example, if our application is an accounting system, then the

```
acc094:{
     balance := 2094.
     audit := [inv('Plumbob merchants',-90),
          ..., cash('Jones Bros',300)]
     }.
```

Program 4.2 The description of `account` number 94

dynamic objects would include the various accounts that are held in the system. Typically an account will have an identifier– which we shall use as the label of the class template – and also a balance and an audit trail of recent activity in the account. Program 4.2 shows how we might organize this as a class template.

This `account` object has a balance of 2094 associated with it and an audit trail recording that recently an invoice was issued to Plumbob merchants for $90 and cash was received from Jones Bros for $300.

There will often also be many different types of data that are manipulated in the abstract database with different operations defined over them. We can differentiate different types of data object by means of class rules (which may also be dynamically asserted):

```
     acc094<=sales_account.
```

This rule identifies the object `acc094` as a sales account. The `sales_account` program in Program 4.3 defines the methods, predicates and functions which are valid for sales accounts. Other data objects in the system will have similar definitions in their defining class templates.

Tools and tool programs
The role of a tool in an abstract database application is to perform a given function or operation over one, some or all of the objects in the database. In fact, each tool greatly resembles a single function application albeit in simplified form. Thus

```
sales_account:{
     balance := 0.        % dynamic variable
     audit := [].         % audit is initially empty

     report=balance.      % find balance of a/c

     new_object(Name):-
          assert((Name<=sales_account))
     }.
```

Program 4.3 The `sales_account` class template

```
tools:{
    trial_balance(List)=trial_b(List,0).
    trial_b([],Total)=Total.
    trial_b([Ac|List],Sub)=
        trial_b(List,Sub+(Ac:report)).
}.
```

Program 4.4 The `trial_balance` tool

an abstract database can be seen as a way of aggregating a collection of single function applications – all of which operate over a common set of data – into a single super application. We can expect that a tool will be used for analogous purposes on any data object in the database; even if the objects are of different types. For example, the accounts database is likely to have several different types of account and yet an edit account tool would be used by the user to edit any account. Thus such a tool must be generic with respect to the types of data objects it can handle.

We have already encountered this kind of situation with the generic sort program. Recall that, on page 60, we parameterized the **simple** program to use a parameter theory to indicate individual ordering relations. In our dynamic data objects, the name of the object serves also to identify the theory associated with it (usually via a class rule). So, we can construct our tools to be generic with respect to the data objects that the tools manipulate. When a tool needs to perform a specific operation on a data object it invokes the appropriate services from it in the same way that **simple** invokes the ordering predicate **less** from its host modules.

For example, suppose that we had a tool (**trial_balance** say) in our accounts application whose role is to check the balances of a set of accounts, (which accounts to check need not be predetermined). The **trial_balance** tool in Program 4.4 would typically be invoked with a list of account identifiers. It reports the net balance of these accounts (i.e., it adds up the the balances of the objects in its list).

A typical use of the **trial_balance** tool occurs in the expression:

```
tools:trial_balance([...,acc094,...])=?
```

During the evaluation of this expression we will get the sub-expression which relates to the **acc094** account:

```
acc094:report=?
```

which, because **acc094** is a sales account is reduced to:

```
acc094:balance=?
```

or

2094

Thus the trial balance tool can compute the trial balance of a set of accounts without knowing in detail the type of each account. The collection of tools in an abstract database application can be encapsulated within an *L&O* program – as in this case where we have the tools program. Where the library of tools is large, or where the individual tools are complex, we might prefer to structure the tools library differently. For example, we could split the tools library for the accounts package into three components – the accounts creation and editing sub-library, the reporting sub-library and the transactions sub-library. We can reflect this structure in the layout of the tools library as shown in Program 4.5.

Within each sub-library, we collect together those tools which are related; thus the **trial_balance** tool is likely to be located in the **reporting** library shown in Program 4.6.

```
tools<=accounts.
tools<=reporting.
tools<=transactions.
```

Program 4.5 The structure of a library of tools

```
reporting:{
    trial_balance(List)=trial_b(List,0).

    trial_b([],Total)=Total.
    trial_b([Ac|List],Sub)=
        trial_b(List,Sub+(Ac:report)).
}.
```

Program 4.6 The reporting library

Building an abstract database shell

The final link in the structure of an abstract database application is the shell. The role of the shell module is to provide a use interface to the abstract database application. In essence, a user interface program has to allow the user to select a command and a set of data to operate on with the command. There can be

```
shell:{
    operate:-
        select_data(O),          % select data
        select_command(C),       % select command
        self:O(C),               % apply command
        operate.                 % next command
    }.
```

Program 4.7 The skeleton of a shell program

any number of ways of achieving this, from a graphical multiple windows style of system to a more prosaic character based command language. Given a command, and given the data to operate over, the shell invokes the appropriate *L&O* program to perform the desired operation.

The abstract database shell is a single-function application – its single function is to dispatch the various commands in the library and to control the user's interaction. We can construct an abstract database shell quite simply in class templates. The main part of the shell is a program (**operate**) which repeatedly cycles to obtain the data and command selections from the user and invokes the selected command (see Program 4.7).

The programs **select_data** and **select_command** respectively determine the data and command to execute. The sub-program **select_command** within Program 4.7 relies on the list of available commands to verify that a selected command is actually available in the accounts application. This specific information must be supplied by the programmer when building the application.

A complete accounts application is a special case of a shell; thus its top-level is defined in terms of the shell together with a list of the available commands. In Program 4.8, we see a pair of class rules indicating the library of tools that goes with the application as well as the fact that it is an abstract database application. The class body of **account** contain the specific program information needed to

```
accounts<=shell.
accounts<=tools.
accounts:{
    available(report).
    available(new_object).
    ...
}.
```

Program 4.8 A complete accounts package skeleton

link the shell to the application proper.

With this organization we can see that the natural structure of the standard abstract database is reflected in the structure of class templates used to implement it. Furthermore, the modularity of the system is such that we can replace parts of it – including the user interface itself – without unduly affecting other parts of the system.

In practice, there may be many such shells, for example we might have a command language shell which reads in text strings and issues the appropriate commands or we could have a graphically based shell where the commands and data are indicated by means of graphical concepts. An example of a graphical shell for implementing abstract databases is given in Chapter 5.

4.2.3   Abstract pipelines

As the name suggests, an abstract pipeline application involves data moving through a system. The characteristic hallmark of abstract pipelines is their modality: not all the operations and commands implemented within the system are available at any one time. As the data flows from one stage in the pipeline to the next so the actions that are appropriate change also.

Many commercial applications have a pipeline structure. For example, a data entry system – such as an order entry system – will allow the operator to enter new orders (and possibly edit some existing orders also) but, once entered, the orders are transmuted into jobs to be scheduled within the factory and are no longer accessible as orders.

Abstract pipelines are rarely single-functional; more often, at each stage of the pipeline there will be a suite of functions which are applicable to that stage. To this extent an abstract pipeline is similar in structure to a sequence of abstract databases.

We can use a variant of the abstract database shell to control a given stage of an

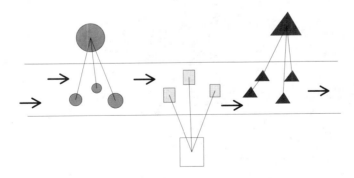

Figure 4.4 *Abstract pipeline*

abstract pipeline. We augment this at the top-level by constructing a higher level shell to glue the pipeline's stages together. Again, many commercial applications recognize this structure and use a single menu-driven shell to both select a pipeline stage (such as order entry versus statement reporting) and to control the available functions within a given stage (create a new order or edit an existing one say). As before, with the abstract database, we can use the *L&O* formalism to build each stage of the pipeline; and we can construct the super shell which allows the operator to select the appropriate stage.

Although we have characterised the data as flowing down a linear pipeline, there is no actual requirement for this simple structure. The pipeline may be a network, possibly including feedback of data. We use the term abstract pipeline to emphasise the notion of data flowing around the system.

4.3   Composite applications

Many applications are primarily oriented towards a single overall function, or as we have seen with the abstract database style of application, towards a single type of data. For example, a word processor is specialised to editing documents and to processing text, a diagram editor is specialised to producing diagrams and a spreadsheet program is designed to work with tables of figures.

All these applications have something in common: not only are they specialised towards one particular style of data, but they are also designed to enable a user to construct various forms of document: a word processor is used to produce a letter or a book, a diagram editor is used to produce a picture and a spreadsheet is used to compute a financial projection.

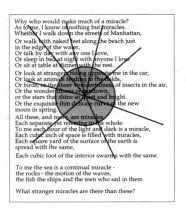

Figure 4.5 *A composite document*

In practice, however, many real documents are neither purely text nor purely diagrams. Many text documents contain pictures, tables and other non-textual components, and many pictures also contain text if only to label components of the diagram. For example this book consists mostly of words, however there are a number of pictures and diagrams interspersed in the text. A financial presentation to a venture capitalist (say) will consist of a mixture of text (explaining the nature of the proposed business) some diagrams and photographs (of prototype products) and tables (containing the cash-flow projections).

Desktop publishing systems are another good case in point: a complete publication consists of text, pictures and other items laid out in a integrated manner. The relationship between the various items in a publication is at least as important as the individual items themselves. Any desktop publishing program must be able to deal with a large variety of objects. The challenge is to build applications which can be used to form such composite documents.

One approach is to construct a single program which can, at the same time, be used to edit text, draw diagrams and whatever else we can think of that might go into the document. Such a program would inevitably be large, have many features, and would probably be quite complex to use. Also, we have not said how such a large program might be built without bugs.

Apart from the difficulty of building such large integrated applications, it is not really possible to cater for every user's needs in a single application. Different users have different needs; whereas one might like to use the diagram editor from one supplier another may need the features of another. One user might not need a diagram editor at all whereas another might need access to a high quality imaging system. If all users must use a single integrated application then some compromise is inevitable.

Another approach to building an integrated document processor is to enable different specialist applications programs to cooperate with each other to produce a document. If we are publishing a newsletter, for example, we can use a picture editor to draw the diagrams which can then be incorporated within the document; similarly a word processor can be used to generate the text and a spreadsheet to generate tables. The function of the desktop publisher program is then limited to arranging these elements in a suitable fashion without necessarily being able to inspect or edit them with any great subtlety.

All that remains is to identify how all these various applications can communicate with each other. One simple way of achieving this is to have a standard format for text and pictures, and to allow applications to transmit data in the standard format.

This approach has been used with some success in the Apple Macintosh series of computer: a standard convention allows applications to 'Cut and Paste' text and pictures amongst themselves. There is a standard format for both text objects and picture objects which is supported by library functions that can display pictures as well as text. In this way, many word processors operating in the Macintosh environment can incorporate pictures in documents. Furthermore, with multi-tasking it is possible to have all the relevant applications resident at the same time and so speed up the intercommunication.

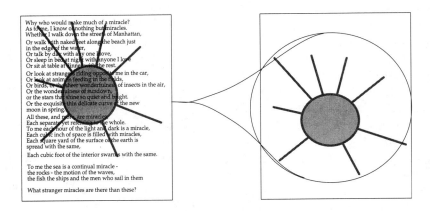

Figure 4.6 *Cutting and pasting between applications*

Multi-tasking between composite document managers and other applications can be made more convenient if the composite document manager can automatically start up the picture editor (say) using a picture from the composite document as initial input when required. There are limitations to this file-based approach however. The link between a composite document and its various components must be maintained manually. If a picture is updated then the author of any composite document which refers to it must ensure that it is updated also. Furthermore, the links between applications are restricted to importing static objects such as diagrams. It is not possible to link in dynamically changing data such as moving pictures, or even demonstration executions of other applications using a purely file-based approach.

A composite application shell

If we permit, for the sake of argument, that the applications which are to be linked together are all *L&O* programs, and that they are all examples of the abstract database style of program, then we can quite simply extend the standard shell that we saw above to include composite documents. Recall that an abstract database can be built by combining an appropriate shell, a set of prototype classes which defines the data objects in the database and the tools which define the operations over the objects in the database. A standard application will consist of a single set of tools and a single set of data objects. The shell will provide a method of viewing, editing and printing the objects in the database (possibly involving the use of some tools).

In a composite document we no longer have a single set of objects but a collection of sets of objects. Overall, the document is divided into regions; each of which contains objects of a single type. All we need to do to extend the shell to be able to manage a composite document is to be able to have several sets of tools and to be able to switch between sets of tools when the user wishes to move between regions of the composite document.

So, when a user wishes to edit a picture in a composite document, the act of selecting a picture region in the document (by clicking on the picture) can be intercepted by the shell which can then automatically switch to the set of tools which are appropriate to editing pictures. This switching process can be completely transparent to the sub-applications associated with the composite document – each sub-application is constructed as though it is the 'only' application manipulating the document.

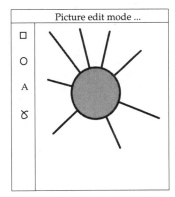

Figure 4.7 *Switching tool sets in a composite document*

Notice that with this style of system it is no longer necessary for the word processor to be able to 'handle' pictures and other non-text objects. The editor will only ever be required to process words; and the picture editor will only be required to handle pictures and so on.

So, by providing standard shells for the use of abstract database style applications the task of building those applications is made much simpler (a fact which will encourage application developers to use it). Furthermore, by the simple expedient of using a slightly different shell which can also organise multiple types of databases within a single document we can handle composite documents without needing to alter the individual specialist applications. We have seen this effect before with generic modules: the simple sort module was able to sort lists without needing to know exactly what kind of lists needed to be sorted.

4.4 Summary

In this chapter we have looked at the problem of building complete applications in the *L&O* language. This is a problem which goes beyond simple issues such as those relating to syntax and small scale functionality, and is more to do with larger scale issues such as program structuring and program design.

The standard 'divide and conquer' approach used in logic programming is not sufficiently strong to solve all the problems; neither is the classic 'browse and edit' methodology as used in object oriented programming.

We have suggested that, in practice, most programmers 'learn their trade' as a result of both their own experience and most especially by observing more experienced 'master' programmers. This can be either directly or, more commonly, by inspecting the programs written by others. In order to fully exploit this kind of knowledge, we propose a library of applications and application modules. This library is structured according to the content of the application and according to the form of the application. This structure also suggests support tools which by themselves can greatly reduce the burden of introducing new applications.

CHAPTER FIVE

$L\&O$ graphics

In this chapter we look at a significant application of $L\&O$ programming, namely the implementation of a graphics sub-language. Apart from being a significant application in its own right we also adopt a novel approach to graphics itself. We use recursive term structures to denote pictures. Common operations, such as drawing pictures and testing to see if a point is inside a picture, are described using $L\&O$ programs. The same combination also forms a sound basis for graphically oriented applications.

5.1 Introduction

Graphics and graphics-based applications are important primarily because a good graphical interface to an application makes the application much easier to use. However there is a great deal more to graphics than simply being able to draw pretty pictures on a screen or on a plotter. The construction of systems with a graphical style of interface is also important and rather harder to achieve. For example, in modern window based systems, such as X-windows, Microsoft windows and in the Apple Macintosh system, icons are used to represent programs and files, and the graphical operations of pointing at an icon with a mouse and clicking the mouse button is interpreted as the logical action of invoking the program represented by the icon. From the point of view of a user interacting with a complex system, graphical operations are quite intuitive and easy to use and learn.

It follows that any attempt to link the visual world of graphics to the symbolic world of logic programming must go further than simply drawing pictures. Apart from a language in which to describe pictures logically we also need a language in which the interaction between a user and an application can be described.

In this chapter we examine one such language for describing pictures based on a simple term representation. We show how these terms can be manipulated to compute drawing sequences and to perform other graphical operations. We also look at graphics windows and see how they form a suitable basis for constructing a certain class of graphic applications.

5.1.1   Objects versus command sequences

A key aspect of the way graphics facilities are embedded into programming languages is the sub-language in which pictures are described and manipulated. Some languages are completely dedicated to graphical applications. The page description language is a good example of this: Postscript [Int91] is a development of FORTH [Bro81] which has been specialized to perform graphics. However, for the most part, a graphics capability is embedded as a sub-language within a more conventional host programming language such as 'C' or Pascal.

Programming languages often contain sub-languages, for example arithmetic expressions in Prolog or data pictures in COBOL can also be seen as examples of sub-languages. Like any other sub-language there is the problem of integrating the graphics sub-language into the host programming language; in this case the host is logic programming, or more accurately the *L&O* language based on Prolog. The choice of notation for describing pictures affects the ease of integration and the ease of constructing graphical applications. We aim to produce a notation which is natural for both pictures and logic.

There are fundamentally two styles of graphical sub-language: the procedural or command oriented approach and the object oriented approach. A good example of the former is turtle graphics in the LOGO language [Pap80]. Turtle graphics was expressly designed to be easy to use so that young children could use graphics as an introduction to mathematics and computing. However turtle graphics is heavily oriented towards drawing pictures, in particular line drawings. It is not as strong in describing interactive graphics applications.

Given the preponderance of procedural languages we should not be too surprised that most graphics sub-languages are also procedural. Also, the low-level graphic primitives, as understood by hardware, are always command based. However a procedural/command based model is not appropriate for a symbolic declarative language such as Prolog.

An alternative approach is the object oriented approach (not to be confused with object oriented programming). In this approach data objects in the language are used to denote pictures on a screen or plotter. In our case, we use terms to denote pictures.

The relationship between picture terms and the pictures they denote is the same as between symbols and terms in general and objects in the world. For example, the 'symbol' `circle((0,0),10)` has the same relationship to a picture of a circle as the symbol '**3**' has to the number and **peter** to a person. In each case the term can be said to denote the actual object. In addition, we can use logic programs to represent computations over these objects. For example, we can write clauses which describe the laws of arithmetic in terms of 'number terms', and we can use these clauses to perform arithmetic. In the same way, we can write down logic programs which describe 'graphical laws' in terms of 'picture terms' and we can use them to perform graphical calculations. In this chapter we explore this approach to graphics and graphics-based applications.

5.2 Denoting pictures by terms

In our graphical sub-language we use compound terms to denote various kinds of pictures, and we describe relations and functions over those terms to represent graphical operations. For example, the draw function can be used to compute the low-level drawing sequence needed to actually draw the picture, and the pt_in predicate is true of points which occur inside pictures.

We classify pictures into three types, and these are reflected by three kinds of terms: primitive or simple pictures, aggregate pictures and modified pictures.

5.2.1 Simple pictures

A term such as (X,Y) can be used to denote the *point* (X, Y) in some coordinate space. This is the simplest primitive picture. A slightly more complex picture is the straight line segment. This is denoted by the term $P_1 \sim P_2$ where P_1 and P_2 are both terms which denote points. One can allow for a connected sequence of points with a construction such as the term

$$(10,20) \sim (30,40) \sim (50,0) \sim (10,20)$$

which denotes the triangular sequence of line segments shown in Figure 5.1. The

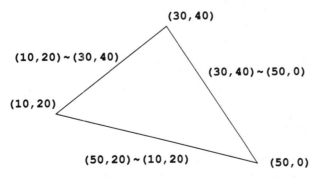

Figure 5.1 *A triangular sequence of lines*

construction P1~P2~P3 is equivalent to a pair of line segments: P1~P2 and P2~P3. This is analogous to the mathematical convention that $x < y < z$ is equivalent to the conjunction $x < y \land y < z$.

Although in principle (and in practice at the level of graphical display hardware) one can construct arbitrary pictures from these two primitive types it is convenient to have a larger library of such primitive types. We would also like to have primitive types to denote circles, text strings, rectangles and so on. We can also use terms to describe these graphical objects: so we can use `circle(C,R)` to denote a circle with centre at the point C and with radius R, and we can use `text(P, F, T)` to denote the textual display of the term T with origin at the point P using the font F.

The richness of the library of primitives determines how much effort is required to describe more complex pictures. In MacProlog [CMJS87] we describe a system with 17 different primitive picture types and over 30 picture modifiers. Below we shall see how we can define a primitive picture by means of an *L&O* program, this allows us to have any number of primitive types of picture.

5.2.2   Computing with pictures

It is interesting but hardly sufficient to have a denotation of pictures by terms. What is also required is a method of computing over these picture terms. We shall look in detail at two common graphical operations: the `draw` function which computes the sequence of low-level commands which when executed by a suitable graphics processor will cause the picture to be drawn; and the `pt_in` predicate which determines if a given point is inside or outside a picture.

A simple graphics display processor

Since we are constructing a drawing sequence which will cause a picture to be displayed, we should make some attempt to specify the acceptable command sequence. There are many different varieties of graphics display hardware/software environments, so for the sake of simplicity we shall assume a system which can cope with commands represented by terms such as `m(X,Y)` to move a drawing pen to the location (X, Y), `l(X,Y)` to move the pen while drawing a line, `p(H,W)` to change the size of the pen, `c(C)` to change the pen's colour and so on. Using these commands, the drawing sequence to draw a red square of sides 20 units centred at the point (10, 20) (such as in Figure 5.2) could be represented by the list:

```
[c(red),m(0,10),l(20,10),l(20,30),l(0,30),l(0,10)]
```

Of course in order to actually draw the square this list would have to be interpreted as the appropriate sequence of commands. Furthermore the command letters c, m, l etc. are in practice more likely to be integers or character escape sequences

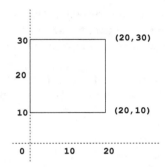

Figure 5.2 *A square centred at (10,20)*

than letters. However neither of these considerations concerns us at the moment. (A real graphics display processor is quite likely to be more sophisticated than we have assumed, and should be able to understand higher level commands such as 'draw a circle' and be able to plot text in various fonts without us having to reduce everything to a sequence of lines and points.)

Drawing a simple picture

In order to draw a picture we have to translate the term which represents the picture into the appropriate list of drawing commands. The output of this 'compiler' can then be executed on a suitable graphics processor. While the actual behaviour invoked by these commands cannot be said to be declarative – since there is no relation or function which is described by the execution of the sequence of graphical commands – there is a function defined by the graphical compiler.

We can use the *L&O* notation to distribute the definition of the **draw** function over different classes, each focussed on describing a particular kind of picture. Each class includes local definitions of methods for drawing, computing interior points and so on. This is in line with the data driven programming technique that we discussed in Chapter 3. For example, the **sq** class template in Program 5.1 contains the equations which define the **draw** function for squares.

```
sq((U,V),L):{
    draw = b_left~b_right~t_right~t_left~b_right:draw.

    b_left=((U-L/2,V-L/2)).        b_right((U+L/2,V-L/2)).
    t_left=((U-L/2,V+L/2)).        t_right((U+L/2,V+L/2)).
    }
```

Program 5.1 A *L&O* program for drawing squares

This program shows how a square is drawn in terms of four line segments. The locally defined functions b_left, b_right, t_left and t_right return the vertices of the square. In order to draw a square one draws a sequence of line segments around these vertices.

For example, if we wanted to construct the drawing sequence for a square which is centred at $(10, 20)$ and has sides of size 20 pixels, then we could use the query:

```
sq((10,20),20):draw=?
```

This query initially reduces as follows:

```
sq((10,20),20):draw=?
(10-20/2,20-20/2)~...~(10-20/2,20-20/2):draw=?
(0,10)~(20,10)~(20,30)~(0,30)~(0,10):draw=?
 ...
```

That is, it reduces to a call to the **draw** method in the line segment class ~. Program 5.2 shows a possible implementation of the **draw** method for line segments, in terms of drawing points and single line segments.

```
P1~P2:{
       ...
    draw=P1:draw              % draw the first point
            <>[l(P2:x_coord,P2:y_coord)]
                              % append a line to the second point
    }
```

Program 5.2 The line segment class

In order to draw a single point we simply move the drawing pen to it – as is shown in Program 5.3, which contains the **draw** function relating to the point class ','.

```
(X,Y):{
    draw=[m(X,Y)].

    x_coord=X.                % define function X coord
    y_coord=Y.                % define function Y coord
    }
```

Program 5.3 The *L&O* program for a point

So, armed with these definitions, the initial drawing expression reduces further, finally resulting in the list of commands to the drawing processor:

```
[m(0,10),1(20,10),1(20,30),1(0,30),1(0,10)]
```

Notice that in Program 5.2 we are using the fact that $\sim$ is left-associative, i.e., the term P1$\sim$P2$\sim$P3 is the same as the term (P1$\sim$P2)$\sim$P3, and we are also using the fact that drawing a line sequence such as P1$\sim$P2 leaves the drawing pen at the point P2. This is a property of the graphics processor that we are constructing the sequence for, not a feature of the language that we are using to describe a graphical object.

Using inheritance to implement a primitive picture

A primitive may *inherit* its drawing method from another primitive rather than defining the **draw** function directly. In Program 5.4, we see that we can quite adequately describe a circle being a special case of an oval; which we do with a class rule.

```
circle(C,R):{
                         % no method for draw in here
...}
circle(C,R) <= oval(C,C,R,R).
```

Program 5.4 A definition of `circle` using inheritance

The inheritance rule in Program 5.4 states that

> 'in order to **draw** (say) a circle of radius R at the centre C, it is sufficient to draw an **oval** with centres at C and with radii R.'

A class rule used in this way amounts to a statement of a kind of *graphical equivalence*: a circle is graphically equivalent to a particular variation of oval. We can use this graphical naming convention to distinguish out the various aspects of objects in a database. For example, suppose that we had a database of stellar information. In this database there would almost certainly be representations of stars (amongst other objects), so we might want to be able to draw stars as well as have more abstract information about them (such as their emission spectra). With a class rule we can show how to draw the star in Figure 5.3:

```
star<=(0,18)~(23,26)~(8,7)~(8,31)~(23,10)~(0,18)
```

whilst in the class body for **star** we would describe the other aspects of **star**dom.

Figure 5.3 *A star picture*

5.3   More complex pictures

Some graphic objects are best regarded as modifications of one or more simpler graphic objects. We have seen a trivial example of this with the connected line sequences that we used to describe squares and stars. In general we need to be able to do more than simply connect pictures together: we also need to be able to modify pictures and distort them in some way as well as simply connecting them together. The most important class of modifier is the geometric transformation operator. Operators such as translate, rotate and scale are analogous to functions over picture terms that describe new graphical objects in terms of other ones; however, geometric transformations should not be confused with functions.

We can denote a modified graphical object quite simply by using a term to name the transformation. For example the term:

    scale(C,X,P)

can be used to denote the picture obtained by scaling the picture denoted by P by the scaling factor X about the centre C. The term

    scale((0,0),(2,0.5),sq((0,0),10))

denotes the flattened square shown in Figure 5.4.

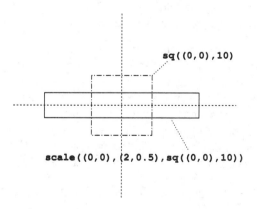

Figure 5.4 *A flattened square picture*

There are many common graphical operations which can be seen as modifying pictures, apart from the traditional operators such as translate, scale, rotate and shear. Other attributes of pictures, such as colour or pen style can also be viewed as the result of applying transformations to pictures. For example one can describe a triangle with a red outline and a light green interior by the term:

```
pen_colour(red,fill_colour(lgreen,P1~P2~P3~P1))
```

Notice that we have actually applied two transformational operators to the triangle. The ability to apply operators to already transformed pictures makes it easy to construct complex pictures.

5.3.1   Aggregate pictures

Often a complex picture contains many separate elements, each of which is a picture in its own right. These are *aggregate pictures*. An aggregate picture is a set of component pictures. It behaves as one picture from the point of view of transformations applied to the picture. We use a list such as:

$$[P_1,\ldots,P_n]$$

to describe the aggregate of the pictures $P_1,\ldots,P_n$. Aggregate pictures allow us to view and manipulate a collection of pictures as a single picture. For example, the graphical description of a table may consist of several distinct parts: the four legs and the table top. These individual components aggregate together to form the table itself. Such a table might be described by the term:

```
[table_top,leg₁,leg₂,leg₃,leg₄]
```

We can link the graphical description of a table to the other aspects of table-ness through the rule:

```
table <= [table_top,leg₁,leg₂,leg₃,leg₄]
```

Of course we also require definitions of these components before we could draw or otherwise use such an aggregate picture.

One relatively arbitrary aspect of aggregations that will concern us is the drawing order. If the elements of an aggregation overlap then we must decide which of the elements is 'on top'. In the case of the table aggregation, we have to decide whether leg_4 is on top of (and therefore obscures) table_top or vice versa. This issue is arbitrary because it does not really matter which we choose so long as we are consistent. We can see the effect of different arrangements of overlapping pictures in Figure 5.5 and Figure 5.6

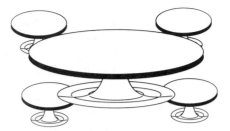

Figure 5.5 *The arrangement* [chair$_1$,...,chair$_4$,table]

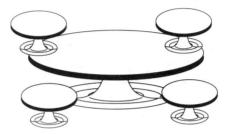

Figure 5.6 *The arrangement* [table,chair$_1$,...,chair$_4$]

5.3.2   Recursively defined pictures

An important class of pictures is the class of *recursively defined pictures*. Included in these are the many fractal images that are common today, as well as objects such as graphics and trees. Whilst we can implement algorithms which generate such images in any language, the fact that our picture language is both recursive and also non-procedural means that is is easy to describe such pictures both from the point of view of drawing them and of manipulating or interrogating them (such as finding a point in a tree). We illustrate this with a program which automatically generates a pictorial tree description of an arbitrary Prolog term. For example, the term

$$f(g(h,[i,[j,k]]),l) \hspace{4cm} \text{(V.i)}$$

might have the generic tree diagram which looks like that in Figure 5.7.

The program which can generate such a pictorial description of a term is less than a page in length. It also forms the basis for similar types of tree and graph drawing programs. The tree diagram in Figure 5.7 is 'sideways' because it is slightly easier to compute sideways trees. With the tree drawn sideways the height of each node in the tree is fixed, and hence the standard 'gap' between nodes is also fixed (by the height of the font used to label the nodes). A 'downward' pointing tree is also possible of course but slightly more complicated to calculate

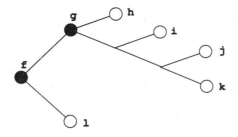

Figure 5.7 *A generic tree diagram of* `f(g(h,[i,[j,k]]),l)`

since we would have to take into account the width of each node, which in turn is determined by the length of the print names of the atoms and function symbols in the tree.

In describing the picture of a term we use three kinds of nodes as shown in Figure 5.8. A leaf node (for an atomic or simple term) consists of a circle with the name of the node alongside; it is denoted by a term of the form `leaf(A)`. A compound term node has the name and its arguments radiating out to the right and is denoted by the aggregation `[node(F),A]` where `F` is the function symbol of the compound term and `A` is the subtree corresponding to the arguments of the term.

Lists are drawn by drawing the elements of the list (one on top of the the other) and drawing a set of connecting lines to a central point. (In this program we ignore the issue of representing lists which are not nil-terminated.)

A call to the **generic** function which calculates the generic tree description is typically of the form:

```
generic(Term,Height)=?
```

which returns the graph of **Term** and its **Height**. The **Height** of the graph gives the vertical height of the tree as it will be drawn, it is actually a measure of

a. The graph of a compound term   b. The graph of an atom

Figure 5.8 *The elements of generic pictures*

```
generic(A,15) = leaf(A):-    % an atom is a leaf node
        atomic(A).
generic(T,H) = [node(F),generic(A,H)]:-
        compound(T),         % a functor is drawn as a node
        T=..[F|A].           % with a list of subterms
generic(L,Height) = put_list(S,H2):-
        S=gen_list(L,Height),
        H2 = Height/2.
```

Program 5.5 Top-level of the **generic** graph drawing function

the number of terminal nodes in the **Term**. The main equations for **generic** in Program 5.5 represent a case analysis of the type of terms one might encounter.

Notice that **leaf** nodes have a fixed height, which we have assumed to be 15, although any height that separates out the leaf nodes would be sufficient. A compound term (other than a list) has two components in its graph: [node(F),List], where **node(F)** is formed from the function symbol **F** of the composite term, and **List** from the list of arguments. The second clause for **generic** in Program 5.5 uses the =.. primitive to dismantle the compound term into the function symbol and list of arguments. The graph for the list of arguments is formed in the same way as the graph of a list of terms.

The height of compound terms is dictated by the height of the graph needed to represent the compound term's arguments. So, we delegate that calculation to the **generic** sub-expression that calculates the graphs of the arguments.

The most complex case of a graph is the list case. We graph a list of terms by drawing each element of the list one on top of the other and then connecting these sub-graphs by a series of connecting lines to a central root point. The **gen_list** function in Program 5.6 computes the sub-graph for each of the elements of the list and **put_list** completes the graph by arranging then together one on top of the other (via the use of the **trans** operator) and also creating lines from each sub-graph to a centred point to the left of the stacked sub-graphs.

The **gen_list** program generates an intermediate structure which consists of a list of pairs, each pair describing the sub-graph of an element of the list and its individual height Once this is constructed, we need to place the sub-graphs in

```
gen_list([],0)=[].
gen_list([E|L],G1+H1)=
             [(generic(E,H1),H1)|gen_list(L,H1)].
```

Program 5.6 The first pass of the generate a list sub-graph

relationship to each other and to construct a set of line segments to join it up to a common root point. If we imagine the root of the whole graph is placed at (0,0), then the sub-graphs must be placed to the right (by 30 points say) and above (by half the total height of the sub-graphs), as is shown in Figure 5.9.

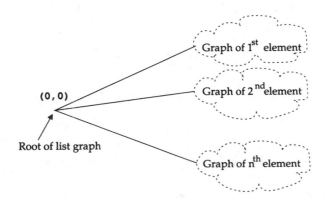

Figure 5.9 *Graphing a list of elements*

The `put_list` function, which is shown in Program 5.7, generates the final graph of the list by picking up each sub-graph/height pair and constructing an appropriate line segment from the root of the list graph to the origin of the sub-graph and returning the sub-graph **trans**lated by 30 units to the right and H2 units up.

The term which describes the graph of a term can be quite complicated; for example, the term which describes the graph of (V.i) as shown in Figure 5.7 is:

```
[node(f),trans(0, -37, [trans(25, 30,
   [node(g),trans(0, -30,
      [trans(25, 7, leaf(h)),(0,30)~(25,7),
         [trans(25, 37, trans(0, -22,
            [trans(25, 7, leaf(i)), (0,22)~(25,7),
               [trans(25, 30, trans(0, -15,
                  [trans(25, 7, leaf(j)), (0,15)~(25,7),
                     [trans(25, 22, leaf(k)),
                        (0,15)~(25,22)]]))),
                  (0,22)~(25,30)]])),
            (0,30)~(25,37)]])]),
      (0,37)~(25,30),
      [trans(25, 67, leaf(l)),(0,37)~(25,67)]])]
```

If we examine this term we can see that our simple program for constructing generic graphic descriptions is a little redundant in the descriptions it produces.

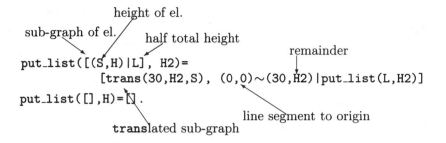

Program 5.7 Connecting a list of sub-graphs

A more careful program could avoid or simplify this redundancy. It also shows that even simple graphics operations can involve manipulating large structures.

Packing sub-graphs more carefully

In a more sophisticated version of the **generic** program we would be more careful about placing the sub-graphs. In our rather naive program we are liable to waste a lot of space when deep terms are placed adjacent to shallow ones. For example, consider the list:

```
[f(k,g(h,i,j)),a(b,c)]
```

The sub-graphs for the first and second elements in this list are shown in Figure 5.10.

According to our placement strategy, the second graph will be placed directly below the j node, as is shown in Figure 5.11. In general this strategy leads to a certain amount of wasted space, especially in deep graphs. A more careful placement strategy would 'notice' that there is room to bring the second graph much closer to the first one. In fact we only need to make sure that we don't clash

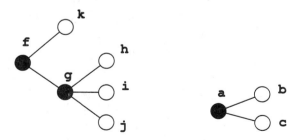

Figure 5.10 *The sub-graphs of* f(k,g(h,i,j)) *and* a(b,c)

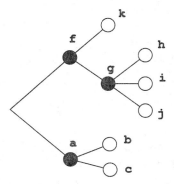

Figure 5.11 *The standard placement for* f(k,g(h,i,j)) *and* a(b,c)

with the **g** node rather than the **j** node. The more compact possibility is shown in Figure 5.12.

To implement this requires a more careful analysis of the space required, looking at the height of the graphs at each level as opposed to the height at the leaf nodes. In particular, if two trees are to be placed one above the other, the effective height of the 'deeper' of the two trees should be calculated as the height of its cross section at the same depth as the bottom of the 'shallower' tree. This is because the deeper layers of the deeper tree cannot clash with any part of the shallower tree and so these layers do not need to be involved in the calculations of the relative positions of the two trees. However, with this generalisation, it becomes necessary to consider non-adjacent sub-trees as well as adjacent ones, since two deep trees can clash even if there are shallow trees in between them. This consideration make the complete algorithm still more complicated.

Whilst there may be no more than passing interest in the **generic** program itself it does represent a class of programs which automatically generate graphs. In MacProlog a similar program is used to display the call-graph. This is a graphical

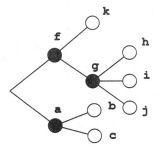

Figure 5.12 *A more compact placement for* f(k,g(h,i,j)) *and* a(b,c)

way of showing the connections in the user's program. By traversing the call-graph the user can traverse his program, showing the source as required. Another potential application of automatic graph generation is in graphical debugging packages. In this case the graph would represent the trace of a query.

5.3.3   Graphics calculations and aggregate pictures

Drawing aggregate pictures
Drawing an aggregate picture involves computing the drawing sequences for each of the component parts of the picture and appending them together. We can quite simply implement this by using broadcasting – in particular **map_cast** – a **draw** message to each element of the aggregation. (In a system in which the **draw** program is expected to perform the low-level drawing operations, rather than just computing the drawing sequence, we would use an 'and-cast' instead; and draw each element of the aggregation separately.)

```
[E|L]:{
    draw=[E:draw|map_cast(L,draw)]. % draw an aggregate picture
    pt_in(P):- [E|L]\:pt_in(P).      % locate a point
    }.
[]:{
    draw=[]
    }.
```

Program 5.8 The *L&O* program for aggregates

Pointwise inclusion in an aggregate picture
Another common operation performed on pictures is a test to see if a given point occurs in them. This is used quite heavily in graphics environments which use a mouse pointing device. When the user clicks on a screen with the cursor 'over' a picture, the application will typically need to know which picture is selected. This is determined by locating the picture(s) which include the cursor 'point' at the time that the mouse is clicked.

For simple types of pictures, each class program defining that picture type should have its own method for determining interior points. For example, to determine if a given point is in a **circle** one might use the following query over Program 5.9:

```
circle((0,10), 20):pt_in((5,4))?
```

```
circle(C,R):{
    pt_in(P):-              % from equation for a circle
        P:sub_pt(C)=P1,     % offset P by centre of circle
        sq(P1:x_coord)+sq(P1:y_coord) < sq(R).
}.
```

Program 5.9 The *L&O* program for circles

where the **sub_pt** function, which is defined in the point class in Program 5.10, subtracts one point from another.

```
(X,Y):{...
    sub_pt((U,V)) = (X-U,Y-V).
    ...}.
```

Program 5.10 The point class template

In order to determine if a point occurs in an aggregation it is enough to check that the point occurs in at least one of the component pictures. We can express this quite simply as

'find an element of the aggregation in which this point occurs'

Program 5.8 shows the implementation of **pt_in** in terms of or-casting.

5.3.4   Drawing modified pictures

We are not restricted to using a single transformation in describing a picture. For example one can stretch a square into a rectangle as well as rotate it. So, the term

```
rot(30, scale((0,0),(2,0.5),sq((0,0),10)))
```

could denote the picture in Figure 5.13.

We can represent the application of an arbitrary combination of geometric transformations by means of a single matrix. We can do this because matrix multiplication is associative:

$$M_1 \circ (M_2 \circ T) = (M_1 \circ M_2) \circ T$$

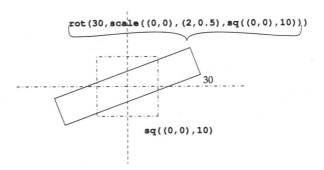

Figure 5.13 *A rotated scaled square*

where M_i are square matrices and T is a vector, i.e., a point. In this case M_1 would represent an outer transformation and M_2 would represent an inner transformation. The transformation induced by first applying M_2 and then M_1 can be encapsulated by the single transformation matrix $M_1 \circ M_2$.

In order to draw a transformed primitive picture the vertices of the picture are multiplied by this matrix, and the picture is drawn around these transformed vertices.

To be consistent, it is convenient to suppose that all graphical operations such as picture drawing and the point inclusion test are performed in the context of a general transformation. In the event that there is no geometric transformation we simply assume the identity transformation. In order to incorporate this, our previously discussed programs for **draw**ing squares and so on must be modified accordingly. We can do this by including the transformation matrix to be applied as an extra argument to **draw**. The standard query to compute the drawing sequence of a picture P becomes:

```
P:draw(M)=?
```

where M is a transformation matrix. If we want to include non-geometric transformations, then we either add another argument or encode it into M; for the moment we shall ignore non-geometric transformations.

Each class program for a primitive picture has to apply the transformation matrix to the relevant vertices before returning the drawing sequence or performing other calculations. For example our point class program which was originally as in Program 5.3 is modified in Program 5.11 by adding the extra matrix argument to the **draw** and **pt_in** programs. **multiply** is a matrix multiplication function used here to multiply the logical coordinates by the mapping matrix to get the actual coordinates.

The class programs for the various modifiers also contain methods for drawing and point finding. However, a typical **draw** method in the **rot**ate class (say) does

```
(X,Y):{
    draw(M)=[m(U,V)]:-
        multiply(M,(X,Y),(U,V)).

    pt_in(P,M)
}
```

Program 5.11 Draw a point taking transformations into account

not compute any actual drawing commands. Instead the incoming transformation matrix is modified and this modified matrix is applied to the picture argument of the modifier. For example the rotation transformation matrix is

$$\begin{pmatrix} \cos\theta & \sin\theta & 0 \\ -\sin\theta & \cos\theta & 0 \\ 0 & 0 & 1 \end{pmatrix}$$

which can be represented by the term

```
m(cos(Th),sin(Th),0,-sin(Th),cos(Th),0,0,0,1)
```

The **rotate** class in Program 5.12 has methods for the **draw** relation, and the **pt_in** relation. These methods invoke the **draw** (and **pt_in**) methods of the transformed picture, but using a modified transformation matrix obtained by multiplying the existing matrix by the rotation matrix. The other geometric transformations can be described using very similar types of programs; the main differences being the transformation matrix to be applied.

In practice, is is convenient to construct a generic template for all geometric transformations and specialise it for the various types of transformation. So, in the class template for **geometric** in Program 5.13, the transformation is given

```
rot(Th,Pi):{
    draw(M,S):-
        multiply(M,m(cos(Th),sin(Th),0,
                     -sin(Th),cos(Th),0,0,0,1),M1),
        Pi:draw(M1,S).
    pt_in(M,P):-
        multiply(M,m(cos(Th),sin(Th),0,
                     -sin(Th),cos(Th),0,0,0,1),M1),
        Pi:pt_in(M1,P).
}
```

Program 5.12 The **rot** program

```
geometric(M,P):{
    draw(N)= P:draw(M:mult(N)).

    pt_in(Pt):- P:pt_in(M:apply(Pt))
    }.
```

Program 5.13 The `geometric` transformation class

as an additional argument in the label, where `M:mult(N)` represents the product $M \circ N$ and `M:apply(Pt)` represents the point `Pt` after M has been applied to it. With this structure we can now use class rules to describe the individual geometric transformations, as we show in Program 5.14.

```
trans((DX,DY),P)<<geometric(m(1,0,0,0,1,0,DX,DY,1),P).
rot(Th,P)<<geometric(m(cos(Th),sin(Th),0,-sin(Th),cos(Th),
                       0,0,0,1),P).
```

Program 5.14 Standard geometric transformations in terms of a general matrix

Just as with other theories, we would like to group together what we know of of matrix multiplication and other matrix manipulations into a single package. We can do this with a matrix module like that in Program 5.15. In a more complete system we also need to know the inverse of transformation matrices and it is also convenient to know when a matrix is 'square' (i.e., does not introduce any rotations). Notice that Program 5.15 also has a special representation of the identity matrix 'i$'.

Of course, we need to include the identity matrix in the top-level queries we use to compute drawing sequences; for example to draw the flattened circle surrounded by a square in Figure 5.14 we would use the query

```
scale((0,0),(2,0.5),
        [circle((0,0),10),sq((0,0),10)]):draw('i$')=?
```

5.4   Graphics and applications

In a complete system it is insufficient to be able to describe and draw pictures. In a complete application graphics forms an integral part of its use – this means that the output, the input and the 'control' of the application can all be expressed in graphical terms. It is the programmer's task to build this environment. In

```
m(A11,A12,A13,A21,A22,A23,A31,A32,A33):{
    mult(m(B11,B12,B13,B21,B22,B23,B31,B32,B33))=
        m(A11*B11+A12*B21+A13*B31,A11*B12+A12*B22+A13*B32,
        A11*B13+A12*B23+A13*B33,A21*B11+A22*B21+A23*B31,
        A21*B12+A22*B22+A23*B32,A21*B13+A22*B23+A23*B33,
        A31*B11+A32*B21+A33*B31,A31*B12+A32*B22+A33*B32,
        A31*B13+A32*B23+A33*B33)
    }.

'i$':{
    mult(M)=M
    }.
```

Program 5.15 The matrix manipulation module

many applications the user interface dominates the application code ; it is not unusual to have more than 75% of the code centred around the implementation of the interface. Any tools and language system which allows the programmer to quickly and easily construct applications is to be greatly appreciated.

Many modern systems employ a desktop metaphor for describing the interaction between the user and the machine. In such a system the screen is divided into a number of different independent areas called windows. Typically windows relate to and are specialized for each application. For example, there may be word processor windows and spreadsheet windows as well as program edit windows and system control windows.

At any one time there may be several different kinds of windows on the screen, depending on the overall task that the user is involved in. The user switches between tasks by the simple expedient of marking one of the windows as the current one; this can be easily accomplished through the use of a pointing device such as a mouse. This should be contrasted with earlier non-graphical multi-

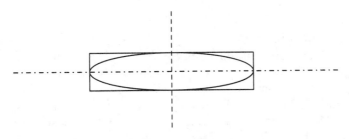

Figure 5.14 *A flattened circle surrounded by a square*

tasking environments (such as Unix) where interacting with more than one task is laborious.

Window based systems consist of several co-existing layers or sub-systems – the collection of applications which are active at the time, a multi-tasking kernel which allows more than one process to be active and a desktop manager program which controls the overall desktop.   The desktop manager program assumes

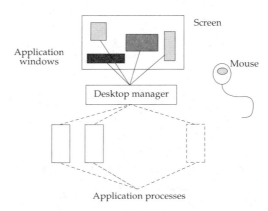

Figure 5.15 *A windowed environment*

responsibility for the screen and for handling events (such as keystrokes) to the appropriate application process. Individual applications can 'concentrate' on ensuring that their individual windows are correctly updated without necessarily knowing where they are on the screen or what other windows are active either. (Indeed, in the X-windows system application processes may not be on the same processor as the one associated with the screen.)

The user is free to resize and shuffle windows as he pleases as the different activities he is involved in assume different importance to him. Moving windows is quite likely to cause windows which were hidden to become visible and to obscure previously visible windows, in much the same way as pieces of paper overlap on a real desk.

The graphic edit window

The *graphic edit window*, introduced in MacProlog, is a generic window which is, in effect, a graphics-based shell for implementing abstract database style applications as we saw in Chapter 4. This shell can be easily specialized to a large class of graphics applications. Each graphic edit window has two drawing areas (see Figure 5.16): the tool pane (usually on the left-hand side of the window) and the drawing pane. The tool pane represents – using a palette of pictorial representations – those tools which can be invoked on data objects in the abstract

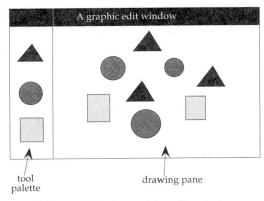

Figure 5.16 *A graphic edit window*

database, and the drawing pane is a visual window on the database itself. The drawing pane is also where application level pictures are drawn.

This abstract database shell is based on a class of applications which we might call picture editors. A picture editor is used to construct and manipulate pictures. There are many varieties of picture editor programs, for example on the Macintosh there are programs such as MacPaint which is a painting program where the system simulates the use of a paint brush. Another well known example of a painting program is PaintBox. This program is used by professional animators to construct cartoons for television. Other programs such as MacDraft and various CAD programs use a similar style of interaction except that their underlying database is more complex than pictures on the screen: a CAD package typically must be able to represent information about the logical structure of components being designed as well as graphical descriptions.

More generally, if our application is an abstract database, we can view the pictures being drawn as being representations of database objects and the tools are implements for querying and manipulating the database. The graphical shell is useful for interfacing to abstract databases because many real databases are as graphical in content as they are textual, for example a database of available flights between cities can be represented on the screen by a map and lines representing available flights between cities. A system which allowed a user to plan an air journey between various cities might have tools to represent different airlines, to select the itinerary and perhaps a route planning device.

In order for a user to plan a route he selects the cities he wishes to go to, and he may also enter other constraints to do with time (say). The system responds with an appropriate schedule, which could be displayed graphically superimposed on the map. The use of a map makes some choices easier to make: alternate routings and destinations can be viewed for example. By extending our view of

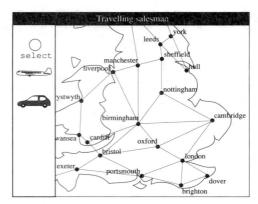

Figure 5.17 *A graphical application*

pictures slightly we can see how a Prolog application can be easily constructed to make use of the graphic edit window style of interface.

By selecting the appropriate tool in the tool palette the user of the application is also selecting the logical tool to use in the abstract database; and the act of selecting an object in the drawing pane becomes an invocation of the tool on the object in the database.

Further input to the system can often be obtained by allowing the user to interact with the picture (selecting cities from the map, for example, rather than by typing city names through the keyboard). The graphical operations of selecting tools and selecting parts of the drawing are simply a graphical syntax for selecting commands and data in the abstract database shell.

When an answer to a query is of the form of a selection of the underlying database, such as a particular flight plan, then the answer can often be given as a graphical overlay to the main view of the database, as in the case of a proposed route being drawn on the map of cities for example.

5.4.1   The link between an application and its tools

We now look in a little more detail at how a Prolog application can be bound into a graphic edit window. The set of tools associated with a window is in effect a tool aggregation : e.g. [tool$_1$,tool$_2$,...]. This tool aggregation is given by the application programmer as part of specifying a graphic edit window.

Each time an event happens in a graphic edit window a query of the form:

    tool$_i$:query?

is executed, where *query* could be **select** or **click** depending on the context, and *tool* is the name of an active tool in the window's tool aggregation. The user interacts with a graphic edit window by clicking in the window with a pointer device such as a mouse . The desktop manager interprets a mouse click as a query to the relevant graphical object. For example if a tool icon in the tool palette is clicked on then it is as though the query

tool:`select`?

were invoked. The intention behind such a query would be to select one of the tools to be the current tool. This tool picture can be highlighted in the tool palette to indicate to the user that this tool is the current tool. This query would normally be paired with a similar query:

oldtool:`deselect`?

to indicate the deselection of another tool before selecting the new one.

If the user clicks in the drawing area of the edit window then a different query is invoked:

tool:`click(P)`?

where P is the point in the window where the mouse cursor was when the mouse button was clicked and tool is the currently selected tool from the palette. Of course if the mouse has more than one button the query would be in the form:

tool:`left_click(P)`?

or

tool:`right_click(P)`?

depending on which button was pressed. Extra arguments might also be added such as the state of various meta-keys, such as the shift or control keys and the time that the button was clicked.

The application program can then interpret a query of this form as a standard entry point. For example, in our airline journey planner, if the user has clicked while the city selection tool is active then the query posed to the database may be of the form:

`select_city:click(P)`?

The *L&O* program for `select_city` in Program 5.16 has a method for `click` which may use the point P parameter to determine if the mouse is over a city. If so then the selected city is added to the user's itinerary and the city highlighted in the window in some way. Naturally, it is difficult to ascribe declarative semantics to the essentially behavioural activity of selecting pictures and running queries. However the *L&O* notation does adapt quite well to the procedural world of user interaction.

```
select_city:{
    click(P) :-
        city(C),
        location(C,P),
        add_to_itinerary(C),
        highlight(C).
}
```

Program 5.16 The *L&O* program for the `select_city` tool

Drawing and selecting tool icons

Apart from the methods for `click`, `select_city`, and so on, which describe the actual query associated with a tool, we also have to design an icon for the tool. The icon for a tool is drawn in the tool palette whenever the window needs to be refreshed. The icon is drawn by drawing the tool object itself – i.e., by posing a query of the form

$$tool: \texttt{draw(M)=?}$$

The reader will recall that the set of tools in a particular window form an aggregation. In order to redraw a window the complete tool aggregation also has to be drawn, using a query of the form of

$$\texttt{[select\_city,\dots,tool}_n\texttt{]:draw(M)=?}$$

The resulting sequence of commands is used to draw the tools in the appropriate part of the window.

Another common activity is selecting tools. If the user has clicked in the tool pane of a graphic edit window then this is interpreted as choosing a tool. In order to be able to determine which tool is selected we can use a broadcast query of this form:

$$\texttt{[select\_city,\dots,tool}_n\texttt{]\textbackslash:pt\_in(P)?}$$

where P is where the mouse is within the tool pane. However, we are more likely to want to know which tool has been selected, in which case a filter-cast expression is more appropriate:

$$\texttt{[select\_city,\dots,tool}_n\texttt{]\^:pt\_in(P)=?}$$

The value of this expression should be a single element list consisting of the selected tool; if it is empty then no tool was selected.

Once the new tool has been determined, the **select** method of the new tool is activated, and the old tool is deselected:

$$\ldots, \text{[T]}=\text{[select\_city},\ldots,\text{tool}_n\text{]}\hat{\ }:\text{pt\_in(P)},$$
$$\text{current\_tool:deselect,T:select},\ldots$$

In order for tools to be drawn and selected there have to be definitions for the standard **draw** and **pt_in** methods in the class programs for each tool. We could do this directly, but if the tool's icon can be represented by a single picture then we can represent a tool's icon through an inheritance rule. For example the icon for **select_city** might be a circle with the word city under it, as in Figure 5.18.   since

select

Figure 5.18 *The* **select_city** *tool icon*

that may be how cities are marked on the airline map. The picture description for this picture is:

```
[circle((0,0),5),text((0,10),courier,city)]
```

and the inheritance rule which allows us to draw the icon for the **select_city** tool, and to determine a mouse hit within it could be:

```
select_city<=[circle((0,0),5),text((0,10),courier,city)]
```

With a single rule we can express both how a tool icon is to be presented in a graphic edit window and also how to select it. Using inheritance rules in this way is analogous to their use for user defined pictures.

5.4.2   Displaying graphic edit windows

In a complete system there may be several graphic edit windows on the user's screen at any one time. Since most windowing systems allow windows to overlap with each other a given window may be partially or completely obscured. If the user brings such a window to the front then the window has to be redisplayed, i.e., it has to be refreshed.

In order to draw a window the system has to be able to draw the various parts of the window: the tool palette and the drawing area. In order for the system to be able to refresh the visible area of a graphic edit window it needs to be able to determine what pictures are associated with the window. This can be done in a similar way to the tool palette: by having an aggregation of all the pictures that the programmer has associated with a window. Then, in order to refresh the graphic window, one merely re-draws the tool aggregate and the picture aggregate.

In practice a graphic edit window may also include display controls such as scroll bars. These would allow the user to scroll the drawing area of the window in case the logical picture area is larger than the physical size of the window. The scroll bars are activated by the user and cause the pictures in the drawing area to shift, bringing different areas of the drawing plane into view. For example, in our airline planner we would use scroll bars to move the visible part of the map to different areas. The scroll bars can be interpreted as being equivalent to a user defined translation applied to all the pictures in the window. This translation is a constant transformation applied to the complete picture aggregation, though not to the tool aggregation.

In a similar vein to scroll bars some systems allow the user to zoom the view of a window. If the user wishes an overall view of the whole logical picture plane of a window he zooms out, to see more detail he zooms in. This user determined zoom can be represented by an implicit outer scale transformation just as scroll bars can be represented by a **trans** transformation.

Thus, to draw the set of pictures in the window we draw the modified aggregation:

```
scale(zoom,trans(scroll_for_shift,Aggregate))
```

Since the desktop manager controls how and when a window is to be refreshed, we can assume that whenever it is to be redrawn it is as though a query of the form:

```
window_x:draw(M)=?
```

were posed. The value of this expression can be used to refresh the screen. Just as with an individual tool icon we can represent how to draw a window by an inheritance rule of the form:

```
window_x<=scale(zoom,trans(scroll_bar,Aggregate))
```

This inheritance rule is quite likely to be very dynamic as the user changing the position and zoom factor in the window. The **Aggregate** also reflects the application's output.

The desktop manager can represent the position of a window on a screen by applying a translation to the window, so that the actual query that is made to draw a window is quite likely of the form

```
trans(windowlocation,window_x):draw(M)=?
```

Other attributes of windows, such as their current size, can also be represented by appropriate transformations.

5.5   Related work

There has not been a great deal of work on relating graphics to logic programming. In fact until recently few Prolog systems offered any kind of graphics. Nowadays many Prolog compilers include some support for graphics. However, they are mostly very procedural and low-level in their orientation. Amongst the most interesting approaches are those discussed by Helm and Marriot in [HM86], and by Julien in [Jul82]. Our approach is effectively an extension of Julian's work, which was itself based on earlier work by the author, combined with class program notation.

5.5.1   Helm and Marriott

In [HM86] Helm and Marriott describe a system for describing pictures by rules. Their system is analogous to definite clause grammars; for example one of their rules, in Program 5.17,   describes a solid red square.   In order to draw such a

```
square((B,L),Len):-
    plus(B,Len,R),
    plus(L,Len,T),
    line([(B,L),(B,R)],red,solid)&
    line([(B,R),(T,R)],red,solid)&
    line([(T,R),(T,L)],red,solid)&
    line([(T,L),(B,L)],red,solid)
```

Program 5.17 The solid red square as a grammar rule

square, or recognize the square, this rule is interpreted with a special purpose interpreter which presumably is modelled on a conventional Prolog interpreter.

The semantics of pictures is based on providing an alternative procedural semantics to an extended form of logic rule. This is similar to the logic grammar formalism except that in this case an alternative procedural semantics is required to describe the effect of drawing pictures on the screen.

This approach is fundamentally different to ours in several aspects. In order to describe complex pictures they introduce new connectives to conventional logic programs: '&' and '{}'. In their formalism a complex picture is represented by a conjunction of simpler pictures, whereas we use term composition and lists to describe complex pictures. Of course it could be argued that we have introduced some new connectives as part of our *L&O* language; however our use of *L&O* programs is primarily for reasons of convenience: it does not affect the underlying semantics of terms denoting pictures.

A graphical transformation, such as translate or rotate, becomes – in Helm and Marriot's scheme – a higher order predicate which contains as an argument the atom(s) which describe the transformed picture. This approach leaves many questions unanswered, for example the logical relationship between formulae which describe pictures and logic programming.

Helm and Marriott suggest that by executing their rules in a bottom-up approach they can *recognise* pictures as well as generate them. Such an ability would have obvious applications in image recognition. This ability of using these 'picture grammars' backwards is reminiscent of the ability to the use DCG's to generate, as well as recognize, strings. However, we feel that in practice it is unlikely to be sufficient to simply run the picture grammars backwards to recognize pictures. Typically, more powerful matching techniques are needed for recognizing pictures in digitized photographs (say).

Finally by concentrating on the problem of drawing (and recognizing) pictures they ignore the other commonly used graphical relationships between pictures such as the spatial relationships of being inside or above a picture. As we have seen these other relationships are important in the construction of graphics applications.

5.6   Summary

In this chapter we have separated out the denotational aspects of graphics from the drawing and behavioural aspects. We use terms to denote graphic entities such as circles and squares. We also use class programs to describe various ways of using these graphic entities. We denote transformed pictures by making the picture term an argument to the transformation factor. This represents a compact yet powerful notation for describing pictures.

Apart from drawing a graphic object, or rather compiling it into a sequence of a graphics driver commands, one can perform other graphic operations such as determining if a point is inside a picture, or whether two objects overlap. The same mechanism is used to describe how a finished graphics application is constructed in terms of tools and graphic edit windows.

We have used the *L&O* notation to describe the various relations denoted by graphics. This formalism allows the programmer to concisely express the essentially object oriented view of denotational graphics.

CHAPTER SIX

The travelling salesman

There is a whole class of problems which are known to be NP-complete. That is, the programs which compute solutions to these problems are 'worse than polynomial' in the time and/or space needed to execute them. A classic example of such a problem is the travelling salesman problem.

Imagine that a salesman has a number of locations to visit; it may be different people to see in a single building or different cities in a country. The problem is to find the shortest route which visits each destination at least once. This problem is known to be exponential in general (no polynomial algorithm is guaranteed always to find the shortest route for all situations).

We set ourselves a two-fold task in this chapter – to build a small application which demonstrates the problem and shows how different algorithms for finding routes might perform – and as a consequence, we aim to demonstrate on a larger scale than before the true potential of $L\&O$ as a programming language.

In our program we envisage two separate parts: a representation of the problem and possible solutions as abstract programs and an environment which allows users to drive the demonstration. Our application also uses a graphical interface since the rather geographical nature of the problem leads to a naturally visual presentation.

6.1 Two solutions to the travelling salesman

The most obvious 'solution' to the travelling salesman problem is to find all the possible routes between all the towns and pick the shortest one. We can express this as a kind of 'ordered permutation', as in Program 6.1.

The **route** function in this program uses the higher order primitive **findall** to find all the possible permutations of the set of towns to form a list of all the possible routes between them. **findall** collects potential routes – as generated by

131

```
permute:{
    route(Towns)=shortest(L):-
        findall((R,route_length(R)),permute(Towns,R),L).

    permute([T],T).
    permute(L,P~D):- delete(L,D,R), permute(R,P).

    delete([E|L],E,L).
    delete([E|L],D,[E|M]) :- delete(L,D,M).

    route_length(T)=0 :-atom(T).
    route_length(R~T1~T2)=
                route_length(R~T1)+(T1:crow_flies(T2)).
    route_length(T1~T2)=T1:crow_flies(T2).

    shortest(L)=shortest(L,null,1000000).

    shortest([],Route,D)=(Route,D).
    shortest([(R,D)|L],RX,DX)=shortest(L,R,D):-D<DX.
    shortest([_|L],RX,DX)=shortest(L,RX,DX)
    }.
```

Program 6.1 A specification of the travelling salesman problem

the **permute** predicate – together with the length of each route – as determined by the **route_length** function.

Once the set of possible routes has been generated, we use the **shortest** function to pick the shortest route in the set. This function is defined in terms of an auxilliary function (**shortest/3**), using the so-called *accumulator* style of definition. As the **shortest/3** function recurses down the list of possible routes, two accumulator arguments of the function (**RX** and **DX**) record the shortest route found so far together with its length. In the course of processing the list of routes, we update these accumulator arguments whenever a shorter route is found; when the last route has been considered the value of the **shortest/3** (and hence the value of **shortest**) function is the the route held in the accumulator argument **RX**. The top-level of the **shortest** functions invokes the auxilliary function **shortest/3** with an initial *dummy* route, together with an initial value of the length of this route as infinity (or near enough infinity for the algorithm to work).

Tail-recursive loops with accumulator arguments are analogous to 'while' and 'for' loops in other programming languages – the variables associated with the loop are represented by accumulator variables in the recursive call, and the value of the 'while' loop is obtained from the final value of the accumulator variables. We will use this style of definition of functions and relations several more times in this application.

Since we are required in this solution to the travelling salesman problem to compute all the possible paths around the towns, the complexity of the algorithm is very high. There are $n!$ ways of permuting a list, therefore the complexity of Program 6.1 is $O(n!)$.

towns	time(secs)	time/$n!$
oxford	0.02	0.02
oxford, london	0.02	0.01
oxford, london, portsmouth	0.1	0.02
oxford, ..., portsmouth,brighton	0.57	0.02
oxford, ..., brighton, exeter	6.37	0.05
oxford, ..., exeter, aberystwyth	177.0	0.25

Table 6.1 *Performance of Program 6.1*

We can see the effect of this in Table 6.1 which shows the steep increase in the execution time with the 4th, 5th and 6th towns. The table also shows that the ratio of the execution time against the theoretical complexity ($O(n!)$) grows only slowly.

Whilst Program 6.1 certainly represents an elegant formulation of the travelling salesman problem, we would not wish to recommend it as a practical method for solving real situations since it is more like a specification of the problem than a real solution.

6.1.1 Incremental algorithms

A more *incremental* approach is to build up the route one town at a time. At each stage we have a 'route-so-far' which represents the route around some of the towns that we are required to visit, together with a list of towns yet to be placed within the route. We then extend the route by adding one of the remaining towns to the partial route, which we can do by inserting the new town in between two towns which are already on the route; or we can add the new town at one of the ends of the route.

So, if the route-so-far contained the segment $\ldots \sim A \sim B \sim \ldots$, then one way of extending the route to include C is to split the route and produce the segment $\ldots \sim A \sim C \sim B \sim \ldots$. Other possible ways of including C are

$\qquad \ldots \sim C \sim A \sim B \sim \ldots$

and

$\qquad \ldots \sim A \sim B \sim C \sim \ldots$

At each stage, we make sure that the next town to be added to the route-so-far is in the best possible place. We can express this by saying that the 'distortion' introduced to the route by adding the next town should result in the smallest increase in the length of the route.

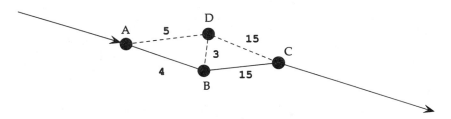

Figure 6.1 *Adding a new town to a partial route*

We can see an example of this in Figure 6.1, which shows an existing route which goes through the towns A, B and C. To include the next town D in the route-so-far, we can either break the segment which links A to B, or we can break the B to C segment. (Since this is a partial route, there may in fact be other places to break the route.)

If we break the A∼B segment, then we replace a segment which is 4 miles (say) long with two new segments A∼D and D∼B which add up to 8 miles, an increase of 4 miles. However, if we replace the B∼C segment, then the new segments add up to 18 miles but, since they replace a 15 mile segment, the additional journey length is only 3 miles. So it is better to break the route between B and C than between A and B. In general, when adding a new town to an existing route, the 'best place' to break the route is the segment which results in the least amount of extra distance when it is split into two segments.

The heart of this algorithm is expressed by the **best_place** function shown in Program 6.2. This function computes the position of the best place to break the route-so-far by comparing the cost of breaking each segment of the route and returning the position of the 'cheapest' segment. The position is used by the **split** function to reform the route with new segments. The top-level of the complete algorithm which builds up the route in this incremental way is shown in Program 6.3.

It is possible to be slightly more clever with this algorithm, and avoid using a numerical index into the route. Instead of accumulating a numerical index, we can accumulate partial routes (actually, it is better to accumulate reversed partial routes). Then, when the optimum break point has been found, inserting the new town is much simpler. However, this requires some complicated list manipulation which detracts somewhat from the clarity of the program.

```
best_place(R~T1,T)=              % try the front first ...
          best_place(R~T1,T,T:crow_flies(T1),0,0).
best_place(T1,T)=0 :- atom(T1).

best_place(R~T1~T2,T,XD,XI,I)=
          best_place(R~T1,T,XT,I+1,I+1):-
     extra(T1,T,T2)=XT, XT<XD.
best_place(R~T1~T2,T,XD,XI,I)=
          best_place(R~T1,T,XD,XI,I+1).
best_place(T1~T2,T,XD,XI,I)=
          best_place(T1,T,XT,I+1,I+1):-
     extra(T1,T,T2)=XT, XT<XD.
best_place(T1~T2,T,XD,XI,I)=
          best_place(T1,T,XD,XI,I+1).
best_place(T1,T,XD,XI,I)=I+1:- (T1:crow_flies(T))<XD.
best_place(T1,T,XD,XI,I)=XI.
```

Program 6.2 Locate the 'best place' to break a journey

6.1.2   Analysis of route in Program 6.3

If we are given a partial route of k towns to which we must add a new town, then we have k segments to try to 'break' when inserting it. Assuming that the calculation of the extra distance involved in breaking a segment is $O(1)$, then we can infer that the additional cost of adding a new town to a partial route of k towns is $O(k)$. The complexity of finding a complete route of n towns is therefore $O(n^2)$, which is considerably less than $O(n!)$.

However, since it is not known that the travelling salesman is subject to a

```
incremental:{
    route([T|Towns])=route(Towns,T).

    route([],R)=R.
    route([T|Towns],R)=
          route(Towns,
                split(best_place(R,T),R,T)).

    best_place( , )=...          % see Program 6.2
    }.
```

Program 6.3 Top-level of the incremental travelling salesman algorithm

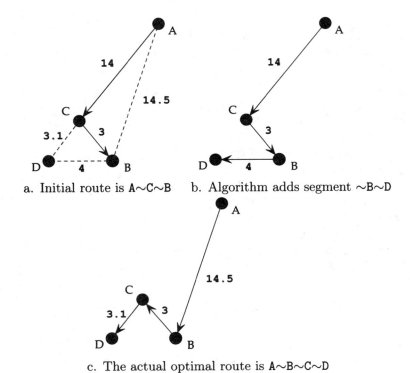

a. Initial route is A∼C∼B   b. Algorithm adds segment ∼B∼D

c. The actual optimal route is A∼B∼C∼D

Figure 6.2 *A sub-optimal arrangement of towns*

polynomial solution, it must be the case that Program 6.3 does not always find the optimal solution. Indeed this is so, and it is instructive to see under what circumstances it generates a less than optimal solution.

Suppose that we have to find the best route between the four towns A, B, C and D as shown in Figure 6.2. In Figure 6.2a, we have already built a partial route consisting of the route A∼C∼B. The algorithm will choose this route over the route A∼B∼C because the length of the second route is 0.5 miles longer. Now, to complete the solution, we need to extend the route by adding the fourth town D to this route. We now have four choices of places where we can split the A∼C∼B at this point:

1. we can add D to the front: D∼A∼C∼B,

2. we can split the A∼C segment: A∼D∼C∼B,

3. we can split the C∼B segment: A∼C∼D∼B or

4. we can add D to the back: A∼C∼B∼D   (VI.i)

which have lengths 34.1, 22.5, 21.1 and 21 miles respectively. Naturally, the algorithm chooses option (VI.i), as shown in Figure 6.2b, since this is the shortest of the possibilities.

However, suppose that we had previously selected the sub-optimal route A∼B∼C (which is 17.5 miles long compared to 17 miles), then our choice of routes when adding D would have been:

1. D∼A∼B∼C,

2. A∼D∼B∼C,

3. A∼B∼D∼C or

4. A∼B∼C∼D   (VI.ii)

which have distances 34.6, 23.5, 22.6 and 20.6 miles respectively. Notice that route (VI.ii), which is shown in Figure 6.2c, is actually shorter than the one selected by the `incremental` algorithm in Program 6.3.

In order for us to be able to find the truly optimal route around a set of towns we need to consider all the towns simultaneously, whereas our route planner only considers the 'local' problem of adding one town to an existing route. This is the real reason that the travelling salesman is non-polynomial – when a new town is added to an existing set of towns we must reconsider *all* the previously possible solutions in order to be sure of finding the best route including the new town. Because we don't re-order a route once established, our incremental algorithm will not always find the optimal solution. However, at least it finds a reasonable solution, which is in many cases also optimal.

6.1.3 The driving salesman

In practice, the travelling salesman may not 'fly' directly between towns. Instead, if he is using a car, then the problem of finding the shortest route is complicated by the fact that journeys between towns need to be planned. As a result, the salesman will be necessarily be visiting other intermediate towns en route between destinations. For example, in order to drive between `birmingham` and `exeter` using the road map in Figure 6.3, it is necessary to go through `bristol`. If `bristol` is added to the itinerary later, then the route can remain unchanged. In general, segments in the route may be split not just between actual destinations but also between intermediate destinations. Our application will consider both the flying salesman and the driving salesman.

6.2 The travelling salesman application

The purpose of our application is to provide a demonstration of the travelling salesman problem. Our vehicle for this is an application which allows the demon-

Figure 6.3 *A 'road map' of Britain and some major cities*

stratee (sic) to select a set of towns to visit and to invoke one of the possible algorithms which have been implemented.

Since this application involves selecting some towns to visit, and seeing the resulting route that is calculated and how it is done, it seems appropriate that we use a graphical user interface. In particular we will use a 'graphic edit window' to implement an 'abstract database' style application. Figure 6.4 shows what such a window might look like.

The data objects that form the abstract database are the towns of Britain – we have selected 25 of the major British towns as an initial collection.

The main components of this application are:

- the collection of places to visit,

- a tool to allow the selection of places to route around,

- a 'road map' giving the possible connections between towns,

- a method of invoking the various routing algorithms,

- the graphic edit window shell program

and, in order to be able to explore the algorithms more carefully:

- a tool to allow the placement of new towns on the map, and

- a tool to allow loading and saving of maps

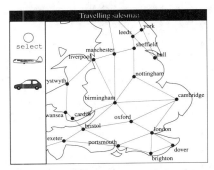

Figure 6.4 *The travelling salesman application as a graphic edit window*

6.2.1   The representation of a town

A 'town' is a location that the travelling salesman might want to visit. Apart from the towns' locations, the other main features of individual towns are the other towns that can be immediately reached from them (i.e., the roads that connect towns together).

So, for example, **bristol** has roads linking it to **oxford**, **exeter**, **cardiff** and **birmingham** (as in Figure 6.5).

We can represent this information as an *L&O* program very easily, as we have represented Bristol in Program 6.4.   In order to facilitate the route planning algorithms, we prefer not to use a relational representation of the **links** between towns; which is why we collect all the destinations which are immediately reachable from a given location into a list. This list is the value of the **links** function, as we can see in Program 6.4.

In the **location** class, which is shown in Program 6.5, we collect together the *generic* knowledge that we have about towns. This includes how to compute the distance metric (which is the geographic distance between towns), how to plan

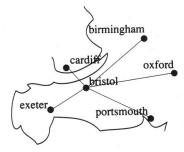

Figure 6.5 *The roads that connect* **bristol** *to other towns*

```
bristol<<location(305, 168).
bristol:{
    links=[(cardiff,44),
           (exeter,76),
           (oxford,71),(birmingham,86)]
    }.
```

Program 6.4 The structure of <code>bristol</code>

a road journey, and how to display towns graphically. This last is done using a class rule which 'rewrites' the town to a picture term.

```
location(X,Y):{
    at(X,Y).                % define where the town is at
    at=(X,Y)                % both a function AND a relation

                            % geographical distance metric
    crow_flies(Town) = sqrt(U0*U0+V0*V0)  :-
        Town:at(U,V),U0=U-X,V0=V-Y.
    ...
    }.
location(X,Y)<<{circle((X,Y),2),
               text(X+5,Y-2,courier,self)}.
                            % note self reference
```

Program 6.5 The class template for a location

Planning a drive

Because it is not possible to drive directly between arbitrary towns, we need to include a simple planner in the `location` program. The planning algorithm we use, which is described as the `plan_drive` predicate in Program 6.6, is quite simple. There are two cases: either the town that the salesman needs to drive to is directly reachable from the source town (see (VI.iii)); or we pick an intermediate town which is reachable from the source and try to plan a journey to the destination from there (see (VI.iv)).

In order to prevent 'looping' in the planning program (i.e., planning a journey using an intermediate town which is already in the plan), we accumulate a list of the towns that are being visited as well as the partial plan. When in (VI.iv) we consider an intermediate town we make sure that it is not on the list of towns

```
drive(To)=(Dist,Route):-
    plan_drive(self,To,[],Dist,Route).

plan_drive(From,To,R,D,From~To):-                                    (VI.iii)
    (From,D) on (To:links).    % direct route

plan_drive(From,To,R,D+DI,Route~To):-                                (VI.iv)
    nearest(To:links,From,Int,DI),
    not Int on R,                    % check not Int not already visited
    plan_drive(From,Int,[To|R],D,Route).

nearest(Links,To,Int,D):-   % sort list according to metric distance
    (Int,D) on simple(metric(To)):sort(Links).
```

Program 6.6 A program to plan a drive in the country

already in the plan.

The planner tries to pick an intermediate town which maximally reduces the distance between the source and the destination towns. This is the reason that we **sort** the links (using the **metric** theory from Program 6.7) before picking the intermediate towns. The **on** predicate is used to non-deterministically select the intermediate town from this sorted list. Of course, the geographic metric is only used as a guide to selecting an intermediate town, the actual length of the route is found by adding up the road lengths from the individual links which make up the complete road plan.

```
metric(Town):{
    less(T1,T2):-
        To:crow_flies(T1)<To:crow_flies(T2)
    }.
```

Program 6.7 A distance metric theory

Pre-sorting the towns

In the driving algorithm, we make use of the locations of the towns to give a crude 'as-the-crow-flies' guess as to which towns to use as intermediate stepping stones as we plan a road journey. The assumption is that the nearer a town is geographically, the shorter the road distance is likely to be as well. Of course, this is not always the case; in the situation of two towns separated by a river with no bridge in the vicinity, a considerable detour may be necessary to drive between the towns, which means that the road distance will be larger than the flying distance.

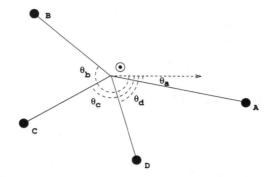

Figure 6.6 *Some towns that we would like to visit*

For many situations the nearest town is likely to be the best town as well when planning the road journey.

We can also use this kind of knowledge to be a little more clever in main travelling salesman algorithm. We can pre-sort the list of towns that need to be visited so that neighbouring towns are next to each other in the list. For example, suppose that we needed to visit the towns A, B, C and D, as shown in Figure 6.6. The algorithm is more likely to get an optimal solution if it considers the list of towns [A,D,C,B] rather than [A,B,C,D]. If we sort the towns first by some kind of geographical ordering we might promote the possibility of an optimal solution.

To sort such a list of towns we can use the **simple** sort program from Program 3.4 on page 60; all we need to do is to define how to 'compare' two towns. One effective way of performing a comparison, especially if the original problem is slightly re-formulated to require a *round trip* around all the towns, is to put

```
presort:{
    route(Towns)=                       % sort according to geographic ordering
        incremental:route(arrange(Towns)).

    arrange(Towns)=
        quick(geographic(centre(Towns))):sort(Towns).

    centre(Towns)=(U/L,V/L):-average(Towns,0,0,U,V,0,L).
    average([],U,V,U,V,L,L).
    average([Town|List],UX,VX,U,V,I,L):-
        Town:at(UT,VT),
        average(List,UX+UT,VX+VT,U,V,I+1,L)
}.
```

Program 6.8 Pre-sort the towns before building the incremental route

```
geographic((OX,OY)):{
    less(T1,T2):-              % when is one town 'less' than another?
        angle(T1)<angle(T2).

    angle(T)=angle(X,Y):-
        T:at(X,Y).

    angle(X,Y)=atan((Y-OY)/(X-OX))   :- X>OX, Y>=OY.
    angle(X,Y)=pi+pi-atan((OY-Y)/(X-OX))   :- X>OX, Y<OY.
    angle(X,Y)=pi-atan((Y-OY)/(OX-X))   :- X<OX, Y>=OY.
    angle(X,Y)=pi+atan((OY-Y)/(OX-X))   :- X<OX, Y<OY.
    angle(OX,Y)=pi/2 :- Y>OY.
    angle(OX,Y)= 1.5*pi :- Y=<OY
}.
```

Program 6.9 The geographic ordering of towns about a centre of gravity

the towns in a 'clockwise' ordering around some point. So, in Figure 6.6, town D is 'more' than A because it is further around the clock relative to the notional origin point ⊙. We can order an arbitrary list of towns in this way; furthermore, once sorted, the list is likely to have geographically adjacent towns also adjacent on the list.

We take as the origin of a set of towns the geographic centre, or the 'centre of gravity' between the towns. We can compute the centre of gravity by computing the average of the X-coordinates and Y-coordinates of all the towns that are to be visited. The program in Program 6.9 contains the theory of this kind of 'geographical' ordering; and there is a special version of Program 6.3, in Program 6.8, which performs this pre-sorting of the towns to visit.

A circular route

A slightly different interpretation of the original problem involves constructing a *circular* route around the towns to visit. It is reasonable to ask that the travelling salesman be permitted to return home after all!

It is a simple matter to modify the programs to allow for this, as we show in Program 6.10 which is a circular version of the incremental version in Program 6.3. The main difference is that the initial route, which is constructed out of the first town in the list of towns to visit, consists of T~T rather than just T; as it happens, the 'circular' program is simpler than the 'straight' version since there are fewer special cases in the shape of a circular route.

It turns out that for many cases this algorithm performs much better, in the sense of generating optimal routes, compared to either the straightforward **incremental** algorithm in Program 6.3 or the pre-sorted version. The reason for this seems to be that when a new town is added to the route-so-far it is as though

```
circular:{
    route([T|Towns])=route(Towns,T~T).
    route([],R)=R.
    route([T|Towns],R)=
        route(Towns,
              split(best_place(R,T),R,T)).
    best_place(R,T)=
        best_place(R,T,10000000,0,0).
    best_place(R~T1~T2,T,XD,XI,I)=
            best_place(R~T1,T,XT,I+1,I+1):-
        extra(T1,T,T2)=XT, XT<XD.
    best_place(R~T1~T2,T,XD,XI,I)=
            best_place(R~T1,T,XD,XI,I+1).
    best_place(T1~T2,T,XD,XI,I)=I+1:-
        extra(T1,T,T2)=XT, XT<XD.
    best_place(T1~T2,T,XD,XI,I)=XI.
    ...}.
```

Program 6.10 A circular version of the `incremental` algorithm

both it and the route when reversed are considered when splitting the route; and that many cases where Program 6.3 would get it wrong because it cannot permute the route Program 6.10 gets it right because it can consider the reversed route as well – although it must be said that Program 6.10 does not *explicitly* consider the reversed route-so-far.

A performance comparison

In Table 6.2, we show the results of running the various algorithms on finding a route between the towns:

[london,brighton,portsmouth,exeter,oxford,aberystwyth]

As we can see, each algorithm seems to find its own way around the towns. Although the **permute** program finds the shortest route, it does so after a very long time (almost 500 times longer than **incremental**).

6.2.2   The application's tools

As we noted earlier, the main tools in our travelling salesman application are the town selection tool, (which we call **select_city**), and the tool(s) which invoke the route finding algorithms.

Algorithm	Route	Distance	Execution time
incremental	oxford~ london~ portsmouth~brighton~ exeter~aberystwyth	304.15	0.2s
presort	brighton~london~ oxford~portsmouth~ exeter~aberystwyth	283.49	0.8s
circular	london~brighton~ portsmouth~exeter~ aberystwyth~oxford~london	273.62	0.2s
permute	oxford~london~brighton~ portsmouth~exeter~ aberystwyth	273.62	230.9s

The indicated route length for the `circular` algorithm does not include the extra leg from `aberystwyth` to `oxford`

Table 6.2 *Summary of routes generated by the travelling salesman*

The `select_city` tool is based on the `select` tool which is used to select pictures in the standard graphic edit window shell. Its function is to allow the selection of towns and to make that list available to the algorithm tools; the only difference is that the tool's icon is different.

The tools which invoke each particular travelling salesman algorithm have a rather straightforward structure. When activated, the 'algorithm' tools compute their routes and display a message giving the resulting length. (By lightly modifying the algorithms themselves, it is also possible to show the progress of the algorithm graphically.) The complete programs which implement these tools are shown in Appendix C.

Since the main purpose of the application is to demonstrate the activity of the various algorithms, we draw the current 'thoughts' of the algorithms dynamically on the screen as the solutions progress.

For the 'permuted order' version of the algorithm, this means drawing each permutation as it is found, and when the final one has been found, and the shortest route calculated, then this route is also marked out on the screen. For the 'incremental' route planner, we draw the route as it is built up. We also highlight the guesses that the algorithm is trying – the possible ways that route-so-far can be broken as each new town is added to it.

In order to do this dynamic drawing we make use of a graphical 'trick': if we draw a line on the screen in 'xor-mode' then, drawing the same line again has the effect of erasing it. We express this behaviour by drawing a picture – in our case the guess the algorithm is making for the route – in a window rather than **adding** it:

```
saleswin:draw_guess(T1~T2~T3)
```

We can use this technique to briefly highlight a choice by drawing the guess in xor-mode and redrawing it to erase it. The effect is to allow the user to see what is happening in the program without cluttering up the display unnecessarily.

6.3   Summary

It is possible to have a lot of fun dreaming up new approaches to solving the travelling salesman problem. Many different techniques have been tried, including one based on neural networks.

Once an application such as this one has been built, it is relatively easy to integrate a new approach – we simply add another tool using the new algorithm. The dynamic graphical view of the algorithms in action provide an effective way of showing them; it can also guide the algorithm designer in finding ways of improving the algorithm.

In this chapter we have concentrated on solving the problem at hand rather than on how to implement the demonstration application. This is how it should be – by using the high-level application shells which are possible in the *L&O* language we can avoid much of the low-level interfacing issues that often dominate the construction of any application.

The complete application, most of which is listed in Appendix C, is not very large. Furthermore, more than 50% of it is 'algorithm' code, not 'interface' code. This was a significant factor in determining how easy it was to build the travelling salesman application.

CHAPTER SEVEN

A general purpose packer/scheduler

Tony Solomonides
School of Computing, Polytechnic of North London

In this chapter we explore a large scale application of $L\&O$ involving problems around the issues of packing, planning and scheduling. At first sight it may appear that the problems of packing boxes into a confined space, scheduling a project, organizing library shelves, and timetabling an academic department have little in common. However, as we shall see, these very different problem areas have enough in common for us to consider the possibility of a single generic application to enable a user to tackle any one of them with more or less equal ease.

We observe that there is good precedent for such *generic applications*: spreadsheets are generic applications which allow such diverse activities as discounted cash flow, matrix algebra and the processing of examination results. Indeed, it will be seen that our 'problem space' resembles a multi-dimensional spreadsheet, but the problems differ in as much as their precise expression in the first place cannot be articulated in terms of entries into cells; cell entries will form the eventual solution, but not the statement of the problem.

There is, in any case, good reason for attempting to tackle problems of this nature through a generic application which allows a dialogue with the user. Most of the problems, at least in their greatest generality, are NP-complete. This means, in effect, that for all practical purposes they are intractable – whilst small scale problems may be practical, large scale problems quickly swamp any available computing resources.

Instead of trying to build a completely automatic solution to these problems, we enlist the aid of the user. We can build a simple and rather unintelligent application which solves simple problems easily and furthermore uses a technique which is not limited by the issues of scale that affect completely automatic solutions. Crucially, it also makes it easy for a user of the application to *intervene* where the computer generated solutions are inadequate and allow the application to continue from that intervention. Indeed, it is suggested here that such a combination of an interactive application which harnesses human intelligence and computational power through an appropriate interface would in large measure solve these problems from the point of view of usefulness to human purposes.

7.1   The problems

What is involved in packing boxes into a confined space, say a truck or van? It may matter that the boxes are grouped together to facilitate unloading or that they be distributed evenly to spread the load; or, if the contents are frozen, that they be packed together as closely as possible to maintain temperature by minimizing surface area; or, if heavy, stacked low so that they are not crushed.

By and large, boxes have a distinguished top and bottom but no special distinction is drawn between front and sides, so in stacking them we are free to turn them round on their base, but not to tip them over on their sides. Although in theory we might consider boxes whose measurements are real numbers, it is more realistic to assume that all measurements will be integer multiples of some unit, be it metres, centimetres or an even smaller unit. This immediately imposes a multidimensional grid or *lattice* on our problem space. All boxes must be anchored at one of the lattice points of the (implicit) measurement system. In practice, of course, boxes cannot be anchored to any lattice point at will – e.g. since they cannot be suspended in mid-air – they can only be placed at a lattice point as they are 'loaded in', hence our observation that the solution to a box-packing problem will consist of 'cell entries' of some kind.

The problem of academic timetabling can be specified in a similar way to the box-packing problem. To specify a simple timetable entry we need to give at least the following information: the course (or unit, module, subject, etc), the teacher (or professor, lecturer, etc), the room and the period. If we imagine the timetable displayed in a four-dimensional grid, we recognize that timetabling constraints are essentially geometric. For example, a teacher can only teach one thing in one place at a time; this can be read as:

> *each plane defined by* Teach = *fixed,* Time = *fixed contains at most one entry which therefore supplies the remaining data* Room = *? and* Unit = *?*

This 'geometrisation' of the timetabling problem is only a good first approximation. There are at least two necessary improvements. The first is to recognize that weeks are not made up of 35, say, otherwise undistinguised periods, but are made up of five days of seven periods each; it may be explicitly required of us not to timetable any given course for more that two periods on the same day, or any given teacher for more than four periods in a day. It is also likely that each teacher will have a relatively narrow specialism, and that the range of courses he or she can teach will be restricted. It is sensible, and indeed common, for the association of teachers with courses to be established first, and for timetabling to

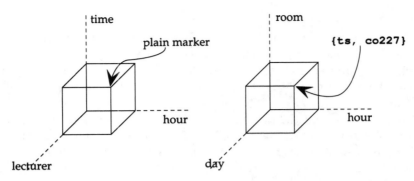

Figure 7.1 *On the left-hand side the dimension 'room' has been omitted*

follow on after that. This transforms timetabling from the distribution of content-less 'boxes' in a five-dimensional grid (recall that periods have been split into days and slots) into boxes with content {`Teacher, Course`} into a three-dimensional space. The constraints still have a geometric flavour, but they also depend on the content of the boxes: e.g. in any given plane *Day* = fixed, there are at most four boxes containing a particular teacher's name. The two styles of representation are contrasted diagrammatically in Figure 7.1.

This also has a parallel with the box-packing problem domain. If boxes have weight and crushing strength, these may be treated as the 'contents' of the boxes, and the relevant constraint is again expressible in geometric terms: the combined weight of boxes stacked above a given box (more precisely, the appropriately computed share of that weight) must not exceed its crushing strength. The idea is illustrated in Figure 7.2 below.

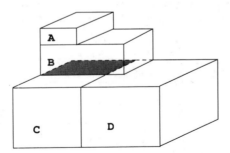

Elementary statics determines the share of the total load from Boxes A and B on the shaded area which is part of the top of Box C. If the crushing strength has been computed on the assumption of an even load distribution and the shaded area is, say, 0.4 of the top of Box C, the share of load on the shaded area must not exceed 0.4× crushing strength of Box C.

Figure 7.2 *Static loading of boxes*

A third domain in which our generic application may be of use is project planning. Project planning is about the task of allocating and scheduling resources. As an activity it bears some similarity to the box-packing and timetabling domains since a planner must 'fit' the sub-tasks and resources of a project together and, once planned, the result is often in the form of a schedule which is similar to a timetable.

For example, consider the task of planning a large programming project. For a large project, we would have a number of programmers, together with some equipment and possibly other resources, with whom to accomplish a certain programming task. Programmers' activities may mutually interact or interfere in at least two ways. First, some will be prerequisites for others, and so must precede them; no task can be commenced if its prerequisite tasks have not been completed. Second, several activities may need access to the same scarce resource – such as an expensive graphics workstation – and so cannot be performed concurrently.

Again we see the possibilities for content-based geometric constraints to have a geometric form: each task can be likened to a 'box' with 'dimensions' corresponding to the resources (including programmers) utilised by the task. The function of a project planner is to find the distribution of tasks to programmers which minimizes overall project duration (in other words to find the critical path), consistent with the restricted use of available resources.

Assuming that the duration of an activity (especially estimated duration) will be expressed as an integer multiple of a unit, say days, and that programmers are also allocated in whole numbers, we again see the discrete lattice in which our solution will eventually be drawn. Similarly, other resources (such as personal workstations for the programmers to use) are also allocated to tasks in integral quantities.

Resources could, at a stretch of the imagination, be seen as adding new 'binary' dimensions, one for each resource, with 0 or 1 indicating use or non use. It would seem to be a good deal more natural to include resource demand, or even a fraction

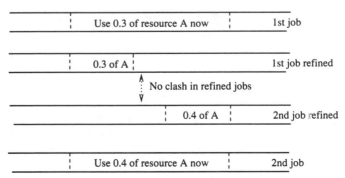

Figure 7.3 *Developing the task in finer detail resolves a potential clash*

estimating the extent of resource use as a proportion of total time, as part of the contents of the task box. This might be of service when the plan is refined subsequently, with gross tasks broken down into detail for fine tuning; if there is a clashing demand for the same equipment, with say two conceivably concurrent tasks making a 0.3 and 0.4 demand on it respectively, we may forgive the clash in the hope that fine tuning will resolve it; this is illustrated in Figure 7.3.

In summary, we have argued that a number of apparently diverse problems have essentially similar 'problem spaces'; and consequently, that they may be amenable to treatment by more or less uniform methods. The argument will be taken further now, to suggest that a generic computer application may be devised which could be used as an *enabling environment* for the solution of all these problems. At this stage we shall reserve the definition of this rather elusive term 'solution'.

7.2   Attributes and features: a wish list

Imagine sitting down at a machine running such an application. You do not see a grid or framework yet, because, as we have discussed, that is the representation of the solution, not the problem. The program knows something about boxes – they may touch each other, but cannot overlap; they extend in some number of dimensions which depends on the problem at hand; their contents may or may not matter; they have to be arranged in accordance with particular constraints. If all this can be represented adequately in the program, the user only needs the means to enter the particular information from the current problem.

A simple and accommodating interface should provide a set of windows in which to enter various aspects of the problem, for example, boxes, sizes and contents in one, constraints in another, specific goals in a third, and so on. Entry may be part text and part graphics; menus and option lists may be used to make the application all the more convenient. The program may have break points at which the user may intervene to modify a solution or to cut off a poor solution still in progress, perhaps to backtrack and restart in a new direction. The solution would certainly be visually available, from different points of view and in different forms, even as it is worked out, so as to provide the user with enough information to make the choice whether and when to intervene.

7.2.1   The nature of boxes

We have spoken of the system 'knowing' something about boxes. In saying that boxes may be placed in contact with each other but may not intrude into each other's space, we are in effect specifying what can happen to a box which is brought into an arrangement of boxes 'in progress'. We may conveniently assume that boxes (of whatever nature) waiting to be included in an arrangement have

no location – they are in limbo. However, they have intrinsic dimensions: the size
of a carton, the probable duration of an activity, a single or double lecture. On
the other hand, the grid into which they will be placed is the means whereby they
acquire – are allocated – 'location'.

Whether a box can be put in a space or not depends on many things, including
the constraints we wish to impose on the overall arrangement, but the primary
requirement, before any other consideration can come into play, is *can the box fit
in that space?* Inevitably then we must look at two aspects of an arrangement
of boxes at the same time; where are the boxes that have already been brought
into the arrangement located, and where (and what size) are the free spaces into
which further boxes can be fitted.

In the particular formulation adopted here, it is convenient to locate a box by
means of a fixed 'anchor' - the corner closest to the origin of the ambient grid.
The coordinates of the anchor give the position of the box, while the coordinates
of other corners, which of course will play a part in determining the spaces newly
made available for the location of further boxes, are deduced because we know
the dimensions of the box. This allows us to express the coarsest question we
might ask at this stage: is a space available; is the room already occupied; is there
another box impeding; is the programmer already occupied on another task?

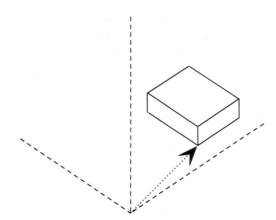

Figure 7.4 *An anchored cell; the anchor is a vector*

To satisfy the requirements of the system so far, then, the user need only specify
the size of each box; of all things this should be the simplest. But the boxes in
question will have many other attributes, and in as much as they impinge on the
solution we seek, they will have to be provided in some form for the use of the
system. We have termed these attributes the 'contents' of the boxes, and we must

now elaborate how the contents are specified a little further.

7.3 Constraints

It is as well to clarify what we mean by the 'contents' of boxes before we proceed
to a discussion of their specification. We certainly are not referring to the *physical*
content of the boxes. Boxes may have physical existence (e.g. they may be
cartons) and they may contain something (e.g. ice cream) which may lead us
to prefer one arrangement rather than another (e.g. we pack ice cream cartons
close together to keep them frozen). However, this influence is only exerted on
the system by the user's specification of the problem. In the first place, the user
will provide the dimensions of the cartons and ask for, say, a compact solution. It
may be that once the problem is solved, the type of problem will be *named* and
the system may at a later stage be told *here are some ice cream cartons* and it
will 'know' what to do.

On the other hand, boxes will have a notional or *abstract* content (weight and
crushing strength of cartons, resource requirements and dependencies of tasks,
course-teacher combinations in timetables) which is used directly by the system
in the solution of the problem. These abstract contents do have to be entered
into the system, and even more, the way they enter into constraint considerations
must also be formulated and entered.

We seek therefore an appropriate way of eliciting this material from the user,
preferably while other pertinent information is being input; it would be undesir-
able for a user to enter details of size about boxes first and then return to each to
enter weight, say. But whereas the system knows to ask about size, it may not yet
know to ask about weight; the user must first specify that as a generic attribute of
importance. That is best thought of in association with constraint specification.

7.3.1 Three kinds of constraints

It is clear from the discussion so far that there are several kinds of constraint
to be considered. We shall distinguish three kinds. The first is intrinsic, and
may, indeed, be viewed as the most fundamental type of constraint: this is the
constraint of 'non-intrusion'. Its effect can only be negative, i.e., to inhibit a
box from being placed in a given location because it would then intrude into the
space occupied by another box.

The second type is that of spatial distribution constraints: we are likely to
specify whether the boxes are to be packed compactly together, distributed evenly
or grouped by size, and so on. These are content-independent constraints. They
are also global, and their simultaneous application may be impossible.

The third kind is the content-dependent constraint which has been most in evidence in the discussion above: they must be stacked so that they don't get crushed, timetabled so that they don't clash, and so on. It is the content of the boxes, rather than their dimensions or the features of any desirable arrangement, which determine whether a box may be put in any given place or not.

Both spatial and content-dependent constraints must be given by the user. We shall make the simplifying assumption that as designers of the system we shall seek to define every conceivable, or at the very least every popular, form of the second type of constraint. This has the advantage – from the user's point of view – that specifying global constraints is just a matter of choosing them from a menu of options; and from our point of view that we don't have to consider the problems of implementing arbitrary global constraints.

There remains the hardest problem of all: how to specify content-related constraint specifications. The question of how to enter the contents of boxes is almost trivial by comparison, or, more accurately, becomes trivial once the constraint entry problem is solved.

7.3.2   Content-related constraints

The varied examples that we have considered so far suggest an approach to the representation of content-related constraints. A content-related constraint is logically a *predicate* which relates the contents – or more generally the *attributes* – of a collection of boxes which are related in some sense geometrically.

For example, if we consider the case of stacking uniform boxes which are all the same size (without loss of generality, unit cubes). The weight of each box is given as an integral number of kg, as is its crushing strength. To ensure that none of the boxes will be crushed, we must sum the weight of all boxes above each box in turn, and check the sum against its crushing strength.

Looking at the column of boxes as a list (topmost first)

$$[\mathtt{b}_n\{\mathtt{w}_n,\mathtt{s}_n\}, \quad \ldots \quad \mathtt{b}_2\{\mathtt{w}_2,\mathtt{s}_2\}, \quad \mathtt{b}_1\{\mathtt{w}_1,\mathtt{s}_1\}]$$

we are in effect asking that for each k,

$$\sum_{i=k+1}^{n} w_i \leq s_k$$

We can express this constraint as the Prolog query:

```
forall(split(Boxes, LBoxes, [HBox|RBoxes]),
       sum(weight, LBoxes) ≤ HBox:strength)?
```

where **split** is true of a partition of a list of **Boxes** into a front part – **LBoxes** – and a remainder – '[HBox|RBoxes]', and **sum** is used to add up all the **weight**s in a list of boxes. This query accomplishes all the required comparisons in the form by partitioning the boxes in every possible way.

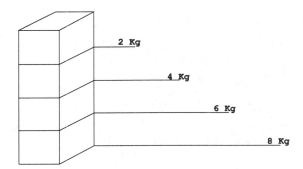

Figure 7.5 *A* $1 \times 1 \times 4$ *box decomposed into a column of four* $1 \times 1 \times 1$ *boxes*

A simple 'vertical' case of this is illustrated in Figure 7.5, but the method can easily be extended to and executed transparently by the system for arbitrary sizes. For boxes of arbitrary size, we would need to extend this by considering an implicit decomposition into unit boxes, with uniform distribution of weight-like parameters and cumulative distribution of strength-like parameters.

In the case of planning a timetable, we have constraints relating to the workload of teachers. For example, to ensure that any teacher does not have to teach more than four classes in one day, we must be able, for any given teacher, to construct a constraint which allows us to:

1. specify 'Any' as a generic teacher name;

2. count occurences of boxes with instantiations of 'Any' to any particular lecturer's name; and

3. compare the count with the desired number; if it is greater, then the arrangement under consideration is rejected.

There are other possible forms of content-related constraint. In the timetabling problem, we have described one of the dimensions as 'room'. We have evaded the issue of room size and whether that matters. Just as with resource requirements discussed above for the project planning problem, we may choose to say that – if class numbers matter, which in most real situations they do – a dimension '*no_of_seats*' must be introduced and the box which represents a particular lecturer-unit combination must have *no_of_seats* magnitude of the anticipated enrolment of that unit. But the problem is still not solved altogether, because we must also find a way to ensure that the room allocated is big enough. Pursuing this line, we would have to superimpose a further constraint in the room/*no_of_seats* plane; this is clearly not a pleasant prospect from the user's point of view.

It is possible to construct a notation for content related constraints which allows us to express these types of constraints in a general way:

$\forall B, B$ is a box, $\Phi(B[x \times y])$

where $B[x \times y] \equiv$ the list of boxes in the $x \times y$ hyperplane which intersects the box B and $\Phi(B[x \times y])$ is some Prolog-style predicate involving the values of one or more attributes of boxes in the list.

Of course, in a practical application, we would choose a more obvious and friendly notation than this to select the boxes involved in a constraint. Perhaps we would use a spreadsheet-style notation. The result is a notation which combines elements of spreadsheets to describe 'solution spaces' on the one hand, and in relational algebra as a database query language on the other.

In general, some of the dimensions associated with boxes' attributes are symbolic or *nominal* (i.e., discrete, almost certainly finite, and without intrinsic order); some are discrete and ordered and some support a whole number structure). The manner in which each kind features in constraints is likely to reflect its nature. Each kind will therefore have some typical operations associated with it. Likewise, the contents of the boxes will be typed in some formal way. Weight and crushing strength, say, are real; duration is integer; lecturer name is symbolic; and so on. Our proposed medium for constraint definition must be able to handle all these types, and yet – as much as possible – should not require the user to understand types in order to use it.

It is a more accurate reflection of the reality we are seeking to represent to accept that the nominal dimension 'room' requires rather more complex terms to describe its 'ordinate points' that simple atomic names; a functional description along the lines of `room(eg,316,25,pc,lab)` readily conveys the necessary information (room 316 in Eden Grove building is a 25-seater PC laboratory) and can as readily be exploited in constraint expressions as our other forms.

There are content-related constraints that we have not considered at all, not because they are insignificant but because we believe that in reality they are likely to be reduced to familiar types by the user, who will wish to pre-process the problem, so to speak, in order to achieve a suitable result. If garments were to be made by cutting from a long roll of material which has weft and warp, which is important, and possibly pattern, which is also important, it is likely that the way in which the designer would choose the orientation of these various pieces would be to circumscribe each in an irregular rectangular figure, and ask for those figures to be located optimally in a long rectangle.

This discussion is not exhaustive, indeed it may fall far short of covering the breadth of content-related constraints that problems or users may require. It offers a general approach and an article of faith, that a language can be found in which a wide variety of constraints will be expressible. The full range of problems that may be tackled in this manner would not, in any case, come to light until a product was available for people to use and, inevitably, seek to extend.

We shall see below that even the simplest of content-independent constraints, i.e., those which are essentially geometric in nature, give rise to fairly complex computational problems.

7.4   The underlying engine

We now turn to the problem of implementing (part of) the general purpose planner/scheduler. We have restricted ourselves to the simplest case of box stacking. Our boxes are 'light' (i.e., weightless) and must be fully supported underneath by another box or the floor. They may be rotated on their base, but no other transformation is allowed.

Our first focus is the implementation of the placing/optimizing machine, rather than the detail of the user interface. As the above discussion suggests, this is not because the latter is thought to be either a trivial or an easy task. From the point of view of applying *L&O*, however, the central engine presents an opportunity to explore its central ideas in a relatively 'pure' form, i.e., without embedding them in specialised issues such as graphics and the uses of windows.

It has been our explicit intention throughout our earlier discussion to geometrize as much as possible. The effectiveness of this approach will become clearer as we proceed with various aspects of the problem. We shall discuss the problem in stages, beginning with the idea behind the overall algorithm, and going on to solve the easier problem of arrangements of boxes (i.e., rectangles) on the floor only; motivating our 'interval algebra' from that simpler case, we finally extend it and apply it to the full three-dimensional problem.

7.4.1   How to stack boxes

Before anything is placed in it, the space into which the boxes may be stacked is itself a rectangular box, referred to for convenience as the 'van', which is simply characterised by its dimensions of length, width and height. As boxes are put in it, the space changes, becoming more awkward. It is not obvious now where boxes may be put; our only guide is that they may not intrude into each other's volume. We may try, therefore, something like the **satisfied** predicate defined in Program 7.1.

The recursive rule for **satisfied** describes how if we already have some satisfactory arrangement of boxes, then we may place a further box into an available space (according to our constraint criterion), provided it actually fits; moreover, the resulting arrangement will be satisfactory. Thus satisfaction of a constraint by an arrangement is controlled by what spaces the methods of the constraint itself make available as the arrangement is built up.

For the moment, this is best read as a partial specification, since we have yet to define how constraints determine what spaces are **available** and how boxes can be made to **fit** into an arrangement.

```
arrangement([Box|Boxes],Constraint):{
    satisfied([Placement|Placements]) :-
        arrangement(Boxes, Contraint):satisfied(Placements),
        Constraint:available(Placements, Patch),
        intervals:fits(Box, Transform, Patch).
    ...
}.
```

Program 7.1 A way of arranging boxes

In fitting a box into a space, the system may have to rotate it on its base before placement; if it fits both ways, then both ways will be tried, and it is seen in practice that this may lead to an optimal solution which might otherwise have been missed. In general, we might wish to have a more permissive interpretation of **fits** than will be given here. Rather than insisting, as we shall, that each box is fully supported by whatever is under it, floor or another box or boxes, we might only ask that the convex hull of contact areas should contain (the xy-projection of) the centre of gravity. We observe in passing that this interpretation can be applied to 'light' boxes as readily as heavy ones, since we would not wish the system to behave as if light boxes can be suspended in mid-air. This interpretation, which gives rise to an interesting geometric constraint problem, is illustrated below in Figure 7.6.

The constraint of interest to us will be described as 'compact'; it requires that arrangements be compactly packed together, in some precisely defined sense. This might simply mean that boxes can only be put next to other boxes, i.e., that even if spaces are available (in the every day sense of the word) away from the arrangement, according to this constraint they are not available in the technical sense. But it could also mean that boxes must be so packed that the final arrangement has a minimal surface area or even a minimal external surface area (i.e., ignoring wholly enclosed gaps).

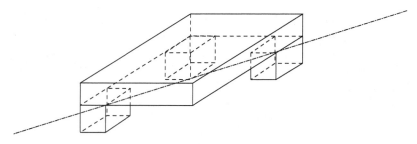

Figure 7.6   *The centre of gravity falls within the convex hull of the areas of contact*

Although it is not part of the immediate problem, we briefly note what additions would have to be made to accommodate a content-dependent constraint, such as a weight and strength constraint. Having established that an arrangement is satisfactory from the point of view of compactness, we need to test that it meets the requirements of the weight and strength constraint. This will be added as a further condition at the end of our definition in Program 7.1:

```
arrangement([Box|Boxes],Constraint):{
        satisfied([Placement|Placements]) :-
               arrangement(Boxes, Contraint):satisfied(Placements),
               Constraint:available(Placements, Patch),
               intervals:fits(Box, Transform, Patch),
               inhibit_crush([Placement|Placements]).
        ...}.
```

It remains to make explicit how a **Placement** is represented. The minimal necessary information for the full support compact problem is the name of the box, the position of the anchor and whether the box has been placed as it was given or was rotated before placement. Thus a **Placement** decomposes into

```
[Box_id,Transformation,Position]
```

where **Box_id** might be an *L&O* label, say **boxA**, whose dimensions are given in an inheritance clause such as

```
boxA <= box([4,5,3]).
```

Transformation will be either **id** for identity or **rot** for rotation, and **Position** will be given by a position vector, say, **(2,5,3)**. We shall then denote the space interval precisely occupied by **boxA** by

```
[(2,5,3),(6,10,6)]
```

since

```
(2,5,3) + (4,5,3) = (6,10,6).
```

7.4.2   The geometry of planar arrangements

If we are packing boxes into a $10' \times 6'$ truck or van, then we might represent the floor of the van as a rectangle of length 10 and width 6 say – or more generally length **VL** and width **VW**. This is essentially the interval [(0,0),(10,6)]. In effect, we begin with the unoccupied interval [(0,0),(10,6)].

The first box, **boxA**, is brought along and anchored at the origin; **boxA** has dimensions 6×3, so we now have the free space shown in Figure 7.7. This view

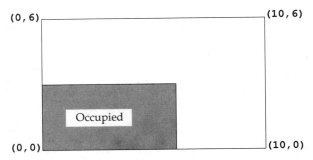

Figure 7.7   *The space* `[(0,0),(10,6)]` `--` `[(0,0),(6,3)]` *is now available for more boxes*

of the free space is not very helpful, however. To begin with, it is an L-shaped space, when we wish to place plain rectangular boxes on the floor.

If we ask what size are the largest boxes we could place in the free space, the answer is readily seen to coincide with the *maximal subintervals* of the set theoretic difference

$$[(0,0),(10,6)] \ -- \ [(0,0),(6,3)]$$

which are

$$[(6,0),(10,6)]$$

and

$$[(0,3),(10,6)]$$

These maximal subintervals correspond to the 'maximal' unoccupied rectangular areas left after `boxA` has been added. They also show the sizes to the largest boxes that can now be loaded into the van.

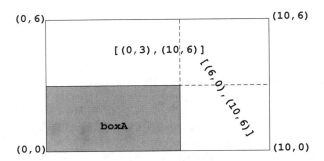

Figure 7.8   *The space* `[(0,0),(10,6)]` `--` `[(0,0),(6,3)]` *in terms of its two maximal subintervals*

The two maximal subintervals overlap, of course, so they cannot both be filled with boxes; but at this stage they represent the available choices for the next box to be brought along. The difference of the two intervals then will be represented by a list containing its two maximal subintervals:

```
[ [(6,0),(10,6)] , [(0,3),(10,6)] ]
```

which are illustrated in Figure 7.8.

The system under discussion does not use any heuristic to optimize the positioning of individual boxes. (This is just as well, for too early an attempt at optimization will preclude some optimal global solutions.) Thus it is possible that the next box to be loaded, boxB, with dimensions 3×4, will be placed as it came, anchored without rotation at (6,0). We now have what appears at first sight a more awkward problem, the representation of the free space following the arrival of boxB.

However, the problem has in effect already been solved. Just as subtracting one interval from another leaves a space which is easily represented by its maximal subintervals, subtracting an interval from a space so represented can be accomplished if the new interval is subtracted from each of the maximal subintervals in turn. Intermediate results comprise the maximal subintervals of the individual differences, and these have to be merged to remove redundancy. This is best seen diagrammatically, as in Figure 7.9 below where we show boxA and boxB together.

The individual differences are:

```
[(6,0),(10,6)] -- [(6,0),(9,4)]
     = [ [(9,0),(10,6)], [(6,4),(10,6)] ]
[(0,3),(10,6)] -- [(6,0),(9,4)]
     = [ [(0,3),(6,6)], [(0,4),(10,6)] ]
```

and, as can be seen in Figure 7.9 also, the interval [(6,4),(10,6)] is wholly

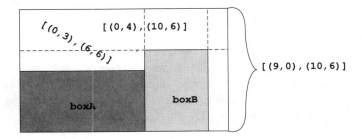

The difference between a set described by its maximal subintervals and another interval is a set which can itself be described by its maximal subintervals.

Figure 7.9 *Differencing maximal subintervals*

```
arrange:{
    satisfied([Box],[[Box,id,(0,0)]]).
    satisfied([Box],[[Box,rot,(0,0)]]).
    satisfied([Box|Boxes],[[Box,Tran,Posn]|Placements]) :-
        satisfied(Boxes,Placements),
        available(Placements,Ints),
        member(Int,Ints),
        iv2:fits([Box,Tran,Posn],Int).
    available([[Box,id,(0,0)]],iv2:cleanup([[(L,0),(VL,VW)],
            [(0,W),(VL,VW)]])):-
        van:length = VL, van:width = VW,
        iv2:fits([Box,id,(0,0)],[(0,0),(VL,VW)]),
        Box:length = L, Box:width = W.
    available([[Box,rot,(0,0)]],iv2:cleanup([[(W,0),(VL,VW)],
            [(0,L),(VL,VW)]])):-
        van:length = VL, van:width = VW,
        iv2:fits([Box,rot,(0,0)],[(0,0),(VL,VW)]),
        Box:length = L, Box:width = W.
    available([[Box,Tran,Posn]|Placements],Ints) :-
        available(Placements,OldInts),
        iv2:lidiff(OldInts,iv2:tran(Tran,Box,Posn))=Ints
}.
```

Program 7.2 Top-level of the two-dimensional arrangment program

contained in [(0,4),(10,6)], and so is redundant. The correct expression for the full difference, then, is

```
[ [(6,0),(10,6)] , [(0,3),(10,6)] ] -- [(0,4),(10,6)]
    = [ [(9,0),(10,6)], [(0,3),(6,6)],[(0,4),(10,6)] ]
```

In the next section we discuss the implementation of this operation. Below, in Figure 7.10, we give an illustration of the two-dimensional **arrange** program (see Program 7.2) at work. Given five boxes, of sizes 6×3, 5×4, 4×3, 4×2 and 3×4 respectively, these are fitted precisely on the van floor which is 10×7. A query which expresses this problem is:

```
arrange:satisfied([box1, box2, box3, box4, box5], P)?
P = [[box1, id, (4, 4)], [box2, id, (5, 0)],
  [box3, id, (0, 4)], [box4, rot, (3, 0)],
  [box5, id, (0, 0)]]
```

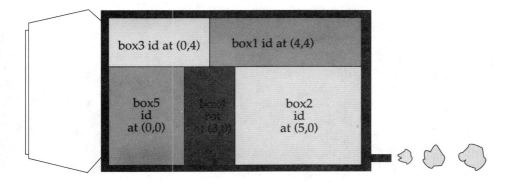

Figure 7.10 *A precise tessellation of the van floor*

The specification of the boxes and the van which form the problem is given in Program 7.3.

Note that our program does not permute the boxes, so it only locates one solution. A moment's consideration will persuade the reader that all other solutions are essentially permutations of this solution and that each can be derived by permuting the boxes in the 'input' list.

For simplicity's sake, both **satisfied** and **available** are treated as methods of one object, **arrange**, in Program 7.2. This simplification obscures somewhat the now implicit adoption of **compact** as the active constraint.

7.4.3 Interval operations and their computation

We have stated the correct answer to a set difference using maximal subintervals, but it is not immediately obvious that the method is well-defined or that it can be expressed as an efficient algorithm. We turn to this formalization now, before

```
rect(L,W):{
    length = L.
    width = W
    }.
box1 <= rect(6,3).         box2 <= rect(5,4).
box3 <= rect(4,3).         box4 <= rect(4,2).
box5 <= rect(3,4).

van <= rect(10,7).
```

Program 7.3 The planar program

```
iv1:{
    diff([A,B],[C,D]) = [[A,B]] :-
        B =< C; A >= D.
    diff([A,B],[C,D]) = [[]] :-
        C =< A, B =< D.
    diff([A,B],[C,D]) =
        cleanup([[A,max(A,C)],[min(B,D),B]]).
    trivial([X,Y]) :-
        Y =< X.
    trivial([]).
    ...
}.
```

Program 7.4 The one-dimensional interval program

going on to show that the full three-dimensional problem brings new challenges in interval algebra in its wake. We begin with the simplest problem, then. What is the difference of two intervals? For reasons which may already be obvious, given the example we have discussed above, we shall allow full generality in our intervals, including the possibility of overlap. Nor need our discussion now be confined to two dimensions, although it is often easiest to illustrate the abstract definitions with two-dimensional diagrams. In any case, the definition is inductive, and the one- and two-dimensional cases are crucial as the base case and an illustration of the inductive step, respectively.

It is evident that in one dimension the definitions are direct, as is shown by `iv1` in Program 7.4. The function `cleanup` is 'imported' from the *L&O* program `list`, and simply removes trivial intervals from the list. The reader may have noticed the odd fact that the empty list can be used to indicate the empty interval without clashing with the notation for proper intervals.

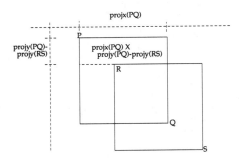

Figure 7.11 *Computation of* `PQ--RS` *as a set of maximal subintervals*

The calculation of intervals in two dimensions is best understood in terms of a diagram, as illustrated in Figure 7.11. Taking the *cartesian product* of one-dimensional intervals is one obvious way to move up one dimension. In `iv2` in Program 7.5, the function `pr` defines the cartesian product in an explicit manner, and `mpr`, for multiproduct, does the same job on lists of intervals. Also explicitly defined are the projections, triviality and containment.

With reference to Figure 7.11, the maximal subintervals of the difference are found by taking the two multiproducts

```
( projx(PQ) -- projx(RS) ) × projy(PQ)
projx(PQ) × ( projy(PQ) -- projy(RS) )
```

and combining them, removing by means of `elim` any properly contained – and so redundant – intervals.

```
iv2:{
    pr([A,B] , [C,D]) = [(A,C), (B,D)].
    pr([] , [_,_]) = [].
    pr([_,_] , []) = [].
    projx([(Px,Py),(Qx,Qy)]) = [Px,Qx].
    projy([(Px,Py),(Qx,Qy)]) = [Py,Qy].
    mpr([],_) = [].  mpr(_,[]) = [].
    mpr([I|Is] , [J|Js]) =chain([[pr(I,J)],mpr([I],Js),
                   mpr(Is,[J]),mpr(Is,Js)]).
    trivial([(A,B),(C,D)]) :- C =< A ; D =< B.
    trivial([]).
    inside([],_).
    inside([(Px,Py),(Qx,Qy)],[(Rx,Ry),(Sx,Sy)]):-
        Px >= Rx, Py >= Ry, Qx =< Sx, Qy =< Sy.
    ...
    }.
```

Program 7.5 Top-level of the two-dimensional interval difference program

7.4.4   Interval problems in three dimensions

It may be thought that with the two-dimensional problem solved, we had exhausted all problems, at least in theory. There is a detail we have deliberately evaded in the two-dimensional case for the sake of smooth exposition: we have said nothing about boxes being fully supported.

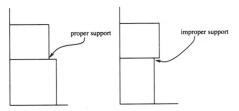

Figure 7.12 *Proper and improper support in two dimensions*

Of course, the way we phrased our problem suggested that the floor was the support. A true two-dimensional analogy for the three-dimensional case would require us to be more careful in analysing proper one-dimensional supports for the two-dimensional boxes. We can see one interpretation of 'proper' and 'improper' support in the case of a vertically stacked two-dimensional example illustrated in Figure 7.12.

The requirement of proper support introduces a complementary problem: we have seen that a properly defined interval difference was needed to ensure that as new boxes were put down on the floor, the remaining free space was so represented as to reflect the availability of suitable sites for new boxes to be deposited. In three dimensions boxes may be stacked on top of each other, provided they are fully supported, so we must provide an adequate representation for the spaces created above floor level. A glimpse of the complexity of this problem is provided by the diagrams in Figure 7.13 below which show the evolution of an arrangement.

What is now striking is that new spaces are created by amalgamation as well as subtraction. If two boxes of the same height are put together, their tops form a rectangular set whose maximal subintervals are available sites for the location of new boxes. This may happen in a more complicated way than our first example above might suggest.

A further example should suffice. One $1 \times 1 \times 1$ boxes and four $2 \times 1 \times 1$ boxes are to be arranged together as compactly as possible. The minimal surface solution to this problem is shown in Figure 7.14a, while in Figure 7.14b we display a possible intermediate arrangement. The tops of the four boxes at this stage form a rectangular annulus, whose maximal subintervals are shown in Figure 7.14c. But this arrangement of subintervals must collapse into one large interval when the

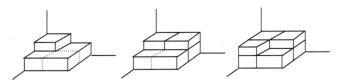

Figure 7.13 *Successive changes as new boxes are brought into the arrangement*

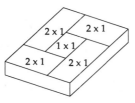 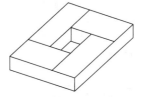

a. The optimal solution   b. An intermediate stage

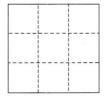

c. Maximal intervals of the square annulus

Figure 7.14 *An annular arrangement*

fifth box is finally placed.

The problem remains, how to express this amalgamation process algorithmically. Our implementation is rather crude in that it forces every interaction and rejects the contained intervals. The algorithm is shown in Program 7.6.

7.4.5   Stacking boxes in three dimensions

We finally use all these procedures to enable boxes to be stacked. The task is relatively simple. Before any box is brought into the van, the floor is the only available space. When the first box is brought in, the remaining free floor space is represented by its maximal subintervals; the other available space is the top of that first box itself. In general, there will be available spaces represented as collections of maximal subintervals at various heights. When a box is placed on a particular site, two things happen to the available spaces: the interval occupied by the newly arrived box has to be subtracted from those at the same height; while the top of the new box (i.e., an interval with the same floor projection as the base) has to be amalgamated with available maximal subintervals at height 'height of base + height of box'.

The only effective change from two to three dimensions, then, is in the notion of availability. How this would be modified to take account of the two base cases is clear – we merely add the top of the box to the available intervals according to the two-dimensional procedure. In the general case, we must take the existing available intervals and divide them up according to height. Those at the same height as the anchor of the last box will have the base of the box subtracted from

```
iv2:{
    mxl(PQ,RS) = append(notriv(PQ,RS),[PQ]).
    notriv(PQ,RS) = cleanup(expel(create(PQ,RS),[PQ,RS])).
    expel([],L) = [].
    expel([H|T],[PQ,RS]) = expel(T,[PQ,RS]) :-
        inside(H,PQ);inside(H,RS).
    expel([H|T],L) = [H|expel(T,L)].
    create(PQ,RS) = [pr(iv1:n(projx(PQ),projx(RS)),
                        iv1:u(projy(PQ),projy(RS))),
                     pr(iv1:u(projx(PQ),projx(RS)),
                        iv1:n(projy(PQ),projy(RS)))].
    remax(L,R) = elim(append(elim(mix(L,R)),R)).
    mix([],L) = [].
    mix([H|T],[I]) = chain([mxl(H,I),elim(mix(T,[I])),[H|T]]).
    mix(L,[H|T]) = mix(elim(mix(L,[H])), T).
    }.
```
Note the union u and intersection n imported from iv1.

Program 7.6 Part of the class iv2 of two-dimensional intervals

them, those at the same height as the top of the new box will have the top of the box amalgamated with them, while those at other heights survive intact.

With some minor simplification for the sake of exposition, this is encoded in Program 7.7.

7.5   The user interface

The essential intentions behind the design for the interface to our generic application are simplicity and openness. We compensate for the fact that the underlying algorithms for arranging boxes are not inherently 'clever' by making it easy and natural for the user to intervene in and collaborate with the system in the problem solving process.

For example, it may be that by reordering the boxes, perhaps removing some from the arrangement and placing them on hold, and so on, the basic algorithms can more easily obtain an optimal solution than either the user on his or her own or by a 'clever' automatic system. In addition, the user is assumed to be interested in choosing from alternative legitimate configurations or to specify criteria by which a configuration may be chosen. The user may also wish to sort the boxes, for example, by height; (this would make sense to a human who recognizes the need for uniform flat surfaces for the next layer of boxes to be placed on).

```
arrange3:{
   ...
   available([[Box,Tran,Posn]|Placements],Ints) :-
       available(Placements,OldInts),
       discr(OldInts,[Box,Tran,Posn]) =
                   [BaseHt,TopHt,OtherHts],
       lidiff(BaseHt,tran(Box,Tran,Posn)) = NewBaseHt,
       remax(top(Box,Tran,Posn),TopHt) = NewTopHt,
       chain([NewBaseHt,NewTopHt,OtherHts]) = Ints.
   ...
}.
```

Program 7.7 The top-level of a three-dimensional arranger

Not all of these are possible here in their full generality, but the following elements of the interface have been implemented:

1. A visually presented 'queue' of boxes showing those boxes which have been placed and those which are 'on hold' waiting to be placed into the arrangement.

2. The graphic entry of each box's attributes; as the image is defined by means of mouse movements and 'clicks', the dimensions are also displayed to ensure accurate entry; each box thus defined is then added to the queue.

3. A visual representation of the current arrangement with the option to extract some boxes from it; boxes thus extracted rejoin the tail of the queue.

4. A facility for trying out alternative placements for boxes which have already been placed; from there the facility to choose one of the offered solutions and to confirm it, thereby producing a new arrangement.

The interface is based on the graphic edit style of window as seen in Chapter 5. The basic tools defined within the **Packer** window, as illustrated in Figure 7.15, are: **create box**, **manipulate queue**, **repack**. Within the drawing pane are displayed a suitably scaled view of the arrangement so far, and a representation of the queue of boxes including those waiting to be arranged.

The **create box** tool gives rise to its own transient *graphic dialog window*, as in Figure 7.16. Within this dialog, the size of the box is defined by means of mouse movements and other fields in the dialog capture the name of the box and any specific constraints that apply to it. A newly created box may be placed anywhere within the queue.

The **repack** tool allows the user to experiment with different arrangements of the boxes which have already been loaded in. Invoking this tool causes the

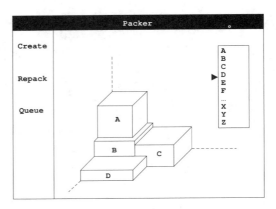

Figure 7.15 *The* `Packer` *application window*

underlying packing system to attempt to find an alternative arrangement for the
boxes which have been packed so far.

The queue of boxes is the structure which identifies those boxes that have been
packed and those which are waiting to be packed. An arrow is used to indicate of
the position within the queue of the next box to be packed.

The queue can be manipulated by applying a standard sort to it – such as
sorting the boxes in it by their height, or in the case of a van being packed for
a delivery round, by their 'unloading' order. Alternatively, the queue can be
manually adjusted by moving entries within it. In this case, the user would 'pick
up' a queue entry with the mouse and 'drop' it into the desired place within the
queue. If a box already in the arrangement is resized, or if its place in the queue
is affected, then the arrangement is undone to that point.

Double clicking an entry in the queue causes a dialog window to open which
enables the user to edit the characteristics of the entry – such as changing its size

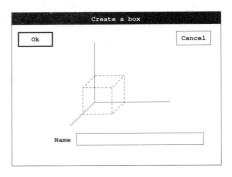

Figure 7.16 *A graphic dialog window for creating a new box*

or altering a constraint.

The queue also uses an arrow to show the 'next' box which is to be packed, and by clicking on the arrow the system attempts to place the next box into the arrangement; showing its location as appropriate. Alternatively, the system may attempt to place all the boxes automatically until no more can be placed within the allocated space; in which case the arrow highlights the first box in the queue that could not be placed.

Generic drawing, text-editing and other tools are invoked by these 'high level' tools via inheritance. At the same time, the visible objects correspond both to real objects in the world and to computational objects in the application itself. The graphical user interface harmonises all three elements in a natural way. *L&O* through its objects and graphics thus facilitates a close correspondence between the user's view of the problem, the computational expression of that problem and the visual solution offered by the system.

7.6 Summary

In this chapter, we have outlined the major components of an application which allows users to solve problems in a range of domains such as packing boxes, planning projects and scheduling timetables. The *L&O* language allows us to express the underlying algorithms employed in the application, to express the graphical interface succinctly and to structure to overall program effectively.

The application as we have developed it is best seen as being a 'skeleton' of a more complete and polished product. We would expect there to be many further features and facilities than we are able to present here, however our `packer` application is certainly adequate to demonstrate the fundamental concepts.

We include a listing of the major components of the program in Appendix D.

CHAPTER EIGHT

Semantics

In earlier chapters we have introduced elements of the *L&O* programming language and we have given it an informal justification. We are now concerned more formally with the semantics of *L&O* programming. Our overall aim is to verify that there is a well-founded basis for understanding *L&O* programs; in particular that our notation is just another variety of logic programming.

However the *L&O* language does have an independent semantics apart from standard logic programming. This is because the language of equations and objects introduces concepts and features which are not needed or explained in basic logic programming which is based on the semantics of relations. Thus we may be able to map our language into logic programming (even onto) but we are nevertheless introducing features which have their own characteristics.

8.1 Semantics of class templates

There are two more or less separate aspects of the *L&O* language that we need to consider – *L&O* programs themselves (with class bodies and class rules etc.) and the equational style of programming. We treat each aspect of the complete language separately. In the case of the equational extension our approach in Section 8.2 is to use the *syntax* of functions and equations as an alternative syntax for standard *semantics* of logic programs.

8.1.1 The fundamental intuition

Conventional object oriented programming cannot be said to have a particularly strong mathematical foundation. This lack of rigour represents both a problem and an opportunity for us. The 'target' which we are trying to reach from logic programming is ill-defined and therefore it is hard to 'know' whether we have captured the intuition behind object oriented programming. However, because of this we also have some freedom in choosing how to integrate logic programming and object oriented programming. This is in marked contrast with the situation we face when attempting to integrate functional programming into logic programming; here, the mathematics of equations is much better founded and when combining logic and functional programming the primary problem is integrating this mathematics with the mathematics of logic programming.

In *L&O* notation we have taken a particular view of objects; the fundamental intuition behind our notation is that an object is characterised by what we know to be true of it. Of course while this view may not encompass the whole of object oriented programming (in particular this does not adequately address issues related to assignment) we have shown in earlier chapters some of the expressive power that the notation gives us.

A complete *L&O* system may have many objects within it; so whereas a conventional logic program consists of a single global set of true facts, a *L&O* program may have many such sets. These sets may be completely independent, weakly linked (via calls expressed as labelled sub-goals) or strongly linked (via inheritance). In this sense the *L&O* formalism takes up where standard logic programming leaves off. We are more concerned with the relationships between whole relations than with individual tuples of relations.

This difference in scale is a key reason why the *L&O* language is so useful. Our object oriented programming view is complementary with conventional logic programming, it is not an alternative. Moreover, simply because we have a change of scale does not mean we wish to abandon logic, perhaps the main result of this chapter is that *L&O* programs are still first order logic programs.

8.1.2   The approach to understanding

After having established the set of allowable formulae in an *L&O* program we introduce a number of *inference rules*. These rules are based on the resolution principle [Rob65] for standard clauses although they are modified in view of the *L&O* syntax. Together, these inference rules form a proof theory which allows us to derive answers to queries.

We can justify this proof theoretic semantics by virtue of a mapping from *L&O* programs into standard first order clauses. We will show the soundness and completeness of our inference procedure in terms of standard resolution. It is important to be able to establish the soundness and completeness of our inference rules, since this gives us one part of the relationship between logic programming and *L&O* programming – it shows that *L&O* is equivalent to a subset of logic programming. Finally, we see that we can embed logic programs into *L&O* programs; in effect we can 'replace' standard logic programs by *L&O* programs.

We show the soundness and completeness of our inference rules by constructing a mapping from *L&O* programs to a subset of standard clausal form and showing that, under this mapping, resolution is preserved by our inference rules.

After having established the main result we also show that we can embed a set of standard clauses in a *L&O* program whilst preserving the meaning of those clauses. This property distinguishes our *L&O* formalism from other extensions to logic programming which may only have a purely one-way semantics – from the new notation to logic programming.

In this chapter, we specifically avoid attempting to address the semantics of the 'extra-logical' features of Prolog and *L&O*. In particular we do not address the semantics of dynamic variables, nor do we address issues relating to input and output and the special Prolog control primitives such as 'cut'. Understanding assignment adequately is a hard problem not confined to the context of *L&O*-style object oriented programming.

L&O programs

An *L&O* program consists of a set of *class templates*, each of which consists of a *class body* and/or a set of *class rules*. A class body is a set of axioms enclosed by '{}'s and prefixed by an identifying label term:

$$label: \{$$
$$axiom_1.$$
$$axiom_2.$$
$$\ldots$$
$$axiom_n.$$
$$\}$$

The *label* term may be a constant or a complex term. In the case of a complex term variables in the label may be shared with the axioms enclosed in the body. Any variables occurring in the label are universally quantified across all the axioms in the class body. Other variables are universally quantified across the individual axioms. Each *axiom* in the class body is of the form:

$$H : -B.$$

where H is a predication and B is a sub-goal. Axioms can be either normal clauses or equations; however we shall see how equations can be incorporated separately – for the moment we assume that any axioms in class bodies look like normal clauses that define relations. In the case that the body of an axiom is empty then we can use the shorter form:

$$H.$$

A *sub-goal* is one of:

- a predication of the form

$$\ldots ,p(t_1,\ldots ,t_n),\ldots$$

where all the t_i are normal terms or expressions which might include the **self** keyword.

- a conjunction of sub-goals of the form

$$\ldots ,(C_1,C_2),\ldots$$

- a disjunction of sub-goals of the form

$$\ldots ,(C_1;C_2),\ldots$$

- a *negated* sub-goal of the form

$$\ldots ,\neg C,\ldots$$

- a labelled sub-goal of the form

$$\ldots ,L:C,\ldots$$

Class rules are used to describe inheritance between *L&O* programs. There are two types of class rule: a normal rule written as:

$$l(l_1,\ldots ,l_l) <= m(m_1,\ldots ,m_m)$$

or the *overriding* class rule which is written as:

$$l(l_1,\ldots ,l_l) << m(m_1,\ldots ,m_m)$$

This second form of the class rule includes an overriding or *default* interpretation: relations defined locally in a class body override any relations with the same name which might be inherited with the class rule.

A class rule can have attached to it a *differential inheritance* filter. This is of the form:

$$l(l_1,\ldots ,l_l) <= m(m_1,\ldots ,m_m) - [template_1,\ldots ,template_n]$$

where each filter *template$_i$* denotes a range of atoms which must not be inherited, it can be either of:

$$pred(t_1,\ldots ,t_n)$$

or

$$pred/arity$$

although the second form is really just a short form of the first where all the t_is are anonymous variables.

Finally, there are two special keywords in our notation: **self** and **super**. The **self** keyword always refers to the original label (prior to the application of any class rules) associated with any sub-goal, and **super** refers to those definitions which result from inheritance rather than the complete class template.

8.1.3   A proof theory for $L\&O$ programs

Given an $L\&O$ program and a query over that program we wish to be able to determine instances of the query which are logical consequences of the program (or *completed program* in the case of a program with negated sub-goals). In order to do that we introduce a proof procedure based on a number of inference rules which allows us to derive new queries from old ones. The proof procedure is an extension of the standard logic programming proof procedure embedded into the context of $L\&O$ programming.

Since an $L\&O$ program consists of a collection of labelled programs rather than a set of clauses in conventional logic programming any top-level query of an $L\&O$ program *must* take the form of a labelled sub-goal:

$$L : C?$$

where C is a sub-goal. Any sub-goals which arise as part of solving such a query may not directly have a label; however as we shall see we have rules which allow us to assign a label to any unlabelled sub-goal. This allows us to declare that every sub-goal that can arise in an $L\&O$ proof is associated with a label which defines where to find the clauses to solve the sub-goal.

In order for us to be able to handle the **self** keyword we actually assign *two* labels to every sub-goal: the explicit or actual label and the self label which is usually identified implicitly. We write the complete labelled sub-goal by subscripting the actual label with the self label. So every $L\&O$ sub-goal may be represented as:

$$L_S : Q$$

where L is the actual label, S is the self label and Q is a sub-goal. In the case of a sub-goal which is a top-level query, or one which is explicitly labelled, then the self label is the same as the actual label:

$$L_L : Q?$$

We will also use the notation

$$H : -B \in L$$

to denote that the axiom $H : -B$ is in the class body associated with label L.

An *initial $L\&O$ query* is a labelled sub-goal. Notice that it is important for the sub-goal to be labelled since in a class template all the individual axioms are associated with a label, and if we do not have a label for our initial query then we cannot identify which class template to invoke.

An *$L\&O$ sequent* is a sequence of sub-goals starting with an initial $L\&O$ query such that each sub-goal (apart from the initial $L\&O$ query) is derived from the previous sub-goal using one of the inference rules outlined above.

An *$L\&O$ proof* is an $L\&O$ sequent which is terminated by the empty query.

The distribution of labels

Our first group of inference rules relate to the distribution of labels in a sub-goal. Given a labelled sub-goal of the form $L : C$ we can redistribute the label L across the connectives that appear in the sub-goal C. Ultimately this may mean that the only labelled sub-goals within the query are labelled predications. We actually have five rules which allow us to distribute labels in a query:

$$I_1 \vdash \frac{L_S : (A, B)}{L_S : A, L_S : B}$$

$$I_2 \vdash \frac{L_S : (A; B)}{L_S : A; L_S : B}$$

$$I_3 \vdash \frac{L_S : (\neg A)}{\neg L_S : A}$$

$$I_4 \vdash \frac{L_S : (\mathbf{super} : A)}{\mathbf{super}(L)_S : A}$$

$$I_5 \vdash \frac{L_S : (M : A)}{M_M : A}$$

Inference rule I_5 captures the notion that explicitly labelled sub-goals retain their explicit labels and that it is only in unlabelled sub-goals that predications are assigned labels via an inference rule. It also shows how the **self** label is identified from an actual label. Inference rule I_4, which is for distributing a label across the **super** label, leaves a special 'marker' label which is interpreted by a variation of the class rule inference rule I_8 that we shall see below.

Given these inference rules we can rewrite any labelled query into an equivalent one where the only labelled formulae are predications and moreover each predication has exactly one label. For example, given the labelled sub-goal

$$\ldots, L_S : (A, \neg(M : B; C)), \ldots$$

where A, B and C are predications, we can rewrite it thus:

$$\ldots, L_S : A, L_S : \neg(M : B; C), \ldots \qquad \text{by } I_1$$
$$\ldots, L_S : A, \neg L_S : (M : B; C), \ldots \qquad \text{by } I_3$$
$$\ldots, L_S : A, \neg(L_S : (M : B); L_S : C), \ldots \qquad \text{by } I_2$$
$$\ldots, L_S : A, \neg(M_M : B; L_S : C), \ldots \qquad \text{by } I_5$$

Class body inference rule

Given a sub-goal in the form of a labelled predication we can reduce it in one of two ways: by replacing the label or by replacing the predication. The class body inference rule shows how we can use an axiom from a class body to replace the predication by a simpler sub-goal. The class rule inference rule (see I_8 below) shows how we can replace the label. The class body inference rule is a variation on the standard resolution principle [Rob65]. We have to extend it slightly to allow for unifying labels and to incorporate **self**.

$$I_6 \vdash \frac{H : -C \in L \wedge Q_1, \ldots, M_S : P, \ldots, Q_n}{(Q_1, \ldots, M_S : C[\texttt{self}/S], \ldots, Q_n)\theta}$$

provided that θ is a m.g.u. and that $(L : H[\texttt{self}/S])\theta \equiv (M : P)\theta$, where $E[X/T]$ means the expression E with each occurrence of X replaced by T; in particular, $C[\texttt{self}/S]$ means replace all occurrences of the **self** keyword by the self label S. In effect there is an 'extra' substitution of the form $\{\texttt{self}/S\}$ at the beginning of the unification (and of course which is still there at the end) between the head of the axiom and the predication.

A simple variation of the I_6 inference rule allows us to reduce sub-goals using axioms which have no body:

$$I_7 \vdash \frac{H \in L \wedge Q_1, \ldots, Q_{i-1}, M_S : P, Q_{i+1}, \ldots, Q_n}{(Q_1, \ldots, Q_{i-1}, Q_{i+1}, \ldots, Q_n)\theta}$$

provided that θ is a m.g.u. and that $(L : H[\texttt{self}/S])\theta \equiv (M : P)\theta$ where H is an assertion in the class body for L.

Class rule inference rules

The class rule inference rules state how we might use the various kinds of class rule in an $L\&O$ program to replace the label in a labelled predication. Recall that there are two types of class rule: the normal class rule and the overriding class rule. These give rise to two class rule inference rules. The normal class rule is the simpler to describe:

$$I_8 \vdash \frac{L <= K \wedge Q_1, \ldots, M_S : P, \ldots, Q_n}{(Q_1, \ldots, K_S : P, \ldots, Q_n)\theta}$$

provided that $L\theta \equiv M\theta$ where θ is a m.g.u. and P is a predication. Notice that the **self** label is not changed by using this inference rule. In fact one may have to use several of these rules before being able to reduce the predication using a class body inference step; and we must be able to recover the original label with **self**.

With the overriding class rule we have to add an extra constraint on the predicate symbol of the predication to make sure that any locally defined programs are not inherited:

$$I_9 \vdash \frac{L << K \wedge Q_1, \ldots, M_S : P(t_1, \ldots, t_m), \ldots, Q_n}{(Q_1, \ldots, K_S : P(t_1, \ldots, t_m), \ldots, Q_n)\theta}$$

provided that $L\theta \equiv M\theta$ where θ is a m.g.u. and that there does not exist an axiom of the form $P(a_1, \ldots, a_m) : -C \in L$.

There are two further variations of the class rule inference rule which handle the **super** label. Recall that when a sub-goal is labelled with **super** then an inheritance step *must* be applied to reduce the sub-goal. We therefore have the following rules for reducing **super** which complement the label distribution rule I_4:

$$I_{10} \vdash \frac{L <= K \wedge Q_1, \ldots, \mathbf{super}(M)_S : P, \ldots, Q_n}{(Q_1, \ldots, K_S : P, \ldots, Q_n)\theta}$$

provided that $L\theta \equiv M\theta$ where θ is a m.g.u. and P is a predication.

$$I_{11} \vdash \frac{L << K \wedge Q_1, \ldots, \mathbf{super}(M)_S : P(a_1, \ldots, a_m), \ldots, Q_n}{Q_1, \ldots, K_S : P(a_1, \ldots, a_m), \ldots, Q_n)\theta}$$

provided that $L\theta \equiv M\theta$ where θ is a m.g.u. and that there does not exist an axiom of the form $P(a_1, \ldots, a_m) : -C \in L$.

Differential inheritance   If a class rule has a differential inheritance filter attached to it then extra constraints are applied to the inference rule prior to its use. In particular we must ensure that no atom which 'matches' a template in the filter may be inherited:

$$I_{12} \vdash \frac{L <= K - [f_1, \ldots, f_k] \wedge Q_1, \ldots, M_S : P, \ldots, Q_n}{(Q_1, \ldots, K_S : P, \ldots, Q_n)\theta}$$

provided that $L\theta \equiv M\theta$ where θ is a m.g.u., P is a predication and that P doesn't match any filter template f_i. A predication can be said to *match* a filter template of the form $pred(t_1, \ldots, t_n)$ if the predication P is identical to it. The predication P will also match a filter of the form $pred/arity$ if P is of arity *arity* and P's predicate symbol is *pred*. Technically, a predication matches a filter if it is *subsumed* by the filter.

There is a similar version of this inference rule for the overriding class rule:

$$I_{13} \vdash \frac{L << K - [f_1, \ldots, f_k] \wedge Q_1, \ldots, M_S : P(t_1, \ldots, t_m), \ldots, Q_n}{(Q_1, \ldots, K_S : P_1, \ldots, t_m), \ldots, Q_n)\theta}$$

provided that $L\theta \equiv M\theta$ where θ is a m.g.u. and that there does not exist an axiom of the form $P(a_1, \ldots, a_m) : -C \in L$ and that $P(a_1, \ldots, a_m)$ doesn't match any filter template f_i.

The logical connective inference rules

We allow in our queries and axioms sub-goals which may be complex, including disjunction and negations. We must therefore also have inference rules to allow us to solve queries containing these complex sub-goals. However these are essentially standard inference rules recast in terms of labelled sub-goals; we shall not dwell on them unduly.

$$I_{14} \vdash \frac{Q_1, \ldots, (A; B), \ldots, Q_n}{Q_1, \ldots, A, \ldots, Q_n}$$

$$I_{15} \vdash \frac{Q_1, \ldots, (A; B), \ldots, Q_n}{Q_1, \ldots, B, \ldots, Q_n}$$

$$I_{16} \vdash \frac{Q_1, \ldots, (A, B), \ldots, Q_n}{Q_1, \ldots, A, B, \ldots, Q_n}$$

As for negated sub-goals we shall assume (though not necessarily rely on) negation-by-failure.

$$I_{17} \vdash \frac{Q_1, \ldots, Q_{i-1}, \neg C, Q_{i+1} \ldots, Q_n}{Q_1, \ldots, Q_{i-1}, Q_{i+1} \ldots, Q_n}$$

if C reduces to `false`, assuming that C is ground.

The importance of being atomic

We have stated earlier that inheritance is of an atomic nature (i.e., when we inherit via a class rule we import the relations defined in the class template rather than the definitions themselves). We have not really justified this interpretation. It must be said that some rather unexpected consequences flow from this decision. For example, we could have the following axiom in the class body for **person**:

```
person(A):{...
      childish :- likes(toys).
      ...}
```

Given our definition above of a child being a young person, a sub-goal of the form:

```
...,child(10):childish,...
```

would fail (unexpectedly?) since the proof of the sub-goal

```
...,likes(toys),...
```

which is necessary to establish childishness takes place in the context of the person class not the child class. For our rule to be correct we have to write it with a **self** keyword as:

```
childish :- self:likes(toys).
```

With this version of the `childish` definition the question of whether a child likes toys is forced, via the `self` keyword, to be relative to the `child` class (and is therefore true in this case).

This 'problem' is a direct result of our interpretation of inheritance, which relies on the rather subtle definition of inheritance that only atomic consequences of a theory are inherited via class rules. If all the consequences of the theory were inherited then we would have to include the original axioms of the host theory; in particular the `childish` rule from `person` would also be a rule for the `child` class and we would not need to use the `self` keyword here (indeed it becomes almost completely redundant). In fact this form of inheritance amounts to unioning the set of axioms belonging to the host theory with the local axioms defined in the class body. This unioned set forms the basis of the complete set of consequences of the theory.

Unfortunately other unexpected results flow from an interpretation of inheritance which is based on unioning sets of axioms. Two programs in separate class templates may start to interact in unexpected ways through being inherited. This is especially inconvenient in the case of stratified programs involving negated sub-goals where the stratification may break down. In Program 8.1, we have two *L&O* programs `t1` and `t2` each of which is stratified[1], but a further *L&O* program `t3` which is defined solely in terms of inheritance of `t1` and `t2` is only stratified if inheritance is defined as inheritance of atomic consequences.

```
t1:{...
      p :- q, ¬r.
      r.
      ...}
t2:{...
      r :- s, ¬p.
      p.
      ...}
t3 <= t1.
t3 <= t2.
```

Program 8.1 A program defined only through inheritance

Under the 'all consequences' view of inheritance we effectively *union* the axioms of `t1` and `t2` to obtain a set of axioms for `t3`, so we could just as well have defined `t3` directly, as in Program 8.2. The clauses for `p` in Program 8.2 contain negated sub-goals which mention `r`. However the definition of `r` also refers to a negated `p`

---

[1]i.e., no predicate depends, for its definition, on a negated recursive call to itself.

```
t3':{...
    p :- q, ¬r.
    p.
    r.
    r :- s, ¬p.
    ...}
```

Program 8.2 A program defined by clause union

sub-goal. Thus p and r rely on each other via negated sub-goals and by definition are not stratified. That a program is stratified is a fundamental property of safety that many systems rely on.

The damage caused by this kind of unexpected interaction is potentially far worse than not being able to derive all non-atomic consequences of inherited theories since the former affects the safety of programs involving negation. In any case we have seen how the judicious use of the self keyword can have the effect of inheriting all the necessary consequences; furthermore this is under programmer control. As we shall see below the translation of the **self** keyword is itself relatively straightforward.

8.1.4   Mapping *L&O* programs into clausal form

As we map *L&O* programs into conventional clauses we simultaneously provide a semantics of our programs: the meaning of a *L&O* program is defined by the translated clauses. However our main purpose in introducing this mapping is to justify the inference rules that we have developed above. We shall look at a mapping where we map each axiom inside a class body into a separate first order clause, and we similarly map class rules into clauses.

The reader will recall that formulae such as

$$\ldots, L_S : P, \ldots$$

where L is the actual label, S is the self label and P is a predication or sub-goal, are central in our inference procedures. The fact that there are three components suggests that a reasonable characterization of a labelled sub-goal in terms of classical clausal form is as a triple, with each element being represented by a term. So we might, for example, represent the labelled predication:

$$\ldots, \texttt{person(30)}_{tom} : \texttt{likes(john)}, \ldots$$

as a triple in the **lano** relation:

$$\ldots, \texttt{lano(person(30),tom,likes(john))}, \ldots$$

In general, given a labelled sub-goal of the form $L_S\!:\!C$ we represent it as the triple

   $\ldots,$`lano`$(L,S,C),\ldots$

In this representation we are using terms to denote labels (both actual and self labels) and we are also using terms to denote sub-goals and predications. We shall also use the special function symbols ',', ';' and '¬' within C to denote conjunctions, disjunctions and negations respectively. For example, an *L&O* query such as

   `tom`$_{tom}$`:(likes(X),X:likes(logic))?`

is represented by the conventional query over `lano`:

   `lano(tom,tom,(likes(X),X:likes(logic)))?`

Mapping class bodies

L&O programs can be represented by clauses which define the `lano` predicate, with one clause for each axiom in each class body, together with further clauses for class rules and some standard auxiliary clauses as defined below. Given an axiom in a class body such as:

   `lab(`$l_1,\ldots,l_k$`):{`$\ldots$
   $\quad$ `p(`$p_1,\ldots,p_H$`):-C`$_1,\ldots,$`C`$_n$`.`
   $\quad\ldots$`}.`

we construct a clause for `lano` of the form:

   `lano(lab(`$l_1,\ldots,l_k$`),Self,p(`$p_1,\ldots,p_H$`)):-`
   $\quad$ `lano(lab(`$l_1,\ldots,l_k$`),Self,(C`$_1,\ldots,$`C`$_n$`)).`

where `Self` is a new variable not occurring elsewhere in the class body axiom. If the body of the class body axiom is empty then the body of the `lano` clause is also empty:

   `lab(`$l_1,\ldots,l_k$`):{`$\ldots$
   $\quad$ `p(`$p_1,\ldots,p_H$`).`
   $\quad\ldots$`}.`

becomes:

   `lano(lab(`$l_1,\ldots,l_k$`),Self,p(`$p_1,\ldots,p_H$`)).`

The rewrite to `lano` clauses involves bringing the quantified variables associated with the class label to the individual axioms inside the class body. Those variables which were quantified by the whole class body are now simply quantified within the individual `lano` clause. We can do this because of the equivalence:

$$\forall x, y[[\forall u, v\Psi_1] \wedge \ldots \wedge [\forall u, v\Psi_n]] \Leftrightarrow [\forall x, y, u, v\Psi_1 \wedge \ldots \wedge \forall x, y, u, v\Psi_n]$$

where Ψ_i are sentences in which x,y,u and v are free variables. If the class body axiom contained any occurrences of the **self** keyword then these are represented in the **lano** clause as further occurrences of the **Self** variable. So, for example if the class body axiom was of the form:

```
lab(l₁,...,lₖ):{...
    p(p₁,...,pₕ):-
        C₁,...,self:Cᵢ,...,Cₙ.
    ...}.
```

or if a given sub-goal mentioned the **self** keyword as a term as in:

```
lab(l₁,...,lₖ):{...
    p(p₁,...,pₕ):-
        C₁,...,pⱼ(tⱼ₁,...,self,...,tⱼₙ),...,Cₙ.
    ...}.
```

then the corresponding **lano** clauses would be

```
lano(lab(l₁,...,lₖ),Self,p(p₁,...,pₕ)):-
    lano(lab(l₁,...ₖ),Self,(C₁,...,Self:Cᵢ,...,Cₙ)).
```

and

```
lano(lab(l₁,...,lₖ),Self,p(p₁,...,pₕ)):-
    lano(lab(l₁,...,lₖ),Self,
        (C₁,...,pⱼ(tⱼ₁,...,Self,...,tⱼₙ),...,Cₙ)).
```

respectively.

Mapping class rules

A class rule is represented by a pair of clauses for **lano**. These clauses implement inheritance by 'calling' the inherited program with the goal to be attempted. In the case of a normal class rule such as:

```
lab(l₁,...,lₖ)<=mab(m₁,...,mₙ)
```

we would get the pair of clauses:

```
lano(lab(l₁,...,lₖ),Self,Atom):-
    lano(super(lab(l₁,...,lₖ)),Self,Atom).                    (VIII.i)
lano(super(lab(l₁,...,lₖ)),Self,Atom):-
    lano(mab(m₁,...,mₙ),Self,Atom).
```

where **Self** and **Atom** are new variables not occurring elsewhere in the original class rule. We only need one copy of **lano** clause (VIII.i) even if there are several class rules, although the extra clauses will do no harm they are redundant. We shall see later that we need to split a class rule into two **lano** clauses in order to correctly implement **super** inheritance.

Mapping overriding class rules   The translation of the overriding form of class rule is a little more complex since we must incorporate the tests required to filter out the locally defined relations. So if a label had the 'local predicates' $l_1, l_2, \ldots, l_x$ of arities $a_1, a_2, \ldots, a_x$ respectively then an overriding class rule for the label of the form:

```
lab(l₁,...,lₖ)<<mab(m₁,...,mₘ).
```

would be mapped to the `lano` clause:

```
lano(super(lab(l₁,...,lₖ)),Self,Atom):-
    lano(mab(m₁,...,mₘ),Self,Atom),
    functor(Atom,P,A),
    ¬member(P/A,[l₁/a₁,l₂/a₂,...,lₓ/aₓ]).
```

(Recall that there will also be at least one clause for `lano` equivalent to clause (VIII.i) above). `functor` is a predicate which is found in many Prolog systems. It behaves as though it were defined by a set of assertions as in Program 8.3. There is a tuple in the `functor` relation for each constant symbol, function sym-

```
functor(likes(_), likes, 1).
functor(likes(_,_), likes, 2).
...
functor(constant,constant, 0).
...
```

Program 8.3 The logical structure of the `functor` primitive

bol and predicate symbol in the program. `functor` is commonly regarded as a 'meta-logical' predicate although in our view it is easily justified in purely first order terms via a finite axiom schema. The `member` predicate is standard list membership.

   The filter sub-goal

```
¬member(P/A,[l₁/a₁,l₂/a₂,...,lₓ/aₓ])
```

is true if the term `P/A` which represents the relation being inherited is not on the list $[l_1/a_1, l_2/a_2, \ldots, l_x/a_x]$ (i.e., it is not a locally identified predicate).

   Clearly we are relying on negation for the definition of overriding inheritance. Given the intention to use the *L&O* programs as a programming language, we are likely to prefer the use of negation-by-failure as our negation. Moreover we are guaranteed the safety of this negated sub-goal since the variables in the `member` sub-goal are all governed by the `functor` sub-goal (under Clark's [Cla78] completion semantics a negated sub-goal must be ground at the time of the negative proof for negation-by-failure to be equivalent to logical negation).

Mapping class rules with differential inheritance If a class rule has a differential filter associated with it then we must also ensure that no predications which match the filter are 'allowed' in the inheritance. The actual filter test can be seen as an extension to the filter test that we implemented for overriding class rules. So, suppose that we have a class rule of the form:

$$\texttt{lab}(\texttt{l}_1,\ldots,\texttt{l}_k)\texttt{<=mab}(\texttt{m}_1,\ldots,\texttt{m}_n)\texttt{-[f}_1,\ \ldots,\texttt{f}_j\texttt{]}$$

We can split the filter into two lists: one list containing filters of the form *pred/arity* and the remaining filter tests are left on the other list. Then, the first list can be tested using a similar combination of goals to those used for overriding class rules such as:

```
...,functor(Atom,P,A),
      ¬member(P/A,[p₁/a₁,...,pᵢ/aᵢ]),...
```

The second part of the filter test can be expressed as the sub-goal:

```
...,¬member(Atom,[t₁,...,tₗ]),...
```

The main complication that arises here is in ensuring a 'safe' use of the negated **member** sub-goal. First of all, we would note that if the **Atom** which is potentially being inherited is ground then the not-**member** sub-goal is safe even if some of the filter terms in the list are not ground. We can guarantee this safety because, as we did with the *pred/arity* filter, we can re-formulate such filters.

Suppose that we have a differential inheritance filter with some variables in it, such as in the class rule:

```
man(Name)<=person(Name)-[likes(food(X))]
```

In the mapped clauses for this class rule we would get the pair of **lano** clauses:

```
lano(man(Name),Self,Atom):-
      lano(super(man(Name)),Self,Atom).
lano(super(man(Name)),Self,Atom):-
      lano(person(Name),Self,Atom),
      ¬member(Atom,[likes(food(X))]).
```

We can restructure the **member** sub-goal into the equivalent sub-goal:

```
...,Atom¬=likes(food(X)),...
```

Furthermore, by a combination of calls to the '=..' built-in, this sub-goal can be rewritten to:

```
...,Atom=..[P,A|B], A=..[F|C],                          (VIII.ii)
      ¬(P=likes, B=[], F=food, C=[]),...
```

The '=..' primitive (which is pronounced 'univ') which is to be found in most Prolog systems can be viewed as being defined by a finite axiom schema; for every function symbol and constant symbol there is a tuple in the '=..' relation of the form:

$$f(X_1,\ldots,X_n) =.. \quad [f,X_1,\ldots,X_n]$$

This definition of '=..' guarantees that if the left-hand argument is ground then the right-hand argument will also be ground after it is solved. In particular, if **Atom** is ground in (VIII.ii) then the subsequent negated conjunction is ground also and hence we can safely use negation-as-failure to implement this test. Notice that if **Atom** were *not* ground then this reformulation is not equivalent. In particular if **Atom** is unknown when attempting this test then the sub-goal

```
...,Atom=..[P,A|B],...
```

flounders (i.e., it fails because of a lack of data) and in most Prolog systems the whole sub-goal may incorrectly report a failure of the differential inheritance filter. In general, we can always reformulate a filter inequality as a combination of '=..' calls and safe negations. Since the form of the filter is known at 'compile' time this reformulation can be incorporated into the mapping from class templates to logic clauses. In practice, a preprocessor from class templates to Prolog clauses would probably not be so careful to decompose the filter tests to be safe; instead it would rely on the programmer to ensure that inherited sub-goals were always more instantiated than any tests in a differential inheritance filter.

Mapping label distribution   In order to support the various inference rules for label distribution etc. we also need some additional clauses in the `lano` program. The clauses in Program 8.4 must be added to the clauses derived from the *L&O* program itself.

```
lano(L,S,(A,B)) :- lano(L,S,A),lano(L,S,B).              (VIII.iii)
lano(L,S,(A;B)) :- lano(L,S,A).
lano(L,S,(A;B)) :- lano(L,S,B).
lano(L,S,¬(A)) :- ¬lano(L,S,A).
lano(L,S,super:A) :- lano(super(L),S,A).
lano(L,S,M:A) :- lano(M,M,A).
```

Program 8.4 The label distribution clauses for `lano`

The semantics of variable labels

A great portion of the expressive power of the *L&O* language comes from the ease of using variable labels. This should not be too surprising since it allows us to construct generic programs in the same manner as the variable call allows generic programs in Prolog itself. However, it may not be obvious that variable labels are justifiable in a first order logic programming language. If a labelled predication in a class body has a variable label, as in:

```
...,Order:less(X,Y),...
```

then, as it is translated into the **lano** clause, we obtain the predication:

```
...,lano(Order,Self, less(X,Y)),...
```

The presence of a variable as the first element of this triple is no more remarkable than a variable anywhere else. By interpreting the labelled sub-goal in this way variable labels reduce to terms like any other, hence eliminating the distinction. The meaning of a variable label is compatible with the intuition that the theory identified by the variable label is the same theory as would be identified had the variable been replaced by its value in the original text of the program.

8.1.5 The soundness of *L&O* inference

Our strategy in showing the soundness of our inference procedure is to demonstrate that each inference rule when applied to an *L&O* query is paralleled by normal resolution steps in the mapped set of **lano** clauses. Since we know that resolution itself is sound then if we can show that our inference can be 'reduced' to resolution then it too is sound. In other words given an *L&O* sequent

$$Q_1, \ldots, Q_n$$

then there is a corresponding conventional sequent

$$M(Q_1), \ldots, M(Q_n)$$

where each $M(Q_i)$ is the result of mapping the corresponding Q_i into normal logic queries. Furthermore if there is an *L&O* proof then there must also be a conventional proof in the mapped clauses. To show this we proceed by induction on the length of the sequent. We take for the base case the original query Q_0 and the mapping of this initial query into a standard query for class: $M(Q_0)$. Now, suppose that we have a non-empty *L&O* sequent

$$Q_1, \ldots, Q_i$$

and corresponding conventional sequent

$$M(Q_1), \ldots, M(Q_i)$$

then suppose we wish to extend the class sequent with a new $L\&O$ query Q_{i+1}. Then by definition there must be an inference rule I_k within $I_1 - I_{17}$ which we wish to apply to some Q_i. We must show that

$$Q_1, \ldots, Q_i, M(I_k(Q_i))$$

is also a sequent. We do that by showing that $M(I_k(Q_i))$ is a logical consequence of $M(Q_1), \ldots, M(Q_i)$, i.e., that the inference step that we applied was valid – which it will be if we can reduce the $L\&O$ inference to conventional resolution. In general for each of our inference rules I we wish to establish the equality:

$$M(I(Q)) = R^*(M(Q))$$

where R^* represents the application of one or more steps of standard resolution and M is the mapping function defined in Section 8.1.4.

Soundness of label distribution

The label distribution rules take the form:

$$L_S\!:\!(A \odot B) \vdash \ \Phi(L_S\!:\!A, L_S\!:\!B)$$

where $\odot$ is one of ',', ';', '¬' or ':' and Φ is some function (equal to $\odot$ in the cases of ',', ';' and '¬'). These inference rules are reflected by corresponding `lano` clauses.

For example, if we were to map a query of the form $L_S : (A, B)$ into standard form we would obtain the `lano` query:

    lano($L, S, (A, B)$)?

in other words

$$M(L_S : (A, B)) = \texttt{lano}(L, S, (A, B))$$

for all labels L, S and sub-goals A and B . If we now use the `lano` clause (VIII.iii) which matches this query we obtain a new query consisting of a pair of `lano` sub-goals:

    lano(L, S, A),lano(L, S, B)?

However if we apply M to the right-hand side of I_1 we obtain the same pair, i.e., we have shown

$$M(I_1(LS : (A, B))) = M(L_S : A), M(L_S : B)$$

Similar reasoning applies to each of the label distribution rules I_1 through I_5. Of course we should not be too surprised at this since this is how we set up the extra `lano` clauses.

The soundness of the class body inference rules

Recall that there are two inference rules which relate to inference *within* a class body – the main one being I_6 on page 179. In order to justify this rule we shall apply the mapping function to the inputs to the rule, perform the resolution step and show that this is the same (possibly up to the renaming of variables) as the mapped result of the rule. The `lano` clause which results from mapping the class body axiom is:

$$\texttt{lano}(L,\texttt{Self},H) \texttt{ :- lano}(L,\texttt{Self},C). \tag{VIII.iv}$$

and the mapped form of the *L&O* query from I_6 is:

$$\begin{aligned} &\texttt{lano}(L_1,S_1,C_1),\dots, \\ &\quad \texttt{lano}(M,S,P),\dots,\texttt{lano}(L_n,S_n,C_n) \end{aligned} \tag{VIII.v}$$

respectively, where each Q_i is of the form $L_{i_{S_i}} : C_i$. Suppose now that the sub-goal

$$\dots,\texttt{lano}(M,S,P),\dots$$

unifies with the head of (VIII.iv) with m.g.u. θ'. If we perform the resolution with this m.g.u. then we obtain the new `lano` query:

$$\begin{aligned} &(\texttt{lano}(L_1,S_1,C_1),\dots,\texttt{lano}(L,S,C),\dots, \\ &\quad \texttt{lano}(L_n,S_n,C_n))\theta' \end{aligned} \tag{VIII.vi}$$

Recall that under the mapping the `self` keyword is represented by the `Self` variable in clause (VIII.iv). As part of this resolution step therefore all occurrences of the `Self` variable in (VIII.iv) would have been replaced by S. Thus in (VIII.vi) the new sub-goal

$$\dots,\texttt{lano}(L,S,C),\dots$$

has had all occurrences of `Self` replaced by S also. We could equally have rewritten the θ' m.g.u. as a composition of $\{\texttt{Self}/S\}$ and a remainder which we shall call θ, i.e., we have the equality:

$$\theta' = \theta \circ \{\texttt{Self}/S\}$$

Since `Self` is a variable which originally only occurred (after renaming of variables) in clause (VIII.iv) and does not occur in the query (VIII.v) we can rewrite the resolvent (VIII.vi) without loss as:

$$\begin{aligned} &(\texttt{lano}(L_1,S_1,C_1),\dots, \ (\texttt{lano}(L,S,C))\{\texttt{Self}/S\},\dots, \\ &\quad \texttt{lano}(L_n,S_n,C_n))\theta \end{aligned}$$

which is exactly the same as the result of mapping the resultant of our class body inference rule I_6 into a `lano` query.

This shows that the class body inference rule can be justified by a resolution step in standard clausal form. If the inference rule were not sound then it would be possible to perform a class body inference step which forced an incorrect resolution step over the `lano` clauses. The second variety of class body rule is simply a special case of the main one where the body of the class body axiom is empty. The proof of its soundness flows easily from the main proof.

The soundness of class rule inference

There are four inference rules which are used to describe the process of inheritance. These relate to the 'normal' inheritance rule, the 'overriding' inheritance rule and the two '**super**' variations of these. As with the class body inference rules we shall appeal to the mapping into `lano` clauses in order to justify these inference rules. Recall that the normal inheritance rule is I_8 on page 179.

If we apply our mapping to the class rule we obtain the set of clauses for `lano`:

$$\text{lano}(L,\text{Self},\text{Atom}):-$$
$$\quad\text{lano}(\text{super}(L),\text{Self},\text{Atom}). \qquad\qquad\qquad \text{(VIII.vii)}$$
$$\text{lano}(\text{super}(L),\text{Self},\text{Atom}):-$$
$$\quad\text{lano}(K,\text{Self},\text{Atom}). \qquad\qquad\qquad\qquad \text{(VIII.viii)}$$

the $L\&O$ query in the left-hand side of I_8 is mapped into the `lano` query:

$$\text{lano}(L_1,S_1,C_1),\ldots,\text{lano}(M,S,P),\ldots,$$
$$\quad\text{elano}(L_n,S_n,C_n)? \qquad\qquad\qquad\qquad \text{(VIII.ix)}$$

assuming that each Q_i is of the form $L_{i_{S_i}}:C_i$. If we now resolve clause (VIII.vii) with the sub-goal

$$\ldots,\text{lano}(M,S,P),\ldots$$

from (VIII.ix) we obtain the new query (assuming of course that they unify):

$$(\text{lano}(L_1,S_1,C_1),\ldots,\text{lano}(\text{super}(L),S,P),\ldots,$$
$$\quad\text{lano}(L_n,S_n,C_n))\theta \qquad\qquad\qquad \text{(VIII.x)}$$

This resolution step can only be performed if the predications

$$\text{lano}(M,S,P)$$

and

$$\text{lano}(L,Self,Atom)$$

unify (with m.g.u. θ). In practice this means that the terms L and M must unify. This is precisely the condition that the *labels* L and M unify prior to the application of the class rule inference rule (furthermore the m.g.u.s will be the same except for the additional substitutions Self/S and Atom/P). In order to achieve the same effect as the class rule inference rule we must also resolve the sub-goal:

$$\ldots, \mathtt{lano(super}(L), S, P\mathtt{)}, \ldots$$

from the query (VIII.x) with the **lano** clause (VIII.viii). We can guarantee that we will be able to perform this resolution because of the way that we constructed (VIII.viii). Furthermore we can say that there will be no further substitutions for variables in the label term L. The resolvent from this second resolution step is the new **lano** query:

$$\begin{aligned}
&(\mathtt{lano}(L_1, S_1, C_1), \ldots, \mathtt{lano}(K, S, P), \ldots, \\
&\quad \mathtt{lano}(L_n, S_n, C_n))\theta
\end{aligned} \qquad \text{(VIII.xi)}$$

which is also what would be obtained if we applied θ to the labelled query

$$\ldots, Q_1, \ldots, K_S : P, \ldots, Q_n, \ldots$$

and mapped the result into a **lano** query. This shows that the standard class rule inference rule is also sound.

The overriding class rule is similar to the normal class rule (and hence the proof of its soundness), with the extra need to filter out the locally defined predicates. Recall that the translation of an overriding class rule such as

$$L \mathtt{<<} K$$

is

```
lano(L,Self,Atom):-
     lano(super(L),Self,Atom).
lano(super(L),Self,Atom) :-                          (VIII.xii)
     functor(Atom,P,A),
     ¬member(P/A,[l₁/a₁,...,lₓ/aₓ]),
     lano(K,Self,Atom).
```

and that the overriding class rule inference rule is I_9 on page 180. The extra filtering requirement is exactly characterised by the body of (VIII.xii) since, by definition of the mapping into **lano** clauses, the list of pairs

$$[l_1/a_1, \ldots, l_x/a_x]$$

mentions each of the locally defined predicate symbols in the class body for L.

In place of a constraint which controls the application of the overriding class rule inference we have to perform an extra sub-proof in the **lano** query which implements the constraint. Notice that this extra sub-proof relies on negation in the **lano** program. However as we noted above we can show that negation-by-failure (which is the most likely form of negation to be actually used) is equivalent to logical negation in this context. Apart from this extra sub-proof the steps in applying the overriding class rule are identical to the normal inheritance rule. Hence we can also conclude that the overriding class rule is sound. A similar argument can be used to justify the differential inheritance filter on both normal and overriding class rules.

The final class rule inference rules that we must justify are the rules for interpreting the **super** label. Recall that we have split the procedure for handling **super** into two steps: the first step is a label distribution rule (I_4) which leaves a 'marker' for and the second step using I_{10} (or I_{11}) involves applying a class rule to this marker.

If we map the labelled query in the left-hand side of either of these inference rules into a **lano** query we get:

$$\texttt{lano}(L_1, S_1, C_1), \ldots, \texttt{lano}(\texttt{super}(M), S, P), \ldots,$$
$$\texttt{lano}(L_n, S_n, C_n)$$

By resolving the **super** sub-goal with the clause (VIII.viii) (which we obtained as part of mapping the class rules themselves) then we obtain the new **lano** query:

$$\texttt{lano}(L_1, S_1, C_1), \ldots, \texttt{lano}(\texttt{super}(K), S, P), \ldots,$$
$$\texttt{lano}(L_n, S_n, C_n)\theta$$

provided that $L\theta \equiv M\theta$, and in the case of the overriding class rule providing that the sub-proof for non-membership of the locally defined list of predicates is successful. Clearly this new query is the result of mapping the resultant of the inference rule, and hence this rule too is sound.

Incidentally we can now see why we needed to split the translation of class rules into the two **lano** rules. It makes it easy for us to prevent the application of class body axioms to a **super** labelled sub-goal since **super**(L) will never unify with L.

8.1.6 The completeness of $L\&O$ inference

By completeness we mean that any justifiable inference is achievable using our $L\&O$ inference rules. In other words we have sufficiently characterised $L\&O$ inference so that we do not need any ' extra' rules. Since we know that resolution is complete we can show completeness by examining the inferences possible with the translated **lano** programs and show that they are achievable with our rules. However we are not necessarily interested in *all* possible inferences over the mapped **lano** clauses, merely those which are 'reachable' from class queries. Thus a formal statement of the completeness proposition is:

Proposition

'Given an $L\&O$ query $Q_0 \equiv L\!:\!Q$ together with an $L\&O$ program P and their mapped forms $M(Q_0) \equiv \texttt{lano}(L, L, Q)$ and $M(P)$ then if there is a proof of $M(Q_0)$ using $M(P)$ and resolution then there is an $L\&O$ proof of Q_0 using P and the $L\&O$ inference rules.'

We shall prove this by induction on the length of the proof. Trivially, if the initial $L\&O$ query is of the form $L\!:\!\texttt{true}$ then we are already done. Otherwise consider the partial proof consisting of the sequent

$$M(Q_0), \ldots, M(Q_i)$$

where (under the induction hypothesis) query $M(Q_i)$ has a corresponding Q_i which is 'reachable' from Q_0 and P. It follows that $M(Q_i)$ takes the form:

$$\texttt{lano}(L_0, S_0, C_0), \ldots, \texttt{lano}(L_n, S_n, C_n)?$$

since this is the mapped form of any $L\&O$ query. Suppose now that we wish to extend the partial proof to obtain a new query. In order to do so we must resolve one of the $\texttt{lano}(L_j, S_j, C_j)$ $(0 \le j \le n)$ sub-goals with a suitable clause.

Given the mapped program $M(P)$ we can predict the possible input clauses that might match with this query. The possible $\texttt{lano}$ clauses originate from the standard clauses in Program 8.4 which are present in all $M(P)$'s. In addition, we have the $\texttt{lano}$ clauses which were generated from the original $L\&O$ program's class bodies and class rules. If any of the standard $\texttt{lano}$ clauses from Program 8.4 matched then it would follow that the sub-goal

$$\ldots, \texttt{lano}(L_j, S_j, C_j), \ldots$$

must have been one of the following forms:

- $\ldots, \texttt{lano}(L_j, S_j, (C_j, D_j)), \ldots$

- $\ldots, \texttt{lano}(L_j, S_j, \neg C_j), \ldots$

- $\ldots, \texttt{lano}(L_j, S_j, \texttt{super}\!:\!C_j), \ldots$

- $\ldots, \texttt{lano}(L_j, S_j, M_j\!:\!C_j), \ldots$

in which case the corresponding sub-goal in the next query in the proof of $M(Q_0)$ is one of

- $\ldots, \texttt{lano}(L_j, S_j, C_j), \texttt{lano}(L_j, S_j, D_j), \ldots$

- $\ldots, \texttt{lano}(L_j, S_j, C_j), \ldots$

- $\ldots, \texttt{lano}(L_j, S_j, D_j), \ldots$

- $\ldots, \neg\texttt{lano}(L_j, S_j, C_j), \ldots$

- $\ldots, \texttt{lano}(\texttt{super}(L_j), S_j, C_j), \ldots$

- $\ldots, \texttt{lano}(M_j, M_j, C_j), \ldots$

In each of the above cases there is a corresponding $L\&O$ inference rule $I_1 - I_5$ which would have the same effect, i.e., if one of the clauses in Program 8.4 were used to produce the next step in the proof of $M(Q_0)$ then there is a corresponding inference rule $I_1 - I_5$ which induces an analogous step in the $L\&O$ proof of Q_0.

Similar reasoning to this applies to the case where the clause which is used to produce the next resolvent arose from a class body axiom. In this case, we can reflect the `lano` resolution with the use of I_6 or I_7.

The case where a `lano` clause generated from a class rule is used is more complicated. If one of these is used to reduce the sub-goal:

$$\ldots, \texttt{lano}(L_j, S_j, C_j), \ldots$$

then the corresponding sub-goal in the next `lano` query must be of the form:

$$(\ldots, \texttt{lano}(\texttt{super}(L_j), S_j, C_j), \ldots,)\theta \qquad \text{(VIII.xiii)}$$

where θ is the m.g.u. that results from unifying L_j and $\texttt{lab}(\texttt{l}_1, \ldots, \texttt{l}_k)$ together with the additional substitutions $\{\texttt{Self}/L_j, \texttt{A}/C_j\}$.

In this case we cannot say that the new query is directly the result of mapping an $L\&O$ query, and hence that the resolution step can be mirrored by an $L\&O$ inference rule. However we know that, in order for the proof of $M(Q_0)$ to successfully terminate, the (VIII.xiii) sub-goal must eventually be selected for further reduction. Furthermore we know (by the independence of the order of selecting sub-goals) that if a proof of $M(Q_0)$ exists then an equivalent proof exists in which the *next* step involves the successful resolution of the (VIII.xiii) sub-goal with some input clause. In other words we can assume that the next step in the proof of $M(Q_0)$ involves resolving

$$\ldots, \texttt{lano}(\texttt{super}(L_j), S_j, C_j), \ldots$$

with some input clause.

There are only two possibilities for this: using one of the clauses which was generated from a normal class rule or one generated from an overriding class rule. If one of the former then, as with the other inference rules, the resolution step can be mirrored by the application of the class rule inference rule I_8. If one of the latter clauses was used to reduce the sub-goal then the next `lano` query will contain sub-goals of the form:

$$
\begin{aligned}
&(\ldots, \texttt{lano}(\texttt{mab}(\texttt{m}_1, \ldots, \texttt{m}_m), S_j, C_j), \\
&\quad \texttt{functor}(C_j, \texttt{P}, \texttt{A}), \\
&\quad \neg\texttt{member}(\texttt{P}/\texttt{A}, [l_1/a_1, \ldots, l_x/a_x]), \ldots)\theta
\end{aligned}
$$

By a similar argument to that above concerning the re-ordering of any proof of $M(Q_0)$ we can assume that the next few steps in the proof involve the solving of the sub-goals

$$\ldots, \texttt{functor}(C_j, \texttt{P}, \texttt{A}), \ldots$$

and

$$\ldots, \neg \texttt{member(P/A}, [l_1/a_1, l_2/a_2, \ldots, l_x/a_x]), \ldots$$

and (since we know that we have a proof of $M(Q_0)$) we know that we will be able to solve these two sub-goals. The resulting query will look like:

$$(\ldots, \texttt{lano(mab(}\texttt{m}_1, \ldots, \texttt{m}_m), S_j, C_j), \ldots) \theta$$

which can also be mirrored in the proof of Q_0 by a successful application of the class rule inference rule I_9. This completes the proof of the completeness of $L\&O$ inference.

8.1.7   Conventional logic programs and $L\&O$ programs

We stated at the beginning of this chapter that we could map conventional logic programs into an $L\&O$ program without affecting their meaning. It is instructive to see how this can be accomplished in a little more detail. A logic program consists of a set of clauses, each of which is of the form:

```
predₕ(h₁,...,hₖ) :-
    pred₁(t₁₁,...,t₁ₖ),
    ...
    predₙ(tₙ₁,...,tₙₖ).
```

We can take our collection of clauses and put them into the special class body of the label Φ shown in Program 8.5. (Φ is only special in the sense that it is only going to be used for this purpose.) A query to this $L\&O$ program would be

```
Φ:{
    predₕ(h₁,...,hₖ) :-
        pred₁(t₁₁,...,t₁ₖ),
        ...
        predₙ(tₙ₁,...,tₙₖ).
    ...}
```

Program 8.5 A logic program embedded in an $L\&O$ program

represented by the labelled query of the form:

$$\Phi\texttt{:pred}_q(\texttt{tq}_1, \ldots, \texttt{tq}_k)?$$

where

```
pred_q(tq_1,...,tq_k)?
```

is a query over the original set of clauses.

If we apply our translation to the Φ program we would get a set of lano clauses each of which is of the following form:

```
lano(Φ,Self,pred_h(h_1,...,h_k)) :-
     lano(Φ,Self,pred_1(t_{1_1},...,t_{1_k})),
     ...
     lano(Φ,Self,pred_n(t_{n_1},...,t_{n_k})).
```

where Self and Φ do not occur anywhere apart from where we have explicitly indicated. Our *L&O* query also has an lano form:

```
lano(Φ,Φ,pred_q(tq_1,...,tq_k))?
```

where the original query was

```
pred_q(tq_1,...,tq_k)?
```

Since the original class template was constructed by enclosing a set of conventional clauses within a class body we know that there are no class rules for Φ, nor are there any explicitly labelled sub-goals. It should be obvious that these two programs are very similar; they differ in the presence of the Self variable and the Φ label. Each clause in each program has an exactly corresponding clause in the other program (there are no extra clauses in either program). In fact these programs are equivalent in the following sense:

$$P \vdash Q \iff CP \vdash \Phi : Q$$

where P is the original logic program, Q is a query over that program, and CP is the *L&O* version of P. We can show this by mapping our *L&O* query

$$\Phi : Q?$$

into the standard clausal form

$$M(\Phi : Q)?$$

and showing that

$$P \vdash Q \iff M(CP) \vdash M(\Phi : Q)$$

which we can do by examining the possible proofs of one query and showing that there are corresponding proofs in the other query. We leave the details of this to the reader.

This result illustrates how it is the case that *L&O* programming is still logic programming when BASIC and DCG's (say) are not strictly logic programming even though they may both have a defensible semantics. In neither BASIC nor DCG's can we embed standard logic programming programs in such a way as to preserve the meaning of the logic sentences. We also know now that the *L&O* language is sufficiently expressive that any logic program (and hence any program) can be expressed within the formalism.

8.1.8   A model theory for *L&O* programs

The theoretical framework that we have outlined so far is one which is based on a mapping from *L&O* programs into logic programs. Such a method for providing a well-founded semantics is encouraging since it enables us to 'lift' many of the theoretical results generated in the pure logic programming field and apply them more-or-less straightaway to *L&O* programming. However, it is instructive to consider whether an alternative more direct approach to *L&O* semantics is possible.

Gurr [Gur90] has investigated such an independent semantics for *L&O* programming. In this thesis, he explores the concepts of a model of an *L&O* program independently from any translation into the standard logic programming model theory.

Gurr's interpretation of an *L&O* program has two phases: loosely corresponding to the class bodies and class rules. A complete interpretation of an *L&O* program involves assigning truth values to individual tuples embedded in class bodies and then using a higher-level truth mapping from collections of class templates to the individual interpretations for each label. This structure manages to capture the intuition of an *L&O* program consisting of a collection of more-or-less independent programs which cooperate to produce a complete program.

Gurr has shown that the standard notions of interpretation, model, minimal models and logical consequence all carry over quite naturally into this scheme. Furthermore, he has also shown that this model theoretic semantics is compatible with the rules of inference and mapping functions introduced in this chapter.

As further evidence of the power of having a well-founded semantics, Gurr shows how some of the more advanced theoretical frameworks in logic programming – in particular the concepts and results underlying 'Stable model semantics' for handling negation [GL88] – can also be lifted into his semantic scheme for *L&O* programs.

Gurr's results, taken with the results developed in this chapter, lay a strong foundation for the semantics of *L&O* programs. We trust that this will encourage the logic programmers (as opposed to Prolog programmers?) to use our notation in the confidence that it is just a conservative extension to logic.

8.2   The logic of functions

There is a simple mathematical relationship between relations and functions, namely that a function is a set of pairs (i.e., a relation) with an extra uniqueness sub-goal:

> 'A set of pairs F is a function iff whenever $(X,Y){\in}F$ and $(X,Z){\in}F$ then $Y{=}Z$'

Furthermore a relation can be viewed as a function from tuples to the finite set {`true`, `false`}. This latter interpretation of relations does not adequately relate to their use in logic programming where we routinely use these functions in the inverse sense: from the value `true` to those tuples which satisfy the predicate.

In giving a sound semantics to a combined functional and relational system we would aim to capture the semantics of both relations and functions in as natural a way as possible. In [vEY87] various possible ways of interpreting equations are considered. These divide into two approaches: the *interpretational* approach and the *compilational* approach.

In the former approach an interpreter for expressions is constructed using the explicit equations supplied by the programmer to reduce expressions into canonical forms. Expressions in canonical form can then be unified with other terms in the conventional logic programming sense. Narrowing [GM84] can be seen as a particular flavour of this approach.

In the compilational approach, any program which has expressions embedded in it is considered to be *isomorphic* to another program in which the expressions are represented by new *expression variables* together with extra sub-goals which 'govern' the values of the new variables. The extra sub-goals are satisfied when the expression variables have as their values the canonical form of the original expressions. For example, suppose that we have the sub-goal with embedded expression:

        ...,index(E,L,I+1,J),...

Such a sub-goal is isomorphic to the pair of sub-goals:

        ...,+*(I,1,X),index(E,L,X,J),...

With X being a variable that does not appear elsewhere in the clause in which this sub-goal is embedded. The definition of the relation '+*' is such that

        +*(X,Y,Z) $\iff$ X+Y=Z

Sentences such as this one linking the '+*' relation to the '+' function are called *definitional* sentences in [vEY87]. This kind of interpretation is more declarative than that implied in the interpretational approach; it describes functions in terms of their defining relations. Another advantage of the compilational approach is that it is possible to use a standard unification algorithm in a standard Prolog language implementation to achieve the effect of expression evaluation. In systems which rely on interpreting expressions it is necessary to modify the standard unification algorithm. This can make compiling unification more difficult and less efficient.

8.2.1   Functions, terms and canonical forms

In standard functional programming, evaluating expressions is viewed as a process of reducing expressions in order to compute canonical values. An expression is viewed as being reducible if there is an equation whose left-hand side matches (unifies) with a sub-term of the expression. Such an expression is reduced by replacing the matched sub-term by the corresponding right-hand side of the equation. The irreducible canonical representation of a term is viewed as the value of the expression.

This is an inherently operational use of the declarative information in an equation: a statement that two terms are equal does not mean that they are only equal when viewed from left to right! In attempting to combine logic and functional programming it is necessary to relate the declarative nature of equations (which state which terms are equal) with the operational use of equations for evaluating expressions. The observant reader will note that our conditional equalities are in the standard form of clauses; it is perfectly possible to regard an equation as a clause about the '=' relation. If we can add to, or infer from, the programmer supplied (and system defined) equations the axioms in Program 8.6 together with a substitutivity axiom:

$$\Phi[x] \wedge x = y \vdash \Phi[x/y]$$

where $\Phi[x]$ denotes a formula in which x is free and $\Phi[x/y]$ denotes replacing all occurrences of x by y in Φ, then the resulting = relation is an equivalence relation, furthermore it is a *congruence* relation.

With any equivalence relation there is a set of equivalence classes associated with it: each equivalence class contains all the terms which are equal according to the defining relation. For example, given the expression [1,2,3]<>[] we can construct a set of terms all of which fall into the same equivalence class as this expression:

```
{[1,2,3]<>[], [1,2]<>[3], ..., [1,2,3],
    []<>[]<>[1,2,3],...,rev([3,2,1]),...}
```

Each equivalence class contains all the terms which are equivalent under the relation induced by the = axioms. Of course, as this example shows, equivalence classes are often infinite in size.

```
X=X.
X=Y :- Y=X.
X=Y :- X=Z, Z=Y.
```

Program 8.6 The three equivalence axioms

Equivalence relations are important because they allow us to construct other relations. Given an equivalence relation E, and another relation R, we can construct the *relational quotient* R/E. Where R is a relation over individual terms R/E is a relation over sets, equivalence classes in particular. The definition of R/E is obtained as follows:

'a tuple $(T_1, T_2, \ldots, T_n) \in R/E$, where each T_i is an equivalence class
of $E \iff$ for each $t_i \in T_i$ the tuple $(t_1, t_2, \ldots, t_n) \in R$'

Informally, the quotient relation R/E is a relation which reflects the relation R but whose tuples consist of equivalence classes of E rather than individual terms. Given a set of clauses P (not including any axioms for the predicate symbol '=') and a set of equations E (as defined through axioms for the predicate symbol '='), we can construct a quotient program P/E by a direct extension of the definition above.

We claim that by allowing equality in our programs we are actually interested in the relational quotients of programs rather than the standard relational model of the programs. However we do not need to reconstruct logic programming in terms of relational quotients as we see next. It is a property of congruence relations that in order to determine if a tuple $(T_1, T_2, \ldots, T_n)$ is in the relation R/E it is sufficient to show that the tuple $(t_1, t_2, \ldots, t_n)$ is in R, where each t_i is any term in the corresponding equivalence class T_i. In particular, we do not have to show that $(t_1, t_2, \ldots, t_n)$ is in R for every possible member of the T_i equivalence classes. Instead, we can identify a particular member, the representative or *canonical* member, of a given equivalence class and use that member when trying to determine tuples of R/E. In this way we can formally justify the use of canonical terms in rewriting systems: any term in an equivalence class can be used as the representative element.

For some – well behaved – sets of equations each equivalence class of an expression contains an element which contains no symbol which appears as the principal function symbol on the left-hand side of an equation. Such a term is obviously easily recognizable and forms a good candidate as the canonical representative of the equivalence class. We call such a term the *value* of the expression and evaluation of an expression becomes computing this canonical member of the equivalence class of the expression. This is why [1,2,3] is the 'value' of the expression

[1,2]<>[3]

even though they are both equal according to the system of equations.

There should be at most one of these canonical terms if the equations are to define functions. If the equivalence class of an expression contains more than one canonical term then the 'function' is multi-valued, and therefore is not really a function at all but is a relation. If the equivalence class of an expression contains no canonical terms then the function is partial: there is no value for the expression.

A *reducible* expression is a term of the form

```
f(t₁,t₂,...,tₙ)
```

where there is an equation of the form:

```
f(a₁,...,aₙ) = t :- B
```

or where one or more of t_i are reducible. Note that it is not required for all of the t_i/a_i pairs to unify for $f(t_1, t_2, \ldots, t_n)$ to be reducible.

An *irreducible* expression is a term of the form $f(t_1, t_2, \ldots, t_n)$ where there is no equation for f and furthermore t_i are all also irreducible. A canonical term is irreducible. An expression has a *canonical form* if there is a derivation starting from the goal:

```
X=E?
```

where X is a new variable not occurring in E, using only the axioms in the program (including the programmer's axioms for the '=' relation, and the axioms for reflexivity and transitivity of '=' but not symmetry) ending in a goal of the form:

```
X=C?
```

where C is irreducible.

This definition of canonical form coincides with the notion of a canonical representative provided that we can show that '=' is an equivalence relation, i.e., provided that '=' is symmetric. With the existing formulation of the axioms for the '=' equivalence relation (reflexivity, symmetry and transitivity) represented as object level axioms along with the programmer's axioms it is quite easy for an evaluator to indulge in useless loops during execution. This is especially true of the symmetry axiom. However we can use the properties of reducibility and canonicality to establish symmetry as a theorem.

Suppose that we have the fact that two expressions f and g are in the '=' relation:

$$f = g$$

then since g has a canonical form r(say) we know (by definition) that $g = r$; it follows (from transitivity) that $f = r$. If it was the case that $g\neg = f$ then since each expression has exactly one canonical representative then by transitivity it would follow that

$$g\neg = r$$

which is a contradiction. Notice that if an expression has no canonical form then symmetry may break down. If we have

$$f = g$$

where g is not canonical and furthermore no equation for g applies (i.e., there is no equation whose left-hand side unifies with g), then there may not exist a term h such that

$$g = h$$

let alone

$$h = f$$

In summary, when we augment a set of clauses by a set of equations which have the property that if any expression has exactly one canonical form then the relation induced is an equivalence relation. We can use the fact that it is an equivalence relation together with the substitutivity property to prove that two terms are equal iff they have the same canonical representative. We next look at a simple program which can be used to compute the canonical representative of an equivalence class.

8.2.2 A simple evaluator for canon

The skeleton Prolog program below in Program 8.7, called canon, computes the canonical form of expressions given a set of equations. The predicate canon(E,T) is true if T is a canonical member of the equivalence class induced by the expression E.

```
canon(F,T) :-              % a complex term                    (VIII.xiv)
    reducible(F),          % is the term reducible?
    F=..[Fu|A],
    canon_list(A,CA),
    S=..[Fu|CA],           % rebuild arguments
    S=G,                   % use a programmer's equation
canon(G,T).                % transitive closure
canon(T,T) :-              % Irreducible terms are already canonical:
    not reducible(T).
    canon_list([],[]).
canon_list([S|L],[CS|CL]):-
    canon(S,CS),
    canon_list(L,CL).
```

Program 8.7 The canonical form of an expression

The canonicalizer (sic) program looks for ways of using the equations defined by the user to rewrite progressively – using transitivity – reducible terms into irreducible terms; recursively applying itself to arguments of expressions. If an expression has no canonical form then this process will either fail or loop indefinitely and the expression has no value. The **canon** program can be viewed as a specification for part of a new unification algorithm. In order to unify two expressions we first find their canonical representative and then unify these in the normal manner.

We can produce a modified version of the the unification algorithm by embedding **canon** in a standard unification procedure at the appropriate points. This implements the interpretational view of equations; this modified form of unification is often called narrowing [GM84].

8.2.3   The effect of evaluation order

The order of evaluation of arguments of expressions is determined by the evaluation order in the **canon_list** program and in clause (VIII.xiv) for **canon** itself. A strict Prolog left-right execution of the sub-goals in these clauses gives us the equivalent of strict or call-by-value evaluation. This is because we would be fully evaluating the arguments of an expression before attempting to use any equations. In a system with dataflow co-routining, the evaluation – in **canon_list** – of the arguments of an expression could proceed in parallel, and even with the evaluation of the function (i.e., with any computations arising from the sub-goals in the programmer supplied '=' clauses).

The data dependencies on which dataflow co-routining is based would be those which are implicit in the expression notation: the results of sub-expressions flow in as the arguments of the higher expressions. (A purely random ordering might allow the higher level expressions to guess an answer of the lower level expressions.) There is some correspondence between the concepts of strict/normal ordering in functional languages and left-to-right/dataflow co-routining in logic programming systems. Since logic programming languages such as Prolog have a relational syntax which is apparently neutral to the order of evaluation, the programmer often has to make a separate declaration relating to the desired control flow in his programs, whereas advantage can be taken of the expression notation to give control guidance as well as simply suppressing intermediate variables.

8.2.4   Compiling expressions

In the compilational approach we make use of the definitional sentences implicit in the use of equations to transform programs containing expressions into normal clauses which do not, and therefore we can avoid having to change the unification algorithm and the corresponding resolution rule. For example consider the definition of **palindrome** in Program 8.8, in which we have the reducible term **rev(L)**. We can rewrite the **id** sub-goal to an equivalent conjunction:

```
palin(L):- L id rev(L). % L is palindromic if its it's own reverse
rev([])=[].
rev([E|L])=rev(L)<>[E].

[]<>X=X.
[E|X]<>Y=[E|X<>Y].

X id X.
```

Program 8.8 The `palindrome` program

```
...,rev*(L,Y),L id Y,...
```

where `rev*` is a special predicate symbol which is associated with the rev function symbol by means of the definitional sentence:

```
rev*(X,Y)  ⟺  rev(X)=Y
```

We can systematically replace all reducible terms in the text of a program by new variables, adding extra constraints to the clauses and equations in which the required value of the variable is specified. For example, consider the transformation of one of the `rev` equations, where in each step the underlined sub-expression is rewritten and new sub-goals are added from the corresponding definitional sentence:

```
rev([E|L])    = rev(L)<>[E]
              = X<>[E]  :- rev*(L,X)
              = Y :- rev*(L,X), '<>*'(X,[E],Y)
```

Equations can also be transformed into clauses about the defining predicate, again by invoking the definitional sentences. For each equation of the form

```
f(t₁,...,tₙ)=G:-B.
```

and definitional sentence

```
f*(X₁,...,Xₙ,R)  ⟺  f(X₁,...,Xₙ)=R
```

we generate the clause

```
f*(t1,...,tn,G*):-B*
```

where `G*` and `B*` are themselves the results of transforming `G` and `B`. This last sub-goal ensures that transitive closure of functional expressions is maintained. If we complete the transformation of `rev` in Program 8.8 we get a program which looks rather like the standard formulation of naive reverse in Prolog in Program 8.9. The *L&O* preprocessor given in Appendix A contains the main components of a compiler which compiles equations and expressions into normal clauses.

```
rev*([],[]).
rev*([E|L],Y) :- rev*(L,X), <>*(X,[E],Y)
```

Program 8.9 The transformed **rev** function

8.2.5   Quoted expressions and evaluation

The exact interpretation of ' is quite subtle; consider a first approximation to a definition of ' via the equation:

```
'X=X.
```

An English reading of this equation may be:

'any quoted expression is equal to the expression which is quoted.'

However, this is not sufficient since the '=' relation is transitive, and therefore under this equation we would get '2+3=2+3=5. This is not the desired intention of quote. The correct interpretation has to be expressed by an extra case in the **canon** program (and the corresponding case in the preprocessor):

```
canon('X,X).
```

By defining ' ' in this way we are effectively short-circuiting the transitive closure axiom. The possibility of having quoted terms is an extra complication especially for systems based on the narrowing principle. The (already extended) unification algorithm must now be able to recognise the quote symbol as well as other function symbols. Moreover the system must be careful about when quotes can be removed: if they are removed too early then in subsequent reductions the quoting effect may be unintentionally lost. All this represents further complications in an already complex narrowing algorithm.

Equations and *L&O* programs

We have established how we can translate equations and clauses containing expressions into clauses which do not, and which still 'compute' the same answers. However, equations and expressions occur within *L&O* programs, therefore we should see how the two systems can be integrated. To 'understand' an equation within a class body we can simply combine the equational translation with the translation for class templates. The first will result in a clause within the class body, and the second will translate this into a normal **lano** clause. So, for example, in the class body in Program 8.10, the equations for **x_coord** and **y_coord** would first be translated to generate a purely 'relational' *L&O* program. Then, by applying our *L&O* translation, we obtain the final **lano** clauses shown in Program 8.11.

```
(X,Y):{
    x_coord=X. y_coord=Y.
    }.
```

Program 8.10 A class template with functions

```
lano((X,Y),Self,'x_coord*'(X)).
lano((X,Y),Self,'y_coord*'(Y)).
```

Program 8.11 The `lano` clauses for Program 8.10

An expression may make a reference to a function defined in another class template; recall that we extended the expression syntax to allow a labelled expression which had this rôle:

$$\text{lab}(l_1,\ldots,l_k):\text{fun}(e_1,\ldots,e_n)$$

By a simple extension of the definitional sentence for functions we can construct an equivalent for labelled expressions:

$$\text{lab}(l_1,\ldots,l_k):\text{f}(e_1,\ldots,e_n)\text{=X} \iff \text{lab}(l_1,\ldots,l_k):\text{f*}(e_1,\ldots,e_n,\text{X})$$

8.3   Summary

In this chapter we have given the outline of the semantic foundations of *L&O* programming. The main thrust of this is to show that *L&O* programming is essentially equivalent to normal logic programming; and the extra features that we have added on top of logic programming are simply a kind of syntactic sugar (semantically speaking).

This overall result is crucial since it means that we do not have to repeat all the results obtained in the logic programming context: we can simply lift them into the context of *L&O* programming. It also highlights the scope for using a 'translational' approach for giving logic based programming notations a well-founded semantics.

Apart from the basic semantics of *L&O* programs, we have also looked at various techniques for giving a functional extention to logic programming a semantics. This is somewhat independent of the 'object oriented' extention; although it fits in quite well with it.

CHAPTER NINE

Implementing *L&O*

It is, and always has been, our intention that the formalisms that we have introduced in earlier chapters should form the basis of a practical programming language. In Chapter 8 we gave a mapping from *L&O* programs to standard logic clauses. Whilst this mapping is adequate for the purposes of giving a semantics to class templates; it is not a practical means of implementing a viable programming language.

However, it is possible to give a better translation from *L&O* programs into Prolog clauses [War90] which would allow *L&O* programs to be executed almost as efficiently as normal Prolog programs. Implemented as a preprocessor written in Prolog, such a mapping allows anyone with a Prolog compiler to use our system giving the advantages of class templates to normal Prolog programmers. In this chapter we explore the techniques behind the practical implementation of *L&O* programs in some detail. The salient parts of a MacProlog version of the preprocessor is given in Appendix A; and, as indicated there, a complete version is obtainable via 'anonymous' ftp.

We can divide our treatment of *L&O* programs into two categories – static programs which form the programmer's 'source' code and dynamic programs which are generated during the course of an executing application. Static programs (which we expect to form the bulk of an application's code) are not changed as a result of the *execution* of a program, whereas dynamic programs are dynamically created and modified through the use of **assert** and **retract**.

We look at these two categories of programs separately because we have different criteria when measuring their performance, and therefore the implementation techniques used to implement them, are also different. When we use our preprocessor to translate static *L&O* programs into Prolog clauses we can place the main emphasis on the performance of the translated code. However, when we deal with dynamic programs, then the performance of the translation process must also be taken into account – we cannot afford a slower **assert** since that will impact on the performance of the application itself.

9.1   A preprocessor for *L&O* programs

The task of the preprocessor is to produce Prolog programs from *L&O* programs
that execute as fast as possible on conventional Prolog systems. We aim to ensure
that standard Prolog programs execute with comparable performance 'within'
the *L&O* system and 'outside' it. We shall see that we largely achieve this goal:
Prolog-style *L&O* programs execute with $\approx 95\%$ of the efficiency of Prolog.

9.1.1   Constraints on the translated programs

In order to achieve high performance, it is necessary to know what features of
Prolog programs are used by a typical Prolog compiler in order to generate efficient
Prolog performance. If we can understand this properly, then we can better hope
to achieve good performance from our translated *L&O* programs.

The two most important features that any Prolog compiler focusses on are
indexing and *tail-recursion*.   We would like to ensure that if a set of Prolog-
style clauses is tail-recursive outside the *L&O* system, then it should also be
tail-recursive inside. Similarly, indexing should also be 'preserved' by the preprocessing. In particular, it will not be enough for the Prolog code produced by
the preprocessor to be tail-recursive and well indexed: the *L&O* programmer's
programs must also be tail-recursive and well indexed (if they would be anyway
outside *L&O*).

Space efficiency

A Prolog program can be said to execute in two modes – forward or normal mode
and backward or backtracking mode. In forward mode the sub-goals in a clause
are solved one after the other and when the last goal in the clause has been
successfully completed then the clause as a whole is also successful and therefore
the sub-goal that invoked the clause is also successfully completed. (Forward
mode corresponds to the execution mode of non-logic programming languages.)

Prolog systems often optimize the *last* goal in a clause by not calling it in the
normal way but by *jumping* to it. This replacement of a call by a jump is called the
tail recursion optimization. A purely tail-recursive Prolog program, executing only
in forward mode (i.e., one that does not indulge in backtracking) will execute with
the equivalent space efficiency as an iterative loop in a conventional procedural
programming language.

In order to preserve the tail recursion optimization we must ensure that the
preprocessor does not add any new sub-goals to the end of a clause. If it did, then

any tail recursion optimization that the programmer thought was there would be forfeit.

When a sub-goal fails (which would normally be because an attempt at unification failed) then the program enters into backwards mode. In this mode alternative clauses are tried within the predicate definition one after the other until one of the clauses succeeds, or if none do then the calling sub-goal fails also and a deeper backtracking is attempted.

In order to support backtracking a Prolog system must record a *choice point* each time there may be an alternative way of solving a sub-goal. This choice point record holds sufficient information from the state of the Prolog execution to allow alternative clauses to be tried at a subsequent stage. A choice point record requires a substantial amount of space and time to construct; so most Prolog systems try to avoid creating them whenever possible. In particular, it is possible to optimize the *last* clause in a sequence by not recording a choice point for it. If the last clause in a sequence fails, the system automatically picks up an earlier choice point relating to an earlier sub-goal.

Again, if we want to preserve this optimization, we must not add any extra clauses to the end of the sequence of clauses for a predicate when we translate from *L&O* programs to Prolog programs. Otherwise, there would be a choice point 'left over' when the programmer might have thought otherwise.

Indexing

The two main types of indexing that are common in Prolog systems are *predicate indexing* – where the programmer's clauses are sorted by predicate symbol and arity – and *argument indexing* where the clauses of an individual predicate are indexed by the type and value of some argument (typically the first argument). Predicate indexing means that when a sub-goal is entered, it is possible to locate the clauses that can be used to solve it directly without any form of searching.

Argument indexing is used to eliminate those clauses within a predicate's definition which will not unify when one or more of the arguments of a call are 'obviously' the wrong form. For example, if a call has the atom **peter** in its first argument, then only clauses which also have **peter** in their first argument (together with clauses which are variable in that argument) will be tried. Any clauses which have other atoms, such as **john,** or compound terms or numbers, will be filtered out by the indexing procedure and will not be attempted. Argument indexing usually does involve some degree of searching but this is often several orders of magnitude faster than simply trying the clauses one after the other.

Furthermore, argument indexing reduces the risk of creating redundant choice points. A choice point is redundant if none of the following clauses which it gives access to can be used to solve the sub-goal. There may be many clauses after the one which is being tried but if they are all incompatible (because they have obviously the wrong first argument say) then the choice point is redundant.

The requirement that predicate indexing is preserved by the preprocessor means that individual predicates (and functions) within class bodies should be mapped to different Prolog predicates. Furthermore, in order to be able to make use of any argument indexing that is available, the top-level arguments (especially the first argument) of an axiom in a class body must also be mapped into the *same* top-level arguments in the translation. Any extra arguments that we need to add – for example to support inheritance – must be added *after* the normal arguments in the axiom's predicate and function expression.

Argument registers

One final feature that we need to consider relates to the use of *argument registers* in many Prolog compilers. Whilst it is beyond the scope of this book to consider Prolog compilation techniques in detail, we do need to be aware of the role of argument registers.

Many Prolog compilers, particularly those based on the WAM [War83], use a fixed set of registers to hold the arguments to calls. In these systems, the arguments to a sub-goal are loaded into the argument registers immediately prior to calling the clauses associated with the sub-goal. Unification proceeds by 'reading' and comparing these registers.

The main benefit of using argument registers is that the code generated for the first sub-goal in a clause can often be heavily optimized. Because of the unification with the argument registers and the arguments in the head of the clause, many of the values which are required for this first call are already in argument registers. As a result, the compiler can employ many fewer data movements to set up the first call than the other calls.

In order to preserve *this* optimization we should ensure that we do not add any extra sub-goals to the beginning of a clause. If we do, then the 'first goal' which is encountered by the Prolog compiler will not be the first goal written by the programmer. Some Prolog compilers may be able to cope with some 'built-in' calls at the beginning of a clause without losing this optimization (particularly the '!') but it is safer not to assume this.

In summary, if we want to preserve many of the optimizations that a Prolog compiler applies to Prolog programs then we must ensure that the preprocessor does not add any extra clauses to the end of the clauses, that no extra sub-goals should be added to the beginning or end of a clause, and that any extra arguments that we insert to predicates should be after the existing arguments.

As we shall see, it is not possible to meet all of these constraints for all *L&O* programs; however, it is possible to write *L&O* programs so that all the optimizations which would be available are still there after translation. This is because our preprocessor guarantees all the constraints when the original code is Prolog code. Compiler optimizations are only 'lost' when the extra features are used, and even then as many optimizations as possible are preserved.

9.1.2 A strategy for compiling *L&O* programs

The execution of a *L&O* program could be said to have an additional phase over that of standard Prolog – namely the 'label phase'. In this phase the system is determining which class body is capable of solving a sub-goal; then once that has been determined the system enters into 'body phase' when the individual axioms in the class body are executed.

The label/body distinction is orthogonal to the forward/backwards distinction: the system can be in forward or backward mode whilst in label mode as well as in body mode. Depending on the programming style, we would expect that most of the time the system is in body phase rather than label phase since that is where the 'real' work is done.

Overall, our strategy is to generate two types of Prolog programs as a result of our translation – *label* programs which correspond to the class rules in the class templates and *local* programs which correspond to class bodies. Label programs also determine what is available within a body program. Prolog execution of a query will switch between the two sets of clauses depending on whether the application program is in 'label phase' or in 'body phase'.

Since class bodies contain the actual 'meat' of *L&O* programs, we focus on the efficient translation of programs in class bodies; even if that may be at the expense of inheritance and of features such as variable labels.

9.1.3 The label phase

The label phase of execution is normally entered into when we have an explicitly labelled sub-goal (or expression), such as the top-level query. The other occasion when label phase is entered into is when a local program fails and inheritance must be tried.

The label phase is invoked in two ways:

- when using class rules to select a class body to enter, and

- when entering a class body to execute a local program.

Because it is not possible to predict – at the time that we compile a labelled sub-goal – whether a predicate (or function) is directly defined in a class that has been invoked, we compile all labelled sub-goals in the same way.

Each label symbol of a given arity (such as **simple(Order)** in Program 3.4 on page 60) has associated with it a Prolog program which is 'responsible' for fielding all calls to the label.

So, for example, we associate the Prolog program '**2person:**' as the 'label' predicate for **person** from Program 9.1. When we have defined it, this label program will be responsible for determining if a given sub-goal can be evaluated

```
person(S,A):{
    age=A.
    sex(S).
    likes(X):-
          X:likes(self).
    no_of_legs:=2
    }.
person(S,A)<=animal.
person(S,A)<<citizen(S,A).

tom<<person(male,30).
tom:{
    no_of_legs:=1
    }.
```

Program 9.1 An example *L&O* program

by the **person** class; and if not, then it will attempt to solve the sub-goal using one of the class rules (involving **animal** or **citizen**).

The symbol '2person:' is constructed from the label symbol prepended with the label's arity and suffixed by a ':' character. Constructing the label predicate symbol in this way, rather than just using the label symbol directly, minimizes the possibility of a clash between a compiled *L&O* program and other Prolog programs or system primitives.

A complete call to the **person** class, such as:

```
...,person(male,30):likes(tom),...
```

is compiled to a call to the '2person:' program with the complete call and label represented as arguments:

```
...,'2person:'(likes(tom),person(male,30),
          person(male,30)),...
```

Notice that we have repeated the label twice – once to give the argument of the label to the call and once to pass the value of the **self** keyword (see Section 9.1.4).

The label entry program

The Prolog program generated for the label predicate has two parts: a series of clauses which provides the entry points into the class body and a clause which provides access to the inheritance section of the class. Each entry point clause provides a pattern which matches the calls that an individual body program can solve. (In Section 9.1.5, we explain how class rules are translated; and below, in Section 9.1.4, we explain how axioms from class bodies are translated.)

Program 9.2 shows an outline of the entry point clauses generated for the **person** class defined in Program 9.1.   Notice that each entry point clause has a

```
'2person:'(likes(X),Lb,Sf):-!,...
'2person:'('age*'(X),Lb,Sf):-!,...
'2person:'(sex(X),Lb,Sf):-!,...

'2person:'(C,Lb,Sf):-
      '2person:super'(C,Lb,Sf).
```

Program 9.2 The entry points for **person**

'!' immediately after the ':-'. This 'cut' has the effect of eliminating the other entry point clauses as choice points once one has been successfully selected; it also removes the last clause which would normally be used to enter the class rule portion of the code. We shall see that this technique allows us to implement overriding inheritance at minimal cost.

The functions which are defined in the class body for **person** are also represented in the entry point program – hence the clause mentioning 'age*'. Section 9.1.7 explains how functions and expressions are compiled by our preprocessor.

If a call is made to **person** which is *not* locally defined then none of the main entry point clauses will unify and the last clause in the entry point program will be tried (always successfully) and the class rule portion of the compiled code will be entered – as defined by the '2person:super' program.

Once an entry point has been successfully selected, then the subsequent code that is executed is in body phase involving code generated from a locally defined predicate.

9.1.4   The body phase

The constraints that we discussed in Section 9.1.1 suggest that each clause in a class body should lead – on average – to a single Prolog clause. Furthermore, to separate out the various classes we must ensure that similarly named clauses in different classes lead to separate predicates once translated.

The simplest way of doing this is to generate a new name for each predicate symbol which is defined in a class body. We choose to construct the new name from the label of the class and the predicate symbol and arity of the defining clauses.

So, a locally defined predicate of the form:

$$p(t_1, \ldots, t_n)$$

occurring in the class template with label:

$$lab(l_1, \ldots, l_k) : \{ \ldots$$

will have, as its generated local name:

$$'k\texttt{lab}:n\texttt{p}'$$

where n is the arity of the predicate concerned and k is the arity of the label. This form of predicate symbol maximally distinguishes predicates originating from different classes; furthermore, it is unlikely to be a normally occurring predicate symbol. As a result, we can compile L&O programs knowing that it is unlikely that there will be an accidental clash of names, and therefore we do not need a built-in module system in order to separate out the various programs. In fact, the L&O system can be used as the module system for any Prolog which did not have one.

Translating axioms in class bodies

Each axiom in a class body is translated into a single Prolog clause. An axiom of the form

$$\texttt{lab}(l_1, \ldots, l_k) : \{ \ldots$$
$$p(t_1, \ldots, t_n) : -C_1, \ldots, C_m.$$
$$\ldots$$
$$\}$$

is compiled into a Prolog clause of the form:

$$'\texttt{lab}:\texttt{p}'(t_1, \ldots, t_n, \texttt{Lb}, \texttt{Sf}) : -C_1^\dagger, \ldots, C_m^\dagger.$$

Translating sub-goals   The individual sub-goals $C_i^\dagger$ in the body of the translated clause are obtained from the sub-goals in the body of the axiom in a process which is similar to the way that we generated the head. If a given C_i is a normal unlabelled sub-goal, such as:

$$\ldots, q(a_1, \ldots, a_j), \ldots$$

which is locally defined within the class body, then we generate the sub-goal:

$$\ldots, 'k\texttt{lab}:j\texttt{q}'(a_1, \ldots, a_j, \texttt{Lb}, \texttt{Sf}), \ldots$$

in the translation. The '$k$lab:jq' symbol is constructed in the same way that we built the predicate symbol for the head of the clause.

The **Lb** and **Sf** variables that we use here (and in the head) are new unique variables that do not occur elsewhere in the original axiom. The 'Sf' variable corresponds to the value of the **self** keyword, and the Lb variable is used to hold a term which corresponds to the label term (and hence will give access to the label's arguments).

Any explicitly labelled sub-goal which appears in a clause (or equation) signals that that sub-goal should start in label phase rather than in body phase; and its translation is similar to that of a top-level query. So, for a sub-goal such as

$$\ldots,\texttt{mab(m}_1,\ldots,\texttt{m}_o\texttt{):q(a}_1,\ldots,\texttt{a}_j\texttt{)},\ldots$$

the translated sub-goal is

$$\ldots,\text{`}o\texttt{mab:'(q(a}_1,\ldots,\texttt{a}_j\texttt{)},\texttt{mab(m}_1,\ \ldots,\texttt{m}_o\texttt{)},\texttt{mab(m}_1,\ldots,\texttt{m}_o\texttt{))},\ldots$$

where o is the arity of the label. We shall see the reason for the double occurrence of the $\texttt{mab(m}_1,\ldots,\texttt{m}_o)$ term when we look at the implementation of the **self** keyword and at variables in labels.

In the case that the explicit label associated with the sub-goal is the **super** keyword then we rewrite the sub-goal to a special **super**-local predicate:

$$\ldots,\text{`}k\texttt{lab:super'(q(a}_1,\ldots,\texttt{a}_j\texttt{)},\texttt{Lb},\texttt{Sf)},\ldots$$

Similarly, if a sub-goal is unlabelled, where there is no local definition for it, then we translate it as though the sub-goal were **super** labelled.

The self keyword   The definition of the **self** keyword is that it represents the original label of the sub-goal which 'led' to the occurrence of the keyword. We know that **self** is defined for every sub-goal and expression since all queries to *L&O* programs must originally start with an explicitly labelled sub-goal.

A sub-goal which has an explit label, as in:

$$\ldots,\texttt{label:call},\ldots$$

is used to define the value of the **self** keyword: in this case, it takes on **label** as its value within the proof of **call**. Unless it is overridden in its turn, any unlabelled sub-goals or expressions encountered whilst trying to solve **call**, will have **label** as their value of **self**.

In order to implement this, we have to 'pass the **self**' value to the program invoked by the labelled call. Furthermore, since **self** is unaffected by inheritance through class rules, this value must be passed through them also. We will see this happen when we look at class rules in Section 9.1.5.

We implement **self** by adding an extra variable – the **Sf** variable – to the head and to every unlabelled sub-goal of the Prolog clause generated from class body axiom. The effect is that whatever value is held by the **Sf** variable is shared by every clause which has been translated from the class body. In this way, we can ensure that the value of the **self** keyword is transmitted and held whilst execution is 'within' the class body. In addition, we also replace any occurrences of the **self** keyword in the text of the class body axiom by an occurrence of the **Sf** variable. In this way, the value of the **self** variable can be made available to local programs.

The **self** keyword's value is established in a labelled sub-goal (or expression). A labelled sub-goal is translated into a call to the label program, and the label of the call is included (twice) in the call to the label program. The second occurrence of the label term is the **self** value, and the first is used as a convenient method for passing in the label parameters to the call.

Variable labels   A straightforward translation of a labelled sub-goal is not possible in the case that its label is syntactically a variable. This is because with such a label we cannot know at the time that we compile the sub-goal what label program to call. Instead, we generate a call to '?:?'. So, a call of the form:

$$\ldots, X:q(t_1,\ldots,t_j),\ldots$$

is translated to the Prolog call:

$$\ldots, \text{'?:?'}(X,q(t_1,\ldots,t_j),\text{Sf}),\ldots$$

The '?:?' program, which is part of the support library of the *L&O* system, has to perform the translation from a label to the appropriate label program dynamically. Since variable labels occur quite frequently in *L&O* programs it is important to be able to do this as efficiently as possible.

Perhaps the simplest way of implementing '?:?' is to provide a clause for it for every label that can occur in the *L&O* program, as in Program 9.3 which gives some of the '?:?' clauses for Program 9.1.   The way that the '?:?' program is

```
'?:?'(person(X1,X2),C,S):-!,
    '2person:'(C,person(X1,X2),person(X1,X2)).
...
'?:?'(tom,C,S):-!,
    '0tom:'(C,tom,tom).

'?:?'(L,C,S):-
    '?:?'(S,'?error?'('undefined label',L:C),S).
```

Program 9.3 The '?:?' clauses for **person** and **tom**

built is reminiscent of the way that the entry point clauses are built for individual labels. We can even add an extra *default* case to catch those calls which do not match existing labels.

In fact, we have deliberately arranged the call to '?:?' so that the actual **self** label is passed so that this error reporting procedure can work effectively. Without it, it would not be possible to have specific error handlers associated with individual classes.

Notice that passing in this **Sf** variable in this way violates the principle of **self**. (Since the variable labelled sub-goal has an explicit label, and hence its own value for **self**, the 'outer' value of **self** has no meaning within the sub-goal.) However, we do not actually pass the **Sf** variable into the called program – we only use it within the '?:?' program in the case of an error arising.

This method for implementing variable labels is reasonably efficient; especially in those Prolog systems which support first argument indexing. Our preprocessor actually uses a slightly modified version of this program which enhances the effect of argument indexing and which is easier to maintain by the preprocessor.

Object search   In a final adjustment to our implementation of variable labels, we should allow for *object searching*. An object search is distinguished from a 'normal' variable labelled call by the fact that the label is still unbound at the time of the call. It would be rather unfortunate if at the end of an unsuccessful object search the system reported an error rather than just failed. The simple expedient of preventing the error handler being called when the label is a true variable ensures that an object search would **fail** rather than report an error at the end:

```
'?:?'(L,C,S):-
    nonvar(L),
    '?:?'(S,'?error?'('undefined label',L:C),S).
```

In order to enhance the object search, especially in the context of dynamic programs, we arrange that the preprocessor puts the '?:?' clauses for dynamic clauses ahead of the '?:?' clauses for static programs.

Variables in labels

Recall that any variables which occur in the label are quantified over all the axioms in the class body. Prolog does not directly support this form of two-level quantifiers, however we can get the effect of two-level quantifiers by passing in the label arguments to the translated Prolog program. We do this by passing in the whole label term, and accessing the arguments as we need them. Notice that the 'current' label, which changes when we use a class rule to switch to a different class template, is not necessarily the same as the **self** label.

Variables from labels which occur in a class body axiom are processed into new ordinary Prolog variables, together with extra code for accessing the current label term. So, if we had a label variable **S** occurring in a class body axiom, as in the **sex(S)** assertion in Program 9.1, then this becomes the local variable **S** and we also generate an extra sub-goal of the form:

```
..., arg(Lb, n, S), ...
```

where n is the index of the label variable S in the label. In this case, we actually generate:

```
'2person:1sex'(S,Lb,Sf):- arg(Lb,1,S).
```

as the translation of the **sex** assertion.

The **arg** predicate is a standard Prolog primitive which is usually extremely efficiently implemented in Prolog systems; however, it is possible that the existence of an extra sub-goal like this can compromise some of the optimizations performed by the compiler. (In particular, those optimizations relating to the first sub-goal in a clause.)

An alternative approach to handling labels (and hence variables in labels) is to copy the complete label into every translated sub-goal and head. The normal occurrences of the label variables will then be shared with the label term in a natural way. If we did this for the **sex** assertion, we would get the translation:

```
'2person:1sex'(S,person(S,A),Sf).
```

instead.

This method has the advantage that we don't generate an extra sub-goal to access the label argument; however, if there are no references to label arguments in a particular axiom then copying the label explicitly leads to redundant work for the Prolog system. Furthermore, if there are many sub-goals and few label arguments which are accessed then we might do more work in unifying the label term (and generating extra data movements as a result of building up the label terms for the calls) than we would by using the **arg** primitive to access components.

It is difficult to judge which is the 'best' approach to handling variables in labels. Our preprocessor uses the **arg** technique except in some situations where it is obviously better to copy the label term explicitly (such as when an assertion mentions a label argument).

A complete class body   Program 9.4 shows a more-or-less complete translation into Prolog clauses of the **person** class body from Program 9.1.

9.1.5   Class rules

Class rules are 'methods' for solving queries by replacing the label in a sub-goal rather than the predication. A class rule can be used in a number of different contexts – a 'new' call to a class template may mention a predicate which is not defined locally within the class body (there might not even be a class body); a local program may 'fail' and through backtracking try any inherited definitions; a class body axiom may mention a sub-goal which is not locally defined and finally

% The label entry clauses:-
```
'2person:'(likes(X),Lb,Sf):-!,'2person:1likes'(X,Lb,Sf)
'2person:'('age*'(X),Lb,Sf):-!,'2person:1age*'(X,Lb,Sf)
'2person:'(sex(X),Lb,Sf):-!,'2person:1sex'(X,Lb,Sf)
'2person:'(C,Lb,Sf):-
        '2person:super'(C,Lb,Sf).
```

% The translation of the likes predicate
```
'2person:1likes'(X,Lb,Sf):-
        ?:?(X,likes(Sf),Sf).
```

% The translation of the age function
```
'2person:1age*'(A,person(S,A),Sf):-!.     % See Section 9.1.7
```

% The translation of the sex predicate
```
'2person:1sex'(S,person(S,A),Sf).
```

% See Section 9.1.8 for no_of_legs

Program 9.4 The translation of the **person** class body

a sub-goal may have an explicit **super** label in which case the local programs are not to be tried anyway.

The two types of class rule – normal and overriding – have different behaviours in these situations. A normal class rule is always available: both on initial entry to a class and when a locally defined predicate fails 'out' of the class. An overriding class rule can only be used when there is no local definition of a predicate (or function); therefore, it is only during the 'label phase' that overriding class rules can be activated. A normal class rule can also be used to locate other possible possible solutions for sub-goals of clauses and equations which are within the class body and which fail to find a local solution.

In order to deal with the two types of class rules we generate up to two inheritance programs for each class: one of which consists of an entry for each normal class rule and one which includes both normal and overriding class rules. We will see that this separation allows an efficient implementation of inheritance when there are overriding class rules (especially when there are *only* overriding rules).

Recall that the label entry program will select a locally defined program if one is available; otherwise the **super** label program is entered. This program is generated from all the class rules: both normal and overriding. The fact that the label program (as in Program 9.2) puts a '!' after each of the local entry point clauses ensures that the overriding class rules will not be invoked when the class is called with a program which it defines. (It also seems to prevent access to the normal class rules as well, but see below.) Program 9.5 shows the **super**-label program generated by the preprocessor for the **person** label. Notice

```
'2person:super'(Cl,person(S,A),Sf):-
    'Oanimal:'(Cl,animal,Sf).        % from person¡=animal
'2person:super'(Cl,person(S,A),Sf):-
    '2citizen:'(Cl,citizen(S,A),Sf)% from person¡¡citizen
```

Program 9.5 The '2person:super' program

how the right-hand side of a class rule is translated into a call to the appropriate label program. Furthermore, the Sf variable (representing the value of the self keyword) is passed unchanged into the new label program. This is the means by which self is preserved through inheritance.

The right-hand label term – animal or citizen(...) – is copied into the label argument of the sub-goal which invokes the inherited class – that is the point where the label arguments are defined for the new class. The fact that the left-hand side of the class rule is also copied into the head of this clause ensures that it is only used when the 'current' label unifies with the left-hand side of the class rule.

In the event that there are no explicit class rules for a given class template the preprocessor adds one implicitly. This class rule is used to give *default* access to the system library of built-in primitives. So, the simple class template, which is defined in Program 3.4 on page 60, has a class rule added automatically:

```
simple(Order)<<system
```

Because this is an overriding class rule rather than a normal one, this will have no effect on the translation of axioms from the body of the class. It does mean that the '1simple:super' program will have a proper definition though.

On the other hand, if there is no class body for a label – if it is defined entirely through class rules – then there is no distinction between normal and overriding class rules. The preprocessor optimizes this case, and does not generate programs for both the normal rules and overriding rules. Instead, the label program itself is compiled to give direct access to the classes inherited by the rules.

Normal class rules

Normal class rules are also available to locally defined programs when they backtrack out of their local definitions; whereas the overriding rules are not available in this situation. In order to implement this we generate a Prolog program which consists of the translation of the normal rules only. We call this new program the 'label-inherit' program to distinguish it from the 'label-super' program. The label-inherit program for person is shown in Program 9.6. This program will only be used when a local clause fails; so, in order to access the normal class rules we add an extra clause to the end of all the locally defined predicates generated in

```
'2person:inherit'(Cl,person(S,A),Sf):-
    '0animal:'(Cl,animal,Sf).  % from person¡=animal
```

Program 9.6 The '2person:inherit' program

the body phase. The complete program for **sex** from Program 9.1, including the extra clause which implements inheritance, in given in Program 9.7.

```
'2person:1sex'(S,person(S,A),Sf).
'2person:1sex'(S,Lb,Sf):-
    '2person:inherit'(sex(S),Lb,Sf).
```

Program 9.7 The complete local definition of **sex**

The fact that we have had to add an extra clause to the local programs means that we are potentially adding extra choice points to the program. The *L&O* programmer must be aware of this effect when using normal class rules. If only overriding class rules are used in a class template, then these extra clauses will not be generated.

Class rules with differential inheritance filters

If a class rule has a differential inheritance filter on it then we insert a test in the rule which looks for the atom(s) that may not be inherited. This test is performed (by Prolog) *after* the inherited call. For example, if we have a rule of the form:

```
penguin<=bird-[mode(fly)].
```

The code that is generated for this clause in the 'penguin:super' program is shown in Program 9.8. The **not member** test which makes sure that penguins

```
'0penguin:super'(A,L,S):-
    '0bird:'(A,bird,S),
    not member(A,[mode(fly)]).
```

Program 9.8 The translation of a class rule with differential inheritance

don't fly is performed after a successful computation in **bird**. This is to give the best chance of the inherited atom being ground by the time the filter is applied;

```
animal:{
    mode(walk).
    mode(gallop):-
        self:no_of_legs(4).
    mode(run):-
        self:no_of_legs(2)
    }.
animal<=life_form.
```

Program 9.9 An example *L&O* program

and therefore avoid some atoms being incorrectly filtered out. Of course, it also means that there may be some expensive and redundant computation.

9.1.6   A complete example

We can now look at how a complete class template would be translated. For example the animal program in Program 9.9 is translated by the preprocessor into the list of clauses shown in Program 9.10.

```
'0animal:'(mode(X),Lb,Sf):- !,
    '0animal:mode'(X,Lb,Sf).
'0animal:'(Cl,Lb,Sf):- '0animal:super'(Cl,Lb,Sf).

'0animal:mode'(walk,Lb,Sf).            % The locally defined mode
'0animal:mode'(gallop,Lb,Sf):-
    ?:?(Sf,no_of_legs(4),Sf).
'0animal:mode'(run,Lb,Sf):-
    ?:?(Sf,no_of_legs(2),Sf).

'0animal:mode'(X,Lb,Sf):-              % invoke normal inheritance
    '0animal:inherit'(mode(X),Lb,Sf).

'0animal:super'(Cl,animal,Sf):-        % super inheritance
    '0life_form:'(Cl,life_form,Sf).
'0animal:inherit'(Cl,animal,Sf):-      % normal inheritance
    '0life_form:'(Cl,life_form,Sf).
```

Program 9.10 Program 9.9 translated into Prolog

9.1.7   Equations and expressions

As we have seen in Chapter 8, there are various ways in which we can incorporate equations and expressions into logic programming. One of these –the compilational approach – is particularly suitable in the context of a preprocessor since we are already preprocessing *L&O* programs into Prolog clauses.

We can (and do) integrate the two into a single compilation; this allows us to have equations embedded in class bodies and for class body axioms to contain expressions. In principle there is little difficulty in the combination. If there is an equation in the class body it is first compiled into a clause within the class body and then processed with the other clauses into Prolog clauses. Similarly, any expressions occurring in the class body axioms can be replaced by variables together with the sub-goals that give them the correct value.

So, a *L&O* function such as in Program 9.11, is first translated into the standard class template program with no functions or expressions shown in Program 9.12, and then into the standard Prolog clauses shown in Program 9.13.   The entry

```
llist:{
    app([],X)=X.
    app([E|X],Y)=[E|app(X,Y)].
    }
```

Program 9.11 The app function

```
llist:{
    'app*'([],X,X):-!.
    'app*'([E|X],Y,[E|_1]):-!,
        'app*'(X,Y,_1).
    }
```

Program 9.12 The app* relation

point for the **app** function also appear as a clause in the '0llist:' program.

Notice that we insert a '!' into the Prolog clauses implementing the function. This cut represents a commitment to use the equation when the left-hand side of the equation matches the expression and when the conditional part of the equation has been verified. Committing to the equation in this way implements the functionality property – it 'forces' equations to define functions.

```
'Ollist:2app*'([],X,X,Lb,Sf):-!.
'Ollist:2app*'([E|X],Y,[E|_1],Lb,Sf):-!,
    'Ollist:2app*'(X,Y,_1,Lb,Sf).

'Ollist:'('app*'(_1,_2,_3),Lb,Sf):-
    'Ollist:2app*'(_1,_2,_3,Lb,Sf)
```

Program 9.13 Translated clauses for 'app*'

The local predicate symbol that we generate for functions contains the arity of the function and is suffixed by a '*' to allow adequate differentiation between compiled predicates and compiled functions.

When a class template has functions defined in it, then expressions can mention them both in equations and in clauses. The preprocessor does not insist that functions are defined before they are used within a class body.

Expressions can also occur in class rules. However, for various reasons, the expressions that occur in class rules are restricted to the standard built-in functions (such as '+' and **length**) or explicitly labelled expressions. An unlabelled expression will be simply interpreted as a normal term if it is not a standard function.

9.1.8   Dynamic variables

The *L&O* language includes a simple form of *dynamic variable* which is roughly analogous to the *instance variables* of languages such as Smalltalk and C++. In this section we are interested in how we can implement them using our preprocessor-style technology. There are a number of issues relating to the implementation of dynamic variables which we must address:

- the types of values a dynamic variable can hold,

- how they are stored,

- how the value of a dynamic variable is accessed,

- how dynamic variables are re-assigned and

- how the initial value of a dynamic variable is established

Dynamic and logic variables

As with the normal logical variables, a dynamic variable can have any Prolog term as its value. However, we impose a constraint on the way that *logical variables* are handled within dynamic variables. If a dynamic variable is assigned a term which contains logical variables, then those variables will not be 'maintained' by the assignment; instead they are copied as new logical variables each time the dynamic variable is accessed. Furthermore, if the original logical variables are further instantiated, this will *not* be reflected in the value of the dynamic variable. (This constraint is exactly the same as that imposed by Prolog when using **assert** to add a clause which contain variables.)

This constraint on dynamic variables is important for several reasons: it allows a reasonable implementation strategy, and it avoids potential problems caused when a program which assigns a dynamic variable backtracks over the assignment. If we had to preserve logical variables in a dynamic variable then when the Prolog system backtracked over an assignment we would have no alternative but to undo the assignment since the logical variables involved in the assignment could easily become *invalid* as the system backtracks. It is a major feature of dynamic variables that they are not affected by backtracking.

Basic implementation of dynamic variables

The simplest method of implementing dynamic variables, in standard Prolog systems, is to use the **assert** and **retract** primitives. We can hold the value of a dynamic variable as the single argument to an assertion – the name of the dynamic variable might form the predicate symbol of this assertion. So when a dynamic variable is re-assigned, we could translate this into the sequence:

```
..., '<retract>'(dynamic(Old)), '<assert>'(dynamic(New)),...
```

Notice that when we **assert** the new value of the dynamic variable, any variables which might occur in the **New** value are copied as a natural part of the semantics of **assert**. (Again, we have fabricated a special 'shape' of predicate symbol to hold the value of the variable in order to avoid conflicts with other predicate symbols.)

Whilst this method of implementing dynamic variables is straightforward, it is not exactly cheap. Invoking the **assert** primitive is tantamount to invoking a compiler in many compiler-based Prolog systems; in addition, the **retract** performs a search of the existing database and unnecessarily retrieves the old value (although the chances that the expression which gives the dynamic variable its new value also mentions it are high; in which case we can combine the access with the update). When the existing value is large this can involve a large amount of computation.

A safer version of the re-assignment sequence uses **retractall** rather than **retract** to remove the old value. This ensures that there can never be multiple copies of the assertion which holds the dynamic variable's value should any accident occur with the program.

Other implementation techniques Many Prolog systems offer cheaper means of implementing limited forms of assignment; and in a local version of the preprocessor we would expect them to be used. In our version, we make use of the property management facilites of MacProlog. MacProlog offers several primitives which are useful for implementing assignment:

- The **set_prop** primitive takes three arguments:

    ...,set_prop(Symbol,Prop,Value),...

  which sets the property **Prop** associated with the atom **Symbol** to have value **Value**. If we subsequently **set_prop** same **Symbol/Property** pair then we will *over-write* any previously existing value; which is quite different to the situation with a subsequent **assert** which would *add* a new value unless the old value was specifically **retract**ed.

  Also, **set_prop** does not involve any use of the **assert** compiler, and therefore it is substantially faster.

- The value of a property can be accessed with the **get_prop** primitive. A call of the form:

    ...,get_prop(Symbol,Prop,X),...

  binds the variable **X** to a previously stored value. (If no property has been set before then the **get_prop** call will fail.)

- The **del_prop** primitive is used to delete a property from a symbol. (Which might be useful to clear up the values left over after an aborted execution.)

With these primitives we can implement assignment to dynamic variables very efficiently. A simple implementation of assignment could be in the form of a translation to a sub-goal of the form:

    ...,set_prop(dynamic,'*value*',Value),...

At this point it is important to be slightly more specific about the proper 'ownership' of dynamic variables.

Variable declaration

A dynamic variable is declared by an initialization statement occurring in a class body. We can say therefore, that the dynamic variable 'belongs' to the class in which it is declared. However, if a class inherits programs from a class which also contains dynamic variable declarations then we would expect to inherit the dynamic variables as well. In general, there may be many classes which might claim ownership of a dynamic variable.

We prefer not to have to 'share' this variable amongst all these owners; instead we create copies of the dynamic variable for each sub-class of the defining class. Ultimately, there will be a separate copy of a dynamic variable for all possible values of **self** which can give access to the class containing the variable's declaration. Of course, the different copies of the dynamic variable might have different values; however, they will all be *initialized* using the same declaration statement.

So, the dynamic variable declaration:

```
no_of_legs:=2.
```

which occurs in the **person** class template in Program 9.1 declares the symbol **no_of_legs** as a dynamic variable. This variable has several versions: one in the **person** class, and one in the **tom** class since that is a sub-class of **person**.

If we access the value of the **no_of_legs** variable from the **tom** program, then we would expect the answer:

1

whereas, if we asked the **person** class the same question:

```
person(male,30):no_of_legs=?
```

we should get the answer

2

All this is easily explained if we think of each reference to the **no_of_legs** variable being implicitly prefixed by a **self** keyword. So, whenever a dynamic variable is assigned, it is the version that belongs to the current **self** which is affected.

To implement this requires a subtle change in the way that we represent dynamic variables. Instead of simply using the name of the variable as the key to accessing the value, we must also consider the value of **self**.

In the 'holding assertion' technique, we can simply add another argument to the assertion. So, each assertion which represents a dynamic variable would now look like:

```
'<dynamic>'(Self,Value)
```

and a re-assignment becomes the sequence of sub-goals:

```
...,retractall('<dynamic>'(Sf,_)),
    assert('<dynamic>'(Sf,Value)),...
```

If we are intending to use MacProlog-style properties to hold dynamic variables, then we might use the value of **self** as the symbol and the name of the dynamic variable as the property:

```
...,set_prop(Sf,no_of_legs,2),...
```

However, since **self** is not always a simple atom, and since **set_prop** requires an atom for both the symbol and property names, we have to be a little more careful. Instead, we will use the label predicate that the preprocessor generates for each label as the key to assign the variable. For convenience to avoid a large amount of processing, we access the key as a 'hidden' relation within each class. The re-assignment to the **no_of_legs** dynamic variable is actually implemented as:

```
...,?:?(Sf,'?label?'(L),Sf),set_prop(L,no_of_legs,2),...
```

where '?label?' is defined for each class and which returns the label predicate for the label. We can define '?label?' by adding an extra case in the label entry program:

```
'2person:'('?label?'('2person:')),L,S).
```

This allows us to find the internal name of a label using the same 'interface' as we use for other queries. We know that the dynamic variable's name is an atom since we impose that restriction on the *L&O* language.

Unfortunately, this implementation of dynamic variables is not completely watertight since different *instances* of a class (i.e., with different instantiations of variables in the label) will map to the same key. However, it does adequately distinguish all labels which are atomic which we expect to be the most important case when using dynamic variables. (On the other hand, we *could* have made a 'feature' of this bug by saying that accessing the dynamic variables of a label with variables in it amounts to accessing 'class variables' as opposed to 'instance variables'.)

Accessing a dynamic variable's value
From the point of view of the *L&O* programmer, the value of a dynamic variable is syntactically the same as a zero-argument function. However, our preprocesser can distinguish when the access to a variable is from 'within' the class body in which it is declared or outside it.

If a dynamic variable is referenced from within its defining class, then we can compile code to access it directly, using whatever means we have decided to represent the variable. So, if we are using clauses then to access the **no_of_legs** variable inside the **person** class, we generate a sub-goal of the form:

```
...,'<no_of_legs>'(Sf,X),...
```

where **X** is the Prolog variable which will hold the value of the dynamic variable, and **Sf** is the current self variable.

If we use the property management technique, then the clause which accesses the variable's value will look like:

```
'<no_of_legs>'(Sf,Val):-
        ?:?(Sf,'?label?'(LbL),Sf),
        get_prop(LbL,no_of_legs,Val).
```

If we access the value of a dynamic variable 'outside' the class template in which it is declared then we access it in the same way that we would access a zero-arity function. The value of this function is the current value of the dynamic variable. From the point of view of 'outside' the defining class there is no distinction between dynamic variables and zero-arity functions.

This implies that dynamic variables also have a clause in the label entry program which will give access to them. This entry clause has a 'head' which is as though for a zero-arity function and a body which is as though for a local access to the variable:

```
'2person:0no_of_legs*'(X,Lb,Sf):-
    '<no_of_legs>'(Sf,X).
```

or, where we use properties, we would use:

```
'2person:0no_of_legs*'(X,Lb,Sf):-
    ?:?(Sf,'?label?'(Key),Sf),
    get_prop(Key,no_of_legs,X).
```

in the entry point program.

Initializing a dynamic variable

The declaration statement of a dynamic variable gives its 'first' value before any re-assignments to it take place. This also means that all the separate copies of a dynamic variable must be initialized to the value determined by its declaration statement. (It is possible that different copies of the variable will have different initial values if the declaration statement is sensitive to the value of **self**.) Provided that we make sure that a given copy is initialized prior to its first access, we have some flexibility in the implementation of variable initialization.

We split the implementation of variable initialization into two aspects – a special program (called '#init#') which is responsible for performing the initialization and a 'trigger' which calls the '#init#' program at the appropriate time.

For any class that has at least one dynamic variable we provide a local '#init#' program which is responsible for initializing all the dynamic variables in the class. This program is implemented as an extra clause in the label entry program. The body of this '#init#' clause performs the initialization in the same way that dynamic variables are re-assigned. So, the no_of_legs variable from Program 9.1 is intialized with the program in Program 9.14. The **fail** at the end of the body is important: it will cause any dynamic variables which are inherited by the **person** class to be initialized also (via the class rule for **citizen** for example).

The whole initialization sequence is a failure driven loop (something that we would normally question as it can be dangerous). However, we need to ensure that all the dynamic variables associated with a given label are initialized throughout the inheritance hierarchy; and this means that we have to trigger all the class

```
'2person:'('#init#',Lb,Sf):-
    retractall('<no_of_legs>'(Sf,_)),
    assert('<no_of_legs>'(Sf,2)),
    fail.
```

Program 9.14 The initialization program for no_of_legs

rules. Furthermore, having a failure driven loop allows us to omit the '#init#' clause for any class which does not have any dynamic variables.

The initialization of all the dynamic variables which belong to a class is performed when the first access to any dynamic variable of that class is made. If a dynamic variable has not been initialized then any access to its value will fail (whether because the variable's assertion is not there or because there is no property stored for it). We can use this failure to trigger the initializations of *all* the dynamic variables in a class. The trigger is embedded as a second case in the code for accessing a dynamic variable's value; where we use

```
... , '<no_of_legs>'(Sf,Val),...
```

to access the variable, we define the '<no_of_legs>' program using two clauses as in Program 9.15.   This changes slightly our story about storing and ac-

```
'<no_of_legs>'(S,V):-
    '<<no_of_legs>>'(S,V),!.% Successfully picked up value
'<no_of_legs>'(S,V):-            % trigger initialization
    ?:?('#init#',S,S), fail% initialise all of them
'<no_of_legs>'(S,V):-
    '<<no_of_legs>>'(S,V),!.% Should now have a value
```

Program 9.15 The initialization trigger for no_of_legs

cessing dynamic variables. We re-assign the no_of_legs variable by updating the '<<no_of_legs>>' predicate and we access its value using the '<no_of_legs>' predicate. Each dynamic variable that occurs in the whole L&O program has an access program like this defined for it.

9.1.9   Tracing and debugging L&O programs

The traditional support for debugging Prolog programs is to use a tracer. A Prolog tracer is essentially an interpreter for Prolog which is written in Prolog.

Using the **clause** database to access the programmer's program, the tracer can emulate normal Prolog execution and also report tracing events and allow some control over the execution – such as allowing an inspection of the program or a re-execution of some sub-goal. Many tracers are based on the so-called four port model introduced by Byrd [Byr80] which can allow the user to pause at initial entry to a Prolog predicate, when it succeeds, when it fails or when a re-entry (after a later sub-goal has failed) is called for.

For debugging *L&O* programs, we could also use a Prolog tracer since our preprocessor compiles programs into Prolog. However, a *L&O* programmer would have to understand precisely how *L&O* was translated into Prolog before being able to make much sense of a Prolog-level trace. Tracing a *L&O* program in terms of the Prolog code generated by the preprocessor is much more complicated and unfriendly than tracing at a level which is more like *L&O* itself. It is far more preferable to trace *L&O* queries in terms of *L&O* programs rather than in terms of Prolog programs.

We could also build a *L&O*-level tracer as a Prolog program; in an analgous fashion to the Prolog-in-Prolog tracer. An interpreter for *L&O* programs would consist of at least two phases: the interpreter itself which 'implemented' the *L&O* language and ensured that the traced execution is faithful to the untraced execution; and a reporting/interaction phase which generates tracing information and allows user interaction.

Unfortunately, since we compile *L&O* programs into Prolog, any *L&O* tracer would have to be able to 'de-compile' the Prolog code into the *L&O* original. This is difficult to do for all cases; especially since our aim in building the preprocessor is to produce fast Prolog programs rather than easily traceable programs.

Tracing by hooks

Instead of writing an interpreter, we could borrow some of the techniques used in the tracing of languages like 'C' and compile in tracing information to the *L&O* program as we convert it into a Prolog program.

The basic concept is very simple: wherever a 'traceable event' might occur in a *L&O* program (such as when a class rule is to be used, or when a function returns a value) we add in to the compiled Prolog a call to a special 'hook' procedure. This hook program is then automatically called as the event actually occurs.

So, we might have the '**#q#**' hook when an equation is entered, and the '**#v#**' hook is called when the equation returns its value. A typical translation of a *L&O* function such as the **app** function on page 225, with these hooks embedded in the result is shown in Program 9.16. We arrange the calls to the hooks so that they give sufficient information to enable the source statement to be located in the source file. (In this case the term

```
'@x'('Append function',1056,0,1)
```

```
'Ollist:2app*'([], X, X, Lb, Sf):-
    '#q#'(app([],X), Lb, Sf,'@x'('Append function',1056,0,1)),
    !,
    '#v#'(X, Lb, Sf, '@x'('Append function',1056,0,1)).
'Ollist:2app*'([E|X], Y, [E|_1], Lb, Sf):-
    '#q#'(app([E|X],Y), Lb, Sf, '@x'('Append function',1056,1,2)),
    !,
    'Ollist:2app*'(X, Y, _1, Lb, Sf),
    '#v#'([E|_1], Lb, Sf,'@x'('Append function',1056,1,2)).
```

Program 9.16 The `app` function translated with tracing hooks

gives the name of the window containing the source class, the character offset
within the window for the class body, the number of terms within the body to
skip before this statement and the index of the axiom within the definition of the
function.) The implementation of the trace hook programs themselves is left to
the local implementor of the *L&O* system.

We have arranged the hooks to be as specific as possible, to allow the maximum
differentiation of the traceable events. For example, we can differentiate the initial
entry into a relation or function from outside the class to a re-entry from within
the class body. The set of hooks generated by our preprocessor is:

'#r#'   The initial entry to a relation in a class body.

'#e#'   The entry to a clause in the class body.

'#s#'   The successful completion of a clause in the class body.

'#f#'   The initial entry to a function in a class body.

'#q#'   The entry into an equation of a function.

'#v#'   The completion of an equation.

'#i#'   The use of an inheritance rule.

'#d#'   The initialization of a dynamic variable.

'#a#'   The re-assignment of a dynamic variable.

'#u#'   A user specified print statement. This hook is compiled in when the programmer has inserted a **trace**(*message*) sub-goal into the body of a clause
or equation. The *message* is printed out in the trace of the execution whenever this hook is activated.

The preprocessor allows selective enabling of the tracing information generated.
We can selectively trace only equations, or only inheritance or some arbitrary

combination of traceable events. The actual tracing hook invoked is controlled by
the **tracing** declaration command:

```
:-tracing([equations,clauses,rules,dynamic])
```

Whatever tracing information has been compiled, only those events which are 'in
force' at the time of the execution are actually triggered, (i.e., the tracing hook
programs first of all check to see if they are still valid before activating.)

If all the hooks which can be used are used, then this can result in an amount
of Prolog code which is considerably larger than the normal code generated by
the preprocessor. However, because we are not using an interpreter for tracing
we have a much reduced overhead at run-time. It is not atypical for a Prolog-
in-Prolog tracer to require 10 times as much space and time to execute a Prolog
program over the normal execution; by compiling in tracing information in this
way we can eliminate much of this overhead, and as a result we can debug larger
L&O programs.

9.2 Dynamic *L&O* programs

A dynamic program – in the context of Prolog – is one which has been (or could
have been) loaded into the system via a series of **assert** and **retract** operations.
In this section we outline the approach that we have taken in our preprocessor
based system to dynamic programs; we make a fairly pragmatic choice in the
representation of dynamic programs and in the types of *L&O* programs that can
be dynamic.

The use of Prolog database primitives to build executable programs leads to
a number of uncomfortable compromises. The reason being that in the context of a compiler based language system it is not clear what role the **assert**
and **retract** primitives should have: for example, whether they are intended to
maintain databases efficiently or whether they are intended to edit user programs
efficiently.

In early Prolog language systems, which were interpreter based, the process of
converting a term into an executable representation of a clause was very straightforward and cheap. Furthermore, because of the incremental nature of these
interpreters there was no advantage to be gained by not allowing programs to be
built up one clause at a time. So, typically the **consult** primitive was actually
defined in terms of **assert**.

With a compiler based system many of these considerations change. A whole
relation is typically compiled in one go; and the effort involved in compiling programs in significant. The result being that Prolog programs execute more quickly
at the expense of a more expensive compilation process. Normally, for the main
application clauses in a Prolog program, this trade-off is well worth it.

In order to support the `assert` (and `retract` and `listing` primitives) in a compiler-based system, we have to *compile* the clause being `assert`ed – which is a more expensive operation than simply copying the clause which was all that was required in the old interpreter based `assert`. As a result, it is not atypical for Prolog programs which make heavy use of `assert` to be worse off in a compiler based Prolog compared to an interpreter based system. This might be especially true for database style applications which use `assert` and `retract` to manipulate the database.

On the other hand, a simple minded approach to `assert`ing clauses leads to a disappointing performance of the complex clauses (i.e., those with a non-empty body) when they are asserted compared to compiled clauses. The disparity can easily reach two orders of magnitude in speed between compiled clauses and asserted clauses.

These arguments are magnified in the context of dynamic *L&O* programs. There is inevitably a translational component involved in adding a *L&O* program dynamically since we have to generate an executable Prolog program from the *L&O* program. The amount of processing involved when we convert an *L&O* program into Prolog can be high, and this must be added to the expense of the basic Prolog `assert`.

In order to limit the cost of asserting an *L&O* program we constrain the types of programs that we allow to be dynamic. In particular, we do not permit the use of expressions or equations in dynamic *L&O* programs, nor do we allow the use of `self` except as an explicit label to a sub-goal within an asserted clause. The reason for this is to avoid having to process the arguments to clauses before we can `assert` the result; and also to avoid potential conflicts arising from the order in which equations are `assert`ed.

We can afford to take a relaxed view about the relative order of the declarations of functions in the input to the preprocessor since it accepts the whole of a class body at once – therefore allowing us to determine all the functions' names before translating any clauses or equations. If equations are asserted incrementally then we are faced with the mutual recursion problem – when two functions depend on each other for their definition then it is not clear how to 'order' them.

If we `assert` one equation which contains a function symbol which is only subsequently defined via another `assert` then the interpretation of this function has changed – from being a normal Prolog term to being an 'evaluable' function. We should redo the conversion of the first equation to take this new function into account.

However, reprocessing an already translated program has a tremendous implication for the efficiency of `assert` since we not only have to convert the new equation, but we must potentially also redo *all* the previous work of `assert`ing into the class. This highlights one of the problems in adding features to a language with a compiler or preprocessor. What may be cheap to implement in a preprocessor can become intolerably expensive if the same features have to be supported dynamically.

Given that it must be rare to have a dynamic database involving functions we feel that it is not too great a restriction to impose of dynamic *L&O* programs not to have equations and expressions.

The representation of dynamic *L&O* programs

As with normal pre-processed *L&O* programs we distinguish the label phase of a dynamic program from the body phase. Each clause in the body phase of a class is represented using a Prolog assertion with three arguments:

> `'`*arity*`label:`*arity*`pred'(Head,Label,Body).`

The `Head` and `Body` arguments are the head and body of the dynamic clause and the `Label` argument is a copy of the label term associated with this class. So, for a sub-goal such as:

> `...,assert(foo(U):{bar(X):-foo(X):bar(U),jar(U)}),...`

we would get the Prolog assertion:

> `'1foo:1bar'(bar(X),foo(U),(foo(X):bar(U),jar(U))).`

We still need to distinguish the various local predicates because we need to be able to **assert** at the beginning and end of local relations. The '`1foo:1bar`' is derived in a similar manner to the way that we derived the local predicate symbol for static *L&O* programs.

This representation of local clauses allows us to execute a dynamic program with reasonable performance (i.e., only one order of magnitude slower than compiled programs) and it allows easy manipulation of the program. In order to retrieve the original source of a dynamic clause, we simply access the local predicate directly; whereas if we want to execute the program we access the head and body and interpret the body.

The entry to a dynamic *L&O* program is no different to the entry phase of a compiled program: we have a label entry program which 'knows' about all the locally defined programs within the dynamic class body and which obtains access to the relevant programs. Its structure is a little different to a compiled program; all the locally defined predicates are accessed via a clause of the form:

```
'aritylabel:'(Atom,Lb,Sf):-
    functor(Atom,Pr,Pa),
    'aritylabel:local'(Pr,Pa,LC),!,
    LC(Atom,Lb,Sf,Body),
    execute_local_body(Body,Lb,Sf,'aritylabel:').          (IX.i)
```

Any class rules which have been asserted for a dynamic program are compiled in a similar manner to normal class rules.

The first time that a class rule is **assert**ed (or the first time that any program is added to a dynamic class) an entry clause for the class rules of the label and an entry clause defining the name of the class are generated:

```
'aritylabel:'('?label'('aritylabel:'),_,_):-!.
'aritylabel:'(Atom,Lb,Sf):-
     'arity:super'(Atom,Lb,Sf).
```

we also add a clause to the '?:?' program to give access to the new class:

```
?:?(label(X₁,...,X_arity),Atom,Sf):-
     'aritylabel:'(Atom,label(X₁,...,X_arity),Sf).
```

and, in order to make it easier to manipulate the dynamic program, we also maintain an assertion for the '?dynamic?' Prolog predicate which contains a default name for the **inherit** program which will give access to normal class rules when a local program fails.

Executing a dynamic program

In order to execute the dynamic clause embedded in the local assertions we use a special evaluator program which 'evaluates' bodies of local clauses. The entry point for a dynamic class uses a database of '*arity*label:local' clauses which can be used to give access to the local predicate symbols of a class.

The **execute_local_body** program which is invoked in (IX.i) picks up the body of the clauses which has been stored in the local predicate. This body, which is in the form of a standard Prolog 'comma' conjunction, is evaluated by either using the local predicates in the case of unlabelled sub-goals, or simply by calling the '?:?' program for labelled sub-goals. Program 9.17 gives the outline of the definition for this program.

Tracing dynamic L&O programs

In our discussion about debugging L&O programs in Section 9.1.9 we decided that rather than attempting to implement an interpreter for L&O programs a better approach involves compiling in the tracing information as we generate Prolog programs. In the context of dynamic programs, where in order to implement **clause** and **retract** we need to be able to recover the original form of the program as easily as possible, the interpreter approach is much more suitable.

So, to enable tracing of dynamic programs, we add an extra hook to the entry point of a dynamic class which invokes the interpreter. To be more accurate, the hook simply picks up the current value of the tracing status and passes that to the **execute_dynamic_body** program to generate tracing information.

```
execute_dynamic_body(true,L,S,LbS):-!.
execute_dynamic_body((A,B),L,S,LbS):-!,
    execute_dynamic_body(A,L,S,LbS),
    execute_dynamic_body(B,L,S,LbS).
execute_dynamic_body(self:A,L,S,LbS):-!,
    ?:?(S,'?label?'(SS),S),
    execute_dynamic_body(A,S,S,SS).
execute_dynamic_body(M:A,L,S,LbS):-!,
    ?:?(M,'?label?'(MbS),M),
    execute_dynamic_body(A,M,M,MbS).
execute_dynamic_body(A,L,S,LbS):-
    LbS(A,L,S).
```

Program 9.17 The `execute_dynamic_body` program

9.3   A performance comparison of *L&O* programs

The mapping that we have described from class templates to Prolog programs produces programs which have very little overhead compared to the original programs. If we compare a Prolog program with the translated class template then the primary overhead amounts to two extra arguments in every sub-goal. This will reduce the perceived performance of a program these two arguments have to be allocated, passed as parameters and so on.

The other potential sources of overhead are extra choice points (where none were indicated from the Prolog program), extra resolution steps and extra sub-goals in clauses and a higher memory turnover (i.e., greater amount of garbage needing to be collected).

The local programs have the same number of clauses as the Prolog equivalents except in the case where the class template has a normal class rule. In this case an extra choice point will be needed in case the local program fails and an inherited version is needed to solve the goal. This amounts to an extra overhead, especially in the case where there are no other definitions anyway.

A global analysis of a complete *L&O* program might, by determining which programs are defined in which class templates, be able to determine that a given local program has no alternatives in the class templates which are accessible. In this case then the extra **inherit** linking clause would not be needed and therefore could be omitted. However, such a global analysis would only be worthwhile where the complete program was not evolving since a minor change could mean the re-compilation of the whole. Furthermore, if the programmer has only used overriding class rules then the extra choice point would not be generated in any case thus providing a simple remedy.

Extra resolution steps are introduced into the computation whenever an explicitly labelled call is made and whenever class rules are invoked. A labelled call is compiled into a call to the 'label predicate'; a linking clause for the label predicate establishes an entry point into the 'local predicate' that was actually invoked. The overhead for a labelled call where the label is a variable rather than determinable at compile is higher: a '?:?' sub-goal involves indexing into the set of all labels which may be quite expensive in some Prolog systems.

An inheritance step may involve up to three inference steps depending on the situation. If a local predicate 'backtracks' its way into using a class rule then there are three steps involved before the next local predicate may be tried: one step to access the local class rules, one step to perform the inheritance step and finally the linking rule in the new class template. This overhead can be reduced at the cost of a larger generated code by replicating the class rules with each local predicate for example.

Extra sub-goals are added to the program when a clause references a label argument – a call to the system built-in primitive **arg** – and when a sub-goal has an evaluable function as an argument. Either of these could, in principle, weaken one of the standard optimizations of Prolog compilers where the first sub-goal in a clause is treated specially. If the new sub-goal is added as the first sub-goal is a clause then the programmer' s first sub-goal is no longer optimized in the same way. The importance of this depends on the Prolog compiler itself. Some compilers recognize some system predicates (possibly including **arg**) and deal with them in a special way. In this case the original optimization for the first call in a clause may apply anyway.

A *L&O* program has a similar memory usage profile to a normal Prolog program except where labelled calls are used. In this case copies of label terms are made at the point of an original labelled call, and whenever a class rule is used for inheritance. If an application makes heavy use of inheritance then this might become a significant factor. However since this is an 'extra', and is not incurred in great measure by normal Prolog programs this impacts more on 'native' *L&O* applications than on Prolog applications.

Overall, we feel that the overhead of using a preprocessor to convert *L&O* programs to Prolog is small enough to justify using *L&O* as the programming language in place of Prolog. Appendix B lists a number of simple programs whihc can be used to compare the performance of *L&O* and Prolog. As the measurements in Table 9.1 suggest, there is an overhead of some 5% compared with normal Prolog programs.

9.4   Summary

In this chapter we have not attempted to provide a definitive description of the implementation of *L&O* programs. Instead we have concentrated on a prepro-

Algorithm	Prolog time	$L\&O$ time	$\frac{Prolog}{L\&O}$ time
nrev(100)	0.208s	0.217s	0.96
quicksort(128)	7.92s	7.97s	0.99
q/sort w/par	8.20s	8.71s	0.94

Table 9.1 *Comparative performance of L&O and Prolog programs*

cessor for class templates into Prolog. The performance of this preprocessor is quite adequate; with normal Prolog programs suffering only a marginal loss in performance.

The *L&O* preprocessor

In this appendix, we list extracts from the *L&O* preprocessor and a simple tracing package for *L&O* programs. The full program is available via 'anonymous ftp' at

    `doc.ic.ac.uk`

under the directory

    `languages/icprolog/lo`

The program as listed is designed to be run under MacProlog; although it should be possible to modify it to execute on almost any Prolog. However, the *L&O* pre-processor program takes advantage of a number of special features of MacProlog (for example the ability to have variable function symbols and predicate symbols).

We have made a few changes to the standard Prolog term syntax. The normal dot-space terminator used to signal the end of a term in Prolog is reinterpreted if it occurs within a class body, i.e., if it occurs within a pair of {}'s. In this case the dot-space terminator is interpreted as the symbol '. ' which is also an operator of priority 1201 [1]. We have also adjusted slightly the expected precedence of the term inside {}'s to be 1201 also. This allows us to have terms which represent class bodies without having to force the Prolog programmer to use a different symbol for the end of a clause.

Other changes include the possibility of function symbols of compound terms to be variables or themselves compound; and the ability to have variable predicate symbols. All of these changes have the property that they strictly extend the term syntax of Prolog: the new features would be syntax errors in the standard syntax, and a terms of standard Prolog is the same term in the extended syntax.

---

[1] The maximum priority of a term in Edinburgh Prolog syntax is normally 1200.

A.1   The top-level of the *L&O* preprocessor

A.1.1   Consulting an *L&O* file

```
:-op(699,xfx,':').        % labelled call operator
:-op(699,fx,':').         % super synonym
:-op(700,xfx,'\:').       % or_cast operator
:-op(700,xfx,':=').       % assignment operator
:-op(1201,xfy,'. ').      % clause separator in a class body.
:-op(1198,xfx,'<=').      % class rule operator
:-op(1198,xfx,'<<').      % class rule operator
:-op(698,fx,').           % used for quoting terms
:-op(698,fx,#).           % anti-quote operator
:-op(698,fx,'#).          % quote the function symbol only
```

lo_consult is used to consult an *L&O* program. could be modified to compile them ...

```
lo_consult(File):-
        read_all_formulae(File,Formulae),% read L&O formulae
        keysort(Formulae,Fs),             % sort them
        collect_all(Fs, Classes,File),    % put bodies with rules
        tr_mode(Tr),
        tr_all_templates(Classes, Progs, Labels,Tr),
        disp_prolog(Progs),
        kill_old(File),                   % kill existing code
        compile_all(Progs),               % compile them
        declare_new(Progs,Labels,File),   % declare the new ones

read_all_formulae(File,[LbS-(Class,Pos)|More]):-
        read_a_formula(File, Class, LbS, Pos),!,
        read_all_formulae(File, More).
read_all_formulae(File,[]).

read_a_formula(File, Class, LbS, Pos):-
        seek(File,Ps),                    % where is the formula?
        read(File, Form),
        Form\=end_of_file,
        inspect_formula(Form, Ps, File, Class, Pos, LbS).
```

The **inspect_formula** program looks for the label symbol in a formula that has been read in. In the special case that it is a command, then it just executed it.

In the **collect_all** program, we use terms of the form

```
        '@w'(Id,P,1)
```

to encode the origin of the program fragment, for use in tracing at a later stage.

```
collect_all([LbS-((L<=M),P)|Fs],[tpl(LbS,Id,Pb,Body,
                [['@w'(Id,P,1)|(L<=M)]|Rules])|Progs],Id):-!,
        coll_template(Fs,RFs,LbS,Body,Pb,Rules,2,Id),
        collect_all(RFs,Progs,Id).
```

A.1.2   The translator proper

The data for the main part of the translator is in the form of a list of terms, each of which is of the form

   tpl *(Label, Source-file, Pos of body, Body, Rules)*

The output is a list of relations – i.e., a list of lists of clauses – together with a list of the labels encountered during the translation.

```
/* translate all the templates which occur in a file */
tr_all_templates([],[],[],Tr).
tr_all_templates([tpl(Lb,Id,Pb,Body,Rules)|Ts],
              Rels, [Lb|LbLs],Tr):-
        tr_template(Lb, Body, Rules, Rels, Rs, Tr,Id,Pb),
        tr_all_templates(Ts,Rs,LbLs,Tr).


tr_template(Lb/LbA, Body, Rules, Rls, Rs,Tr,Id,Pb):-
        label_symbol(Lb,LbA,LbS),
        tr_rules(Rules, Ri, Rs, Inherit, LbS, Body,Tr),
        tr_class_body(Body, Rls, Ri, Inherit,LbS,Tr,Id,Pb).
```

A.1.3   A single class body

Generate the clauses for a class body.

```
tr_class_body((L:{Clauses}),[pr(LbS,EntryPs)|R],Rs,
              In, LbS, Tr,Id,Pb):-
        sort_sentences(Clauses,Relations,Preds,Functions,Funs,
              Assigns,IVars,Id,Pb,0,LbS),
        termin(Preds),termin(Funs),termin(IVars),
        Defnd=def(LbS, Funs, Preds, IVars, Tr),
        tr_methods(Relations, R, Ri, Defnd, L, In),
        tr_functions(Functions, Ri, Rj, Defnd, L),!,
        mk_entry_rels(Preds,EntryPs,Ei,Defnd),
        mk_entry_funs(Funs, Ei, Ej,Defnd),
        tr_decls(Assigns, Ej, Ek, Defnd, L),
        mk_entry_vars(IVars, Ek, El, Rj, Rs, Defnd),
        mk_super_rule(LbS, L, El, [], '@w'(Id,Pb,1)),!.
```

```
sort_sentences('. '(Cl,Clauses),Rels,Preds,Functs,Funs,
               Assigns,IVars,Id,Pb,Ix,L):-!,
        sort_sentence(Cl,Rels,Preds,Functs,Funs,
                      Assigns,IVars,Id,Pb,Ix,L), Ix1 is Ix+1,
        sort_sentences(Clauses,Rels,Preds,Functs,Funs,
                       Assigns,IVars,Id,Pb,Ix1,L).
sort_sentences(Cl,Relations,Preds,Functions,Funs,
               Assigns,IVars,Id,Pb,Ix,L):-!,
        sort_sentence(Cl,Relations,Preds,Functions,Funs,
                      Assigns,IVars,Id,Pb,Ix,L).

sort_sentence(Cl,Relations,Preds,Functions,Funs,
              Assigns,IVars,Id,Pb,Ix,L):-
        defining_fun(Cl,F,A),!,           % is this an equation?
        occ(sym(F,A,LP),Funs),
        (var(LP)->local_fun(L,F,A,LP);true), % generate local symbol
        occ(eqs(F,A,Eqs),Functions),
        add_occ(Cl,Eqs,1,Id,Pb,Ix).
sort_sentence(Cl,Relations,Preds,Functions,Funs,
              Assigns,IVars,Id,Pb,Ix,L):-
        defining_ivar(Cl,Var),!,
        occ(Var,IVars),
        add_occ(Cl,Assigns,1,Id,Pb,Ix). % only 1 init. allowed
sort_sentence(Cl,Relations,Preds,Functions,Funs,
              Assigns,IVars,Id,Pb,Ix,L):-
        defining_pred(Cl,Pred,Arity),!,
        occ(sym(Pred,Arity,LP),Preds),
        (var(LP)->local_pred(L,Pred,Arity,LP);true),
        occ(cls(Pred,Arity,Cls),Relations),
        add_occ(Cl,Cls,1,Id,Pb,Ix).
sort_sentence((:-G), _,_,_,_,_,_,_,_,_,_):-
        (call(G)->true;true).
```

Pick out the function symbol and arity of an equation.

```
defining_fun((LHS=RHS:-Body),Fun,Arity):-!,
        functor(LHS,Fun,Arity).
defining_fun((LHS=RHS),Fun,Arity):-
        functor(LHS,Fun,Arity).
```

There are similar programs to **defining_fun** for confirming the existence of a clause (using **defining_pred**) and instance variables (using **defining_ivar**).

The **tr_methods** program maps the *relations* within the class body into Prolog-style clauses.

```
tr_methods([], Rls, Rls, Defnd, L, Super):-!.
tr_methods([cls(Pred,Arity,Clses)|Rels], [pr(P,Cls)|R],
```

```
                  Rs,Defnd, LbL,Super):-
        termin(Clses),
        local_pred_name(Defnd,Pred,Arity,P),
        tr_rel(Clses, Cls, Cli, Defnd, LbL),!,
        inherit_clause(Super, Cli, [], Pred, Arity, Defnd),
        tr_methods(Rels, R, Rs, Defnd, LbL, Super).
```

Map a relation into the appropriate suite of clauses.

```
tr_rel([], C, C, Defnd, LbL).
tr_rel([[Cnt|Cl]|Cls], [(H:-B)|PC], PCls, Defnd, LbL):-
        tr_clause(Cl, H, B, Defnd, LbL,Cnt),
        tr_rel(Cls, PC, PCls, Defnd, LbL).
```

Similar programs are used to the *functions* and *instance variables* within the class body into Prolog style clauses.

The `mk_entry_rels` program generates the clauses that represent the predicate entry points respectively into the class body. Similar programs exist for the function and instance variables in the class body.

```
mk_entry_rels([],OCls,OCls,_).
mk_entry_rels([sym(Pr,Ar,LocP)|Preds],
        [(Head:-!,Goal)|OCls],OCls1,Defnd):-
        defnd_label(Defnd,LbS),
        functor(Atom,Pr,Ar),   % create a skeleton head
        Atom =.. [_|V],
        append(V,[Lab,Self],LocA),
        B=..[LocP|LocA],
        rl_trace(Defnd,Atom,Lab,Self,TGE),
        triple(LbS,Atom,Lab,Self,Head),
        simplify((TGE,B),Goal),
        mk_entry_rels(Preds,OCls, OCls1,Defnd).
```

The `access_rule` program generates a clause for the ?::? predicate to give access to the label for variable labels.

```
access_rule(LbS, Lb, Ar, (?::?(Label,Atom,Self):-Body)):-
        functor(Label,Lb,Ar),
        triple(LbS,Atom,Label,Self,Body).
```

A single class body axiom
In this section we are concerned with the conversion of a single axiom (clause or equation) from the class body.

```
tr_clause((H:-B),Head,Body,Dfnd,L,Cnt):-!,
        label_arg_form(L, H, B, Dfnd, Defnd),
        H=..[HPr|Hargs],
        functor(H,HPr,HAr),
```

```
tr_list(Hargs, Nargs, [], SGH, Defnd),
form_local_pred(HPr, HAr, Nargs, Head, Defnd),
tr_body(B, Bdy, Defnd,Cnt),
cl_trace(Defnd,H,Cnt,GE,GX),
simplify((GE,Bdy,SGH,GX), Body).
```

There is a similar clause for a clause with no body, and similar programs for handling equations and instance variable declations.

The **tr_body** program (which is quite long) is used to handle conditions in clauses and equations which occur in class bodies. In addition to converting sub-goals found within a body axiom, any disjunctions, negations and arrows are also extracted from the body of an axiom, leaving just a conjunction of calls to deal with. At the same time as converting sub-goals, any functional expressions are converted into calls to predicates. We only list the most relevant cases of **tr_body** here.

The first clause in **tr_body** must check for a variable call.

```
tr_body(G, Goal, Defnd,Where):-
        var(G),!,
        label_n_self(Defnd, LbS, LbArg, SelfVar),
        triple(LbS,G,LbArg,SelfVar,Goal).
```

Or a variable predicate symbol ...

```
tr_body(G, Goal, Defnd,Where):-
        functor(G,GP,_),
        var(GP),!,
        tr_unlabelled_body(G,Goal,Defnd,Where).
```

Otherwise we either have a labelled sub-goal...

```
tr_body(LbL:Call, Goal, Defnd,Where):-!,
        tr_term(LbL,Lb,SGL,Defnd),
        tr_labelled_body(Call, Lb, Gl, Defnd,Where),
        simplify((SGL,Gl),Goal).
```

or we have an unlabelled sub-goal.

```
tr_body(G, Goal, Defnd,Where):-
        tr_unlabelled_body(G,Goal,Defnd,Where).
```

The **tr_labelled_body** handles a labelled condition.

```
tr_labelled_body(Call, Lb, Goal, Defnd,Where):-
        var(Call),!,                    % the call is a variable?
        (var(Lb)->self_var(Defnd,Sf),
        Goal= ?:?(Cll,Lb,Sf);
        label_symbol(Lb,LbSymb),
        triple(LbSymb,Cll,Lb,Lb,Goal)).
```

We must also respect the label movement rules, we list the rule for disjunction...

```
tr_labelled_body((E;O),Label, (GE;GO), Defnd,Where):-
      tr_labelled_body(E,Label, G1, Defnd,Where),
      tr_labelled_body(O,Label, G2, Defnd,Where),
      simplify(G1,GE),
      simplify(G2,GO).
```

Other label movement rules relate to the negation operator \+, the implication operator
-> and to the 'higher order' predicates such as setof.

If the condition is an equality, then we handle it specially, hoping to be able to
remove it after translating expressions.

```
tr_labelled_body((LHS=RHS), L, G, Defnd,Where):-!,
      tr_term(L:LHS, NLHS, LG, Defnd),
      tr_term(L:RHS, NRHS, RG, Defnd),
      tr_body_eq(LHS, NLHS, RHS, NRHS, LG, RG, G, Defnd).
```

Before we handle the normal case, we look at the variable labelled call:

```
tr_labelled_body(Call, Lb, Goal, Defnd,Where):-
      var(Lb),!,
      tr_term(Call,Cll,SGC,Defnd),
      self_var(Defnd,Sf),
      simplify((SGC,?:?(Cll,Lb,Sf)), Goal).
```

the super (and self) labelled call:

```
tr_labelled_body(Call, super, Goal, Defnd,Where):-!,
      tr_term(Call,Cll,SGC,Defnd),
      label_n_self(Defnd, LbS, LbArg, SelfVar),
      super_pred(LbS, LocP),
      triple(LocP,Cll, LbArg, SelfVar,GL),
      simplify((SGC,GL), Goal).
```

Finally, we have an explicitly labelled condition:

```
tr_labelled_body(Call, Lb, Goal, Defnd,Where):-
      tr_term(Call,Cll,SGC,Defnd),
      (var(Lb)->self_var(Defnd,Sf),
      simplify((SGC,?:?(Cll,Lb,Sf)), Goal);
      label_symbol(Lb,LbSymb),
      triple(LbSymb,Cll,Lb,Lb,GL),
      simplify((SGC,GL),Goal)).
```

The treatment of unlabelled sub-goals is similar to that for labelled sub-goals.

In the standard unlabelled sub-goal, we process the arguments of the sub-goal to
convert expressions:

```
tr_unlabelled_body(Call, Goal, Defnd,Where):-
      Call=..[Pr|Args],
      functor(Call, _, PAr),
      tr_list(Args, NArgs, [], SGC, Defnd),
      tr_body_call(Pr, PAr, NArgs, SGC, Goal, Defnd).
```

The **tr_body_call** is used to actually generate the translated sub-goal.

```
tr_body_call(Pr, PAr, Args, SGC, Goal, Defnd):-
     form_local_pred(Pr,PAr,Args,LocA,Defnd),
     simplify((SGC,TG,LocA),Goal).
```

The **form_local_pred** program constructs the predicate symbol from the label symbol and the predicate symbols of the su-goal.

```
form_local_pred(Pr,Ar,Args,Atom,
            defnd(LbS,_,Preds,IVs,SelfVar,LbArg,_,Tr)):-
     occ(sym(Pr,Ar,LocP),Preds),      % find local symbol
     append(Args,[LbArg,SelfVar],AArgs),
     Atom=..[LocP|AArgs].
form_local_pred(Pr, Ar, Args, Goal, Defnd):-
     primitive_pred(Pr,Ar),!,         % is it a builtin?
     Goal=..[Pr|Args].
```

If not locally available, nor builtin, then undefined predicates are assumed to be inherited.

```
form_local_pred(Pr, Ar, Args, Goal, Defnd):-
     A=..[Pr|Args],                   % construct a super call
     label_n_self(Defnd, Lb, LbArg, SelfVar),
     super_pred(Lb, LbS),
     triple(LbS,A,LbArg,SelfVar,Goal).
```

The **tr_body_eq** program is used to attempt to eliminate an equality sub-goal, particularly in the situation where one of the arguments is already an expression.

```
tr_body_eq(LHS, NLHS, RHS, NRHS, LG, RG, Goal, Defnd):-
     reduced_term(LHS, NLHS)->   % has the lhs been reduced?
           NLHS = NRHS,
           simplify((LG, RG), Goal);
     reduced_term(RHS, NRHS)->   % has the rhs been reduced?
           NRHS = NLHS,
           simplify((LG, RG), Goal).
tr_body_eq(LHS, NLHS, RHS, NRHS, LG, RG, Goal, Defnd):-
     simplify((LG,RG,NLHS=NRHS), Goal).
```

The **label_arg_form** program analyses the clause or equation to see which of the two methods for handling label arguments to use. If the number of occurrences of label arguments is high enough, then the label term is duplicated in each translated Prolog sub-goal; otherwise, access to label arguments is via the **arg** builtin.

```
label_arg_form(L, H, B, def(LbS,Fs,Prs,IVs,Tr),
            defnd(LbS,Fs,Prs,IVs,Self,L,shared,Tr)):-
     varsin(L, LabVars),
     occurrences(H, LabVars, HO),
```

```
          body_average(B, LabVars, BO),
          shareable(HO,BO),!.      % are label args shareable?
label_arg_form(L, H, B, def(LbS,Fs,Prs,IVs,Tr),
              defnd(LbS,Fs,Prs,IVs,Self,_,LabVars,Tr)):-
          L=..[_|LabVars],
          good_args(LabVars),!.
label_arg_form(L, H, B, def(LbS,Fs,Prs,IVs,Tr),
              defnd(LbS,Fs,Prs,IVs,Self,L,shared,Tr)).
```

The **label_argument** program is used to see if an **arg** condition is to be generated when a label variable is encountered in a term.

```
label_argument(Var,defnd(LbS,Fs,Prs,IVs,Self,LX,L,Tr),Ix,LX):-
          var(LX), L\=shared,
          index_occ(Var, L, 1, Ix).
```

Terms and expressions

tr_term translates a term which may be a functional expression into a regular term, together with a conjunction of goals.

As with **tr_body**, we must first check whether the term to translate is already a variable.

```
tr_term(X, X, arg(Ix,LbArg,X), Defnd):-
          var(X),
          label_argument(X,Defnd,Ix,LbArg),!.   % label argument?
tr_term(X, X, true, _):-
          var(X),!.
```

A quoted expression - again no interpretation.

```
tr_term('X, Y, G, Defnd):-!,
          tr_quoted(X, Y, G, Defnd).      % check for unquotes
```

Other special types of expression include the external class template function call:

```
tr_term(Class:Term, T, Goal, Defnd):-
          Class\==super,!,
          Term=..[Fn|A],
          tr_fun_symbol(Fn,FS,FG),
          tr_term(Class, Lb, SGL, Defnd),
          tr_list(A,B,[T],SGC,Defnd),
          Cll=..[FS|B],
          (var(Lb)->self_var(Defnd,Sf),
          simplify((SGL,SGC,FG,?:?(Cll,Lb,Sf)), Goal);
          label_symbol(Lb,LbSymb),
          triple(LbSymb,Cll,Lb,Lb,GL),
          simplify((SGL,SGC,FG,GL),Goal)).
```

```
tr_term(super:Term, T, Goal, Defnd):-!,
        tr_term('#Term, Trm, SGC, Defnd),
        Trm=..[Fn|A],
        tr_fun_symbol(Fn,FS,FG),
        append(A,[T],B),
        Cll=..[FS|B],
        label_n_self(Defnd, LbS, LbArg, SelfVar),
        super_pred(LbS, LocP),
        triple(LocP,Cll, LbArg, SelfVar,GL),
        simplify((SGC,FG,GL), Goal).
```

When a **self** keyword is used, the **SelfVar** is used instead.

```
tr_term(self,SelfVar,true,Defnd):-!, self_var(Defnd,SelfVar).
```

If a term is atomic - it may be a constant function:

```
tr_term(T, S, G, Defnd):-
        atom(T),
        reducible(T,0,Defnd),!,
        form_fun_goal(T, 0, [S], G, Defnd).
tr_term(T, T, true, Defnd):-
        atom(T),!.                      % similar for numbers
```

A complex term is ripped apart and rebuilt in a new guise

```
tr_term(T, S, (FG,G), Defnd):-
        compound(T),
        functor(T,F,Ar),
        T=..[F|A],
        tr_term(F, F0, FG, Defnd),
        tr_complex(F0, Ar, A, S, G, Defnd).
```

There are two main cases for complex terms – they may be reducible

```
tr_complex(F, Ar, A, S, (SG,G), Defnd):-
        reducible(F,Ar,Defnd),!,
        tr_list(A, B, [S], SG, Defnd),
        form_fun_goal(F, Ar, B, G, Defnd).
```

or they may be a normal free function:

```
tr_complex(F, Ar, A, S, GL, Defnd):-
        tr_list(A, B, [], GL, Defnd),
        S=..[F|B].
```

tr_quoted inspects a quoted term looking for the unquote symbol **#**.

```
tr_quoted(X, X, true, Defnd):-
        var(X),!.
tr_quoted(X, X, true, Defnd):-
        atomic(X),!.
tr_quoted(#X, Y, G, Defnd):-!,
        tr_term(X, Y, G, Defnd).  % unquote part of term
tr_quoted(X, Y, (FG,AG), Defnd):-
        X=..[F|A],
        tr_quoted(F, FY, FG, Defnd),
        tr_quoted_list(A, AY, AG, Defnd),
        Y=..[FY|AY].
```

The `form_fun_goal` program is analogous to the `form_local_pred` program; except it constructs a sub-goal which will generate the value indicated by the expression.

```
form_fun_goal(F, Ar, Args, Goal,
              defnd(LbS,Funs,_,_,SV,LbArg,_,_)):-
        occ(sym(F,Ar,LocP), Funs),!,   % locally defined
        append(Args,[LbArg,SV],AArgs),
        Goal=..[LocP|AArgs].

form_fun_goal(F, Ar, Args, Goal, Defnd):-
        primitive_fun(F,Ar),           % a primitive function?
        Goal=..[F|Args].
```

A.1.4   Class rules

The next section of the preprocessor deals with class rules. Two sets of clauses are generated from the the class rules for each label - those for normal class rules and those for overriding class rules

```
tr_rules(Rules,[pr(LbSuper,Cls)|Rels],Rlo,Inherit,Lb,_,Tr):-
        conc([Lb,super],LbSuper),
        conc([Lb,inherit],LbInherit),
        tr_all_rules(Rules, Cls, LbSuper, Tr),
        tr_over_rules(Rules, Over, [], LbInherit, Tr),
        (Over\=[] ->
                Inherit=present, Rels=[pr(LbInherit,Over)|Rlo];
                Inherit=absent, Rels=Rlo).
```

The `tr_all_rules` program handles both types of class rule; whereas `tr_over_rules` (which is unlisted) only looks for normal class rules.

```
tr_all_rules([],[], _,_).
tr_all_rules([[C|(Lbl<=Mbl)]|Rules], [R|Cls], Lb, Tr):-!,
        tr_rule(Lbl,Mbl, R, Lb,Tr,C),
        tr_all_rules(Rules, Cls, Lb, Tr).
```

```
tr_all_rules([[C|(Lbl<<Mbl)]|Rules], [R|Cls], Lb, Tr):-!,
        tr_rule(Lbl,Mbl, R, Lb, Tr,C),
        tr_all_rules(Rules, Cls, Lb, Tr).
```

The `tr_rule` program translates an individual class rule.

```
tr_rule(LbL, MbL, (Head:-Body), LbS, Tr, Cnt):-
        Defnd = defnd(LbS,[],[],[],Self,L,shared,Tr),
        tr_term(LbL, L, G1,  Defnd),
        tr_mabel(MbL, M, G2, GX, Atom, Defnd),
        ih_trace(Defnd,M,Atom,Cnt,TG),
        triple(LbS,Atom,L,Self,Head),
        (var(M)->
            simplify((G1,G2,TG,?#?(Atom,M,Self),GX),Body);
            functor(M,MbS,MbA),
        (var(MbS)->
            simplify((G1,G2,TG,?#?(Atom,M,Self),GX),Body);
            label_symbol(MbS,MbA,MMbS),
            triple(MMbS,Atom,M,Self,GL),
            simplify((G1,G2,TG,GL,GX), Body))),!.
```

The `tr_mabel` program interprets the RHS of a class rule, handling differential inheritance filters if they are present.

```
tr_mabel(Var, Var, true, true, _, _):-
        var(Var),!.
tr_mabel(Minus(MbL,Diff), M, G, no_occ(Atom,DL), Atom, Defnd):-
        nonvar(Minus),Minus= -,!,   % fix for variable functors
        tr_term(MbL, M, G, Defnd),
        tr_diff(Diff, DL).
tr_mabel(MbL, M, G, true, Atom, Defnd):-
        tr_term(MbL, M, G, Defnd).
```

`tr_diff` handles the differential inheritance list.

```
tr_diff([],[]).
tr_diff([P/A|L], [PQ|LL]):-!,
        functor(PQ, P, A),
        tr_diff(L, LL).
tr_diff([A|L],[A|LL]):-
        tr_diff(L,LL).
```

Examples of $L\&O$ programs

In this appendix, we list some example $L\&O$ programs, including the programs which were used to generate the benchmark figures listed in Chapter 9.

B.1 The benchmark programs

We give both the $L\&O$ and Prolog versions of these programs. Of course, generating any statistics from a Prolog program almost always involves using some non-standard feature. In this case the `ticks` predicate returns the current clock time on the Macintosh to the nearest 60th of a second.

B.1.1 Naïve reverse

This is probably *the* standard benchmark for Prolog systems; so no benchmarking of $L\&O$ would be complete without it. We give the $L\&O$ version first:

```
naive:{
       app([],X)=X.
       app([E|X],Y)=[E|app(X,Y)].
       nr([])=[].
       nr([E|L])=app(nr(L),[E]).

       naive([],[]).
       naive([E|L],R):-
              naive(L,I),
              append(I,[E],R).
       append([],X,X).
       append([E|X],Y,[E|Z]):-
              append(X,Y,Z).
```

```
make(0)=[].
make(N)=[N|make(N-1)].

% the benchmark function computes the actual time for
% N iterations of M elements

bench_naive(N,M)=(End-Start)/(60*N):-
        L=make(M),
        ticks(Start),
        rep_bench_rel(N,L),
        ticks(End).

rep_bench_rel(0,_):-!.
rep_bench_rel(N,L):-
        naive(L,_),
        fail.
rep_bench_rel(N,M):-
        rep_bench_rel(N-1,M)
}.
```

Notice that this program contains naive reverse both in relational form and in functional form. During tests, the functional form executes slightly more slowly due the presence of the cuts which appear in the translated equations.

As we might expect, the Prolog version is quite similar to the L&O version:

```
app([],X,X).
app([E|X],Y,[E|Z]):-
        app(X,Y,Z).


naive([],[]).
naive([E|L],R):-
        naive(L,I),
        app(I,[E],R).

make(0,[]):-!.
make(N,[N|L]):-
        N1 is N-1,
make(N1,L).

naive_bench(N,M,Time):-
        make(M,L),
        ticks(Start),
        rep_bench_rel(N,L),
        ticks(End),
        Time is (End-Start)/(60*N).
```

```
rep_bench_rel(0,_):-!.
rep_bench_rel(N,L):-
        naive(L,_),
        fail.
rep_bench_rel(N,M):-
        N1 is N-1,
        rep_bench_rel(N1,M).
```

B.1.2   Quicksorting a list

There are two versions of this benchmark program – in the first we just have
a standard ordering based on the underlying < predicate, and in the second we
parameterize the program to allow other kinds of elements to be sorted.

As before, we show the *L&O* versions before their corresponding standard Prolog versions. This version of the quick sort program has a fixed ordering. It uses a
difference list to avoid the need of an **append**.

```
qsort:{
        qsort(L)=S:-                    % allow functional access
                qsort(L,[],S).

        qsort(L,S):-
                qsort(L,[],S),!.

        qsort([],S,S).
        qsort([E|L],I,S):-
                split(L,E,L1,L2),
                qsort(L1,[E|S1],S),
                qsort(L2, I, S1).

        split([],_,[],[]).
        split([D|L],E,[D|L1],L2):-
                D<E,!,
                split(L,E,L1,L2).
        split([D|L],E,L1,[D|L2]):-
                split(L,E,L1,L2).
```

A simple harness to benchmark the quick sort program

```
        qbench(N)=(End-Start)/(60*N):-
                make:jumble_list(128,4,L),
                ticks(Start),
                rep_bench(N,L), % invoke qsort N times on L
                ticks(End).
        qbench(N,qbench(N)).
```

```
      rep_bench(0,_):-!.
            rep_bench(N,L):-
            qsort:qsort(L,_),
            fail.
      rep_bench(N,L):-
            rep_bench(N-1,L)
}.
```

The `jumble_list` program in the `make` program below is intended to produce a somewhat chopped up list of integers; the aim being to give a reasonable test for the sort program. `jumble_list` makes a list in 'jumbled' format: it will only reliably make a list of the required length if that length is a power of 2. For example, we might ask for a jumpled up list of eight elements:

```
jumble_list(8,4)= [5, 6, 7, 8, 1, 2, 3, 4]
```

```
make:{
      jumble_list(N,M,L):-
            jumble(1,N,M,L,[]).

      jumble_list(N,M)=L :-
            jumble(1,N,M,L,[]).

      jumble(F,N,M,L,S):-
            N=<M,!,
            make_r_list(N,F,L,S).
      jumble(F,N,M,L,S):-
            jumble(F,int(N/2),M,I,S),
            jumble(F+int(N/2),int(N/2),M,L,I).
```

`make_r_list` makes a list of n integers from m into a d-list

```
      make_r_list(0,_,L,L).
      make_r_list(N,M,[M|L],LS):-
            make_r_list(N-1,M+1,L,LS)
}.
```

In the Prolog version, reproduced below, we have omitted the test harness; as this is very similar to the harness for the naive reverse benchmarks.

```
split([],_,[],[]).
split([D|L],E,[D|L1],L2):-
      D<E,!,
      split(L,E,L1,L2).
split([D|L],E,L1,[D|L2]):-
      split(L,E,L1,L2).
```

```
qsort(L,S):-
        qsort(L,[],S),!.

qsort([],S,S).
qsort([E|L],I,S):-
        split(L,E,L1,L2),
        qsort(L1,[E|S1],S),
        qsort(L2, I,  S1).
```

A parameterized Quick sort

In Program 3.4 on page 60 we have a sorting program which is designed to sort arbitrary lists. The sorting algorithm itself was not especially clever; in this program we combine the quick sort algorithm outlined above with the parameterization technique from **simple**.

```
psort(Order):{
        split([],_,[],[]).
        split([D|L],E,[D|L1],L2):-
                Order:less(D,E),!,
                split(L,E,L1,L2).
        split([D|L],E,L1,[D|L2]):-
                split(L,E,L1,L2).

        qsort(L)=S:-
                qsort(L,[],S).
        qsort(L,S):-
                qsort(L,[],S).

        qsort([],S,S).
        qsort([E|L],I,S):-
                split(L,E,L1,L2),
                qsort(L1,[E|S1],S),
                qsort(L2, I,  S1).

}.
```

The Prolog version of this program uses a similar technique for parameterizing the ordering; although, since Prolog does not have a notion of classes, we cannot use them for this version.

This version of the quick **sort** program has a parameterized ordering. It also uses a difference list representation to avoid the need of an explicit append operation.

```
psort(L,S,O):-
        psort(L,[],S,O),!.
```

```
psort([],S,S,_).
psort([E|L],I,S,O):-
        psplit(L,E,L1,L2,O),
        psort(L1,[E|S1],S,O),
        psort(L2, I, S1,O).

psplit([],_,[],[],O).
psplit([D|L],E,[D|L1],L2,O):-
        O(D,E),!,
psplit(L,E,L1,L2,O).
psplit([D|L],E,L1,[D|L2],O):-
        psplit(L,E,L1,L2,O).


% some possible forms of element ordering...
natural(D,E):- D<E.

descend(D,E):- E<D.
```

B.2   An air-line planner

Going from imperial to aiai

"When planning a journey from Imperial College (imperial) to the
Artificial Intellegence Applications Institute (aiai) in Edinburgh we
have several modes of transport to consider.

Since aiai is in a different city from imperial then we know that
we must use some kind of inter-city transport (say the train or plane).
Once we decide to fly then we can break our plan into two levels:

1.   Planning the journey from imperial to the airport,

2.   then planning the flight from heathrow (say) to edinburgh
     airport (which might have to take in a stop at Manchester's
     airport ringway). Once we are at edinburgh airport then we
     must go to the aiai.

Our planning procedure is very simple in the abstract or generic sense:
we can either go directly from departure to destination or we have to
take in an intermediate point (which we haven's been to yet) and go
from there.

Other places that we might want to go to are Queen Mary West-
field (qmw) in London or Victoria University (victoria) in Manchester
(England).

There are no direct flights from heathrow to edinburgh but there
are direct flights to/from Manchester and Liverpool. There are direct

flights from Manchester to/from Edinburgh and Glasgow (**renfrew**). Within a city the best way of getting anywhere (especially if you don't know your way around) is by **taxi**."

The listing reproduced below gives one possible interpretation of this problem. It shows many of the programming techniques explained within the main text.

```
:-op(900,xfx,on).

plan(S):{
        form(A,B,_,[Step]):-
                S:step(A,B,Step),!.
        form(A,B,L,[Step|R]) :-
                S:step(A,C,Step),
                \+ C on L,
                form(C,B,[A|L],R)
        }.

city:{
        step(X,Y,'P1-P-P2):-
                \+same_city(X,Y),
                plan(fly):form(X:airport,Y:airport,[],P),
                plan(city):form(X,X:airport,[],P1),
                plan(city):form(Y:airport,Y,[],P2).
        step(X,Y,taxi(X,Y)):-
                same_city(X,Y), X\=Y.

        same_city(X,Y):-
                X:airport=Y:airport
        }.

fly:{
        step(From,To, fly(From,To)):-From:fly(To)
        }.

albert_hall<=london.
imperial<=london.
london:{
        airport=lhr
        }.
london<<city.

edin<=edinburgh.
castle<=edinburgh.
aiai<=edinburgh.
edinburgh:{
        airport=edin
        }.
edinburgh<<city.
```

```
victoria<=manchester.
ringway<=manchester.

manchester:{
        airport=ringway
        }.
manchester<<city.

glasgow:{
        airport=renfrew}.
glasgow<<city.

/* the various airports */
lhr<=airport.
lhr:{   fly(edin).
        fly(ringway)}.

ringway:{
        fly(lhr).
        fly(renfrew)
        }.
ringway<=airport.

edin:{  fly(lhr)
        }.
edin<=airport.

renfrew:{
        fly(ringway).
        fly(aberdeen_air)
        }.
renfrew<=airport.

aberdeen_air:{
        fly(renfrew)
        }.
aberdeen_air<=airport.

airport:{
        airport=self
        }.
```

The travelling salesman program

In this appendix we list the key parts of the travelling salesman application, as developed in Chapter 6.

```
:-op(700,xfx,on).
:-op(400,yfx,~).
```

The basic version which just permutes its input for the best route:

```
permute:{
        route(Towns)=shortest(L):-
                findall((R,route_length(R)),permute(Towns,R),L).

        permute([T],T).
        permute(L,P~D):- delete(L,D,R), permute(R,P).

        delete([E|L],E,L).
        delete([E|L],D,[E|M]):-
                delete(L,D,M).

        route_length(T)=0 :-atom(T).
        route_length(R~T1~T2)=
                route_length(R~T1)+(T1:crow_flies(T2)).
        route_length(T1~T2)=T1:crow_flies(T2).

        shortest(L)=shortest(L,null,1000000).

        shortest([],Route,D)=Route.
        shortest([(R,D)|L],RX,DX)=shortest(L,R,D):-D<DX.
        shortest([_|L],RX,DX)=shortest(L,RX,DX)
}.
```

The incremental version of the travelling salesman algorithm:

```
incremental:{
        route([T|Towns])=route(Towns,T).

        route([],R)=R.
        route([T|Towns],R)=route(Towns,NewR):-
                NewR=split(best_place(R,T),R,T).

        best_place(R~T1,T)=    % try the back first ...
                best_place(R~T1,T,T:crow_flies(T1),0,0).
        best_place(T1,T)=0 :- atom(T1).

        best_place(R~T1~T2,T,XD,XI,I)=
                        best_place(R~T1,T,XT,I+1,I+1):-
                extra(T1,T,T2)=XT,
                XT<XD.
        best_place(R~T1~T2,T,XD,XI,I)=
                        best_place(R~T1,T,XD,XI,I+1).
        best_place(T1~T2,T,XD,XI,I)=
                        best_place(T1,T,XT,I+1,I+1):-
                extra(T1,T,T2)=XT,
                XT<XD.
        best_place(T1~T2,T,XD,XI,I)=
                        best_place(T1,T,XD,XI,I+1).
        best_place(T1,T,XD,XI,I)=I+1:- (T1:crow_flies(T))<XD.
        best_place(T1,T,XD,XI,I)=XI.

        split(0,R,T)=R~T.
        split(IX,R~T1,T)=split(IX-1,R,T)~T1.
        split(1,R,T)=T~R.

        extra(T1,T,T2)=(T1:crow_flies(T))+(T:crow_flies(T2))-
                (T1:crow_flies(T2))
}.
```

The presorted version of the incremental algorithm:

```
presort:{
        route(Towns)=
                incremental:route(arrange(Towns)).

        arrange(Towns)=
                quick(geographic(centre(Towns))):sort(Towns).

        centre(Towns)=(U/L,V/L):-
                average(Towns,0,0,U,V,0,L).
```

```
average([],U,V,U,V,L,L).
average([Town|List],UX,VX,U,V,I,L):-
         Town:at(UT,VT),
         average(List,UX+UT,VX+VT,U,V,I+1,L)
}.
```

This version of the algorithm drives between towns rather than driving.

```
driving:{
       route(Towns)=drive_around(presort:route(Towns)).

       drive_around(R~T1~T2)=
                       drive_around(R~T1)~(T1:drive(T2)).
       drive_around(T1~T2)=T1:drive(T2).
       drive_around(T)=T.

       drive_length(R)=drive_length(R,0).
       drive_length(R~T1~T2,X)=
               drive_length(R~T1,X+(T1:road_length(T2)))

}.
```

A version of the incremental algorithm which generates a circular route:

```
circular:{
       route([T|Towns])=route(Towns,T~T).

       route([],R)=R.
       route([T|Towns],R)=
               route(Towns,
                       split(best_place(R,T),R,T)).

       best_place(R,T)=
               best_place(R,T,10000000,0,0).

       best_place(R~T1~T2,T,XD,XI,I)=
                       best_place(R~T1,T,XT,I+1,I+1):-
               extra(T1,T,T2)=XT,
               XT<XD.
       best_place(R~T1~T2,T,XD,XI,I)=
                       best_place(R~T1,T,XD,XI,I+1).
       best_place(T1~T2,T,XD,XI,I)=I+1:-
               extra(T1,T,T2)=XT,
               XT<XD.
       best_place(T1~T2,T,XD,XI,I)=XI.

       split(0,R,T)=R~T.
```

```
split(IX,R~T1,T)=split(IX-1,R,T)~T1.
split(1,R,T)=T~R.

extra(T1,T,T2)=
        (T1:crow_flies(T))+(T:crow_flies(T2))-
                (T1:crow_flies(T2))
```

}.

Here we desribe what it means to be a `location` ...

```
location(X,Y):{
        at=(X,Y).
        at(X,Y).            % both a function AND a relation

        crow_flies(Town) = sqrt(U0*U0+V0*V0) :-
                Town:at=(U,V),U0=U-X,V0=V-Y.

        road_dist(Town) = L :-
                (Town,L) on (self:links).

        drive(To)=Route:-  % plan a road journey
                plan_drive(self,To,[],Dist,Route).

        % go directly
        plan_drive(From,To,R,D,From~To):-
                (From,D) on (To:links).
        % go indirectly
        plan_drive(From,To,R,D+DI,Route~To):-
                nearest(To:links,From,Int,DI),
                not Int on R,
                plan_drive(From,Int,[To|R],D,Route).

        nearest(Links,To,Int,D):-
                (Int,D) on quick(metric(To)):sort(Links)

        }.
```

The graphical description of a location...

```
location(X,Y)<<trans((X+5,400-Y),
        [thick(circle((-5,0),5)),
                string(self,courier,10,[])]).

metric(Town):{
        less((T1,_),(T2,_)):-
                Town:crow_flies(T1)<Town:crow_flies(T2)
        }.
```

Implement the geographic (i.e. circular) ordering between towns:

```
geographic((OX,OY)):{
        less(T1,T2):-
                angle(T1)<angle(T2).

        angle(T)=angle(X,Y):-
                T:at(X,Y).
        angle(X,Y)=atan((Y-OY)/(X-OX)):-
                X>OX,Y>=OY.
        angle(X,Y)=pi+pi-atan((OY-Y)/(X-OX)):-
                X>OX,Y<OY.
        angle(X,Y)=pi-atan((Y-OY)/(OX-X)):-
                X<OX,Y>=OY.
        angle(X,Y)=pi+atan((OY-Y)/(OX-X)):-
                X<OX,Y<OY.
        angle(OX,Y)=pi/2 :-
                Y>OY.
        angle(OX,Y)= 1.5*pi :-
                Y=<OY
        }.
```

A collection of places that we might want to visit in the U.K. Each town lists the places
that it is possible to get to directly

```
aberdeen<<location(194, 340).
aberdeen:{
        links=[(edinburgh,115),
        (glasgow,142)]
}.

aberystwyth<<location(126, 102).
aberystwyth:{
        links=[(birmingham,114),(liverpool,100),(swansea,75)]
}.

birmingham<<location(192, 106).
birmingham:{
        links=[(aberystwyth,114),(bristol,86),(cambridge,97),
                (liverpool,99),(nottingham,48),(oxford,63),
                (sheffield,75)]
}.

brighton<<location(248, 10).
brighton:{
        links=[(dover,81),(portsmouth,49),(london,52)]
}.
```

```
bristol<<location(168, 47).
bristol:{
        links=[(cardiff,44),(exeter,76),
               (oxford,71),(birmingham,86)]
}.


...


swansea<<location(126, 66).
swansea:{
        links=[(cardiff,45),(aberystwyth,75)]
}.


york<<location(218, 184).
york:{
        links=[(leeds,23),(hull,37),(newcastle,80)]
}.
```

The set up corresponding to the exercise on page 136:

```
town_a:{
        crow_flies(town_b)=14.5.
        crow_flies(town_c)=14.
        crow_flies(town_d)=17.1
}.


town_b:{
        crow_flies(town_a)=14.5.
        crow_flies(town_c)=3.
        crow_flies(town_d)=4
}.


town_c:{
        crow_flies(town_a)=14.
        crow_flies(town_b)=3.
        crow_flies(town_d)=3.1
}.


town_d:{
        crow_flies(town_a)=17.1.
        crow_flies(town_b)=4.
        crow_flies(town_c)=3.1
}.
```

Here we outline the graphical shell for the travelling salesman application

```
salesman:{
        tools:=[select_city,permute_route,incremental_route,
                        presort_route,circular_route]
}.
salesman<<graphic_edit.

sales_boot:{
        boot:-
          window_manager:createw('Travelling salesman',
                    Name,salesman),
          add_towns([aberdeen, aberystwyth, birmingham,
                brighton, bristol, cambridge, cardiff,
                carlisle, dover, edinburgh, exeter, glasgow,
                hull, leeds, liverpool, london, manchester,
                newcastle, nottingham, oxford, penzance,
                portsmouth, sheffield, swansea, york],Name).

        add_towns([],_).
        add_towns([T|L],W):-
                W:add(T),
                add_towns(L,W)
        }.
```

Select a city (or cities) to go and visit:

```
select_city<<thick(gray(sq((0,0),16))).
select_city<<select_tool.

circular_route<<thick(circle((0,0),8)).
circular_route<<route_master(circular).

incremental_route<<(-8,-8)~(8,8)~(0,8).
incremental_route<<route_master(incremental).

presort_route<<thick([circle((0,0),8),(-8,-8)~(8,8)~(0,8)]).
presort_route<<route_master(presort).

permute_route<<thick(gray([circle((0,0),8),square((0,0),8)])).
permute_route<<route_master(permute).
```

route_master computes a route over the set of towns:

```
route_master(Type):{
        click(X,Y,Modifier,Selected,Window):-
                Window:draw(thick(lines(
                    Type:route(descriptions(Window:selected)))))),
```

```
        descriptions([])=[].
        descriptions([P|L])=[P:descr|descriptions(L)].

        lines(A~B)=lines(A)~(X,400-Y):-B:at(X,Y).
        lines(A)=(X,400-Y):-A:at(X,Y)
}.
route_master(_)<<icon(1005).
route_master(_)<<standard.
```

The packer algorithms

In this appendix we give the fundamental algorithms of the generic packing and planning application developed in Chapter 7. This is not a complete application since the user interface has not been developed fully.

D.1   Two-dimensional arrangements

An augmented arrangement is satisfactory if the existing arrangement is and the new box fits into an available interval.

```
arrange2:{
      satis([Box],[[Box,id,(0,0)]]):-
             van:length=L,
             van:width=W,
             fits([Box,id,(0,0)],[(0,0),(L,W)]).
      satis([Box],[[Box,rot,(0,0)]]):-
             van:length=L,
             van:width=W,
             fits([Box,rot,(0,0)],[(0,0),(L,W)]).
      satis([Box|Boxes],[[Box,Tran,Posn]|Placements]) :-
             satis(Boxes,Placements),
             avail(Placements,Ints),
             member(Int,Ints),
             fits([Box,Tran,Posn],Int).
```

The first `avail` clauses subtract an interval from the initial interval.

```
      avail([[Box,id,(0,0)]],
                    cleanup([[(L,0),(VL,VW)],
                            [(0,W),(VL,VW)]])) :-
             van:length = VL,
```

```
                  van:width  = VW,
                  fits([Box,id,(0,0)],[(0,0),(VL,VW)]),
                  Box:length = L,
                  Box:width  = W.
         avail([[Box,rot,(0,0)]],
                  cleanup([[(W,0),(VL,VW)],
                           [(0,L),(VL,VW)]]])) :-
                  van:length = VL,
                  van:width  = VW,
                  fits([Box,rot,(0,0)],[(0,0),(VL,VW)]),
                  Box:length = L,
                  Box:width  = W.
```

Otherwise, we subtract an interval from a collection of maximal sub-intervals.

```
         avail([[Box,Tran,Posn]|Placements],Ints) :-
                  avail(Placements,OldInts),
                  lidiff(OldInts,tran(Tran,Box,Posn)) = Ints
     }.
arrange2<<iv2.
```

D.2   Three dimensional arrangments

The three-dimensional version is fundamentally similar to the two-dimensional code above. The first clauses show how a box can be inserted into an empty van:

```
arrange3:{
       satis([Box],[[Box,id,(0,0,0)]]) :-
                  van3:length = L,
                  van3:width  = W,
                  van3:height = H,
                  fits([Box,id,(0,0,0)],
                            [(0,0,0),(L,W,H)]).
       satis([Box],[[Box,rot,(0,0,0)]]) :-
                  van3:length = L,
                  van3:width  = W,
                  van3:height = H,
                  fits([Box,rot,(0,0,0)],
                            [(0,0,0),(L,W,H)]).
```

In the general case an augmented arrangement is satsfactory if the existing arrangement is and the new box fits into it.

```
         satis([Box|Boxes],[[Box,Tran,Posn]|Placements]) :-
                  satis(Boxes,Placements),
                  avail(Placements,Ints),
                  member(Int,Ints),
                  fits([Box,Tran,Posn],Int).
```

```
avail([[Box,id,(0,0,0)]],
                cleanup([[(L,0,0),(VL,VW,VH)],
                         [(0,W,0),(VL,VW,VH)],
                         [(0,0,H),(L,W,VH)]])) :-
        van3:length = VL,
        van3:width  = VW,
        van3:height = VH,
        fits([Box,id,(0,0,0)],[(0,0,0),(VL,VW,VH)]),
        Box:length = L,
        Box:width  = W,
        Box:height = H.
avail([[Box,rot,(0,0,0)]],
                cleanup([[(W,0,0),(VL,VW,VH)],
                         [(0,L,0),(VL,VW,VH)],
                         [(0,0,H),(W,L,VH)]])) :-
        van3:length = VL,
        van3:width  = VW,
        van3:height = VH,
        fits([Box,rot,(0,0,0)],[(0,0,0),(VL,VW,VH)]),
        Box:length = L,
        Box:width  = W,
        Box:height = H.


avail([[Box,Tran,Posn]|Placements],Ints) :-
        avail(Placements,OldInts),
        segregate(OldInts,[Box,Tran,Posn]) =
                [BaseHt,TopHt,OtherHts],
        downdiff(BaseHt,:btm(:tran(Box,Tran,Posn))) =
                NewBaseHt,
        upmerge(TopHt,:top(:tran(Box,Tran,Posn))) =
                NewTopHt,
        chain([NewBaseHt,NewTopHt,OtherHts]) = Ints.
```

The **segregate** program segregates intervals by height, either at the base, the top or otehr heights. This allows collections of boxes at a given height to form a 'floor' for boxes above them.

```
segregate([],_) = [ [],[],[] ].
segregate([[(Ax,Ay,Az),(Bx,By,Bz)]|Ints],
        [Box,_,(_,_,Az)])=
                [[[(Ax,Ay,Az),(Bx,By,Bz)]|BH],TH,OH] :-
        segregate(Ints,[Box,_,(_,_,Az)]) = [BH,TH,OH].
segregate([[(Ax,Ay,Az),(Bx,By,Bz)]|Ints],
        [Box,_,(_,_,Z)])=
                [BH,[[(Ax,Ay,Az),(Bx,By,Bz)]|TH],OH] :-
        Box:height = H,
```

```
                    Az = Z + H,
                    segregate(Ints,[Box,_,(_,_,Z)]) = [BH,TH,OH].
          segregate([Int|Ints],Placement) = [BH,TH,[Int|OH]] :-
                    segregate(Ints,Placement) = [BH,TH,OH].
```

The `flat` program extracts the base profile of a box.

```
          flat([(Px,Py,Pz),(Qx,Qy,Qz)]) = [(Px,Py),(Qx,Qy)].

          flit([]) = [].
          flit([Iv|Ivs]) = [flat(Iv)|flit(Ivs)].
```

The `loft` program raises an interval to the top of the van.

```
          loft([(Px,Py),(Qx,Qy)],Pz) =
                         [(Px,Py,Pz),(Qx,Qy,van3:Height)].

          lift([],_) = [].
          lift([Iv|Ivs],Ht) = [loft(Iv,Ht)|lift(Ivs,Ht)].
```

The `downdiff` program subtracts the base of a box from an interval.

```
          downdiff(IvList,[Iv,Ht]) =
                    lift(iv2:lidiff(flit(IvList),Iv),Ht).
```

The `upmerge` program merges the top of a box to an interval.

```
          upmerge(IvList,[Iv,Ht]) =
                    lift(iv2:remax(flit(IvList),[Iv]),Ht)
                    }.
arrange3<<iv3.
```

D.3   Interval algebra in three dimensions

D.3.1   One-dimensional interval algebra

`iv1:{`

The union of two one-dimensional intervals.

```
          u([A,B], [C,D]) = [min(A,C),max(B,D)] :-
                  max(A,C) =< min(B,D).
          u([A,B], [C,D]) = [] :-
                  max(A,C) > min(B,D).
```

The intersection of two intervals.

```
          n([A,B], [C,D]) = [max(A,C),min(B,D)] :-
                  max(A,C) =< min(B,D).
          n([A,B], [C,D]) = [] :-
                  max(A,C) > min(B,D).
```

The set difference of two intervals.

```
diff([A,B],[C,D]) = [[A,B]] :- B =< C; A >= D.
diff([A,B],[C,D]) = [[]] :- C =< A, B =< D.
diff([A,B],[C,D]) =
          cleanup([[A,max(A,C)],[min(B,D),B]]).
```

The `trivial` program defines what a trivially empty interval is.

```
trivial([X,Y]) :- Y =< X.
trivial([])
}.
iv1<<list.
```

D.3.2 Two dimensional interval algebra

```
iv2:{
```

Form the cartesina product of two intervals.

```
pr([A,B] , [C,D]) = [(A,C), (B,D)].
pr([] , [_,_]) = [].
pr([_,_] , []) = [].
```

Project an interval over the x-axis or y-axis.

```
projx([(Px,Py),(Qx,Qy)]) = [Px,Qx].

projy([(Px,Py),(Qx,Qy)]) = [Py,Qy].
```

Form a cartesian multi-product.

```
mpr([],_) = [].
mpr(_,[]) = [].
mpr([I|Is] , [J|Js]) =
          chain([[pr(I,J)],
                 mpr([I],Js),mpr(Is,[J]),mpr(Is,Js)]).

trivial([(A,B),(C,D)]) :- C =< A.
trivial([(A,B),(C,D)]) :- D =< B.
trivial([]).
```

`elim` removes redundant intervals from a list of intervals. An interval is redundant if it is **inside** another one which is already on the list.

```
elim([]) = [].
elim([H|T]) = [RP|elim(RT)] :-
          select(H,T) = (RP,RT).
```

```
select(P,[]) = (P,[]).
select(P,[H|T]) = select(P,T) :- inside(H,P).
select(P,[H|T]) = select(H,T) :- inside(P,H), P \= H.
select(P,[H|T]) = (PV,[H|NT]) :- select(H,T)=(PV,NT).
```

A two-dimensional interval is contained within another if both its boundaries are contained.

```
inside([],_).
inside([(Px,Py),(Qx,Qy)],[(Rx,Ry),(Sx,Sy)]) :-
        Px >= Rx, Py >= Ry,
        Qx =< Sx, Qy =< Sy.
```

`hdiff` and `vdiff` compute the horizontal and vertical components respectively of the difference of two intervals; this is done in terms of the projections of the intervals on the x and y axes.

```
hdiff(PQ,RS) =
        mpr(iv1:diff(projx(PQ),projx(RS)),[projy(PQ)]).

vdiff(PQ,RS) =
        mpr([projx(PQ)],iv1:diff(projy(PQ),projy(RS))).

diff(PQ,RS) = [[]] :- inside(PQ,RS).
diff(PQ,RS) =
        elim(append(hdiff(PQ,RS),vdiff(PQ,RS))).
```

Find the list of interval differences found by subtracting an interval from a list of intervals.

```
lidiff([],I) = [].
lidiff([H|T],I) =
        elim(append(diff(H,I), lidiff(T,I))).
```

The `mxl` program absorbs new intervals, eliminating redundant intervals.

```
mxl(PQ,RS) = append(notriv(PQ,RS),[PQ]).

mix([],L) = [].
mix([H|T],[I]) =
        chain([mxl(H,I), elim(mix(T,[I])), [H|T]]).

mix(L,[H|T]) = mix(elim(mix(L,[H])), T).

remax(L,R) = elim(append(elim(mix(L,R)),R)).
```

Reject any newly created intervals which are already fully contained in PQ or RS, or are trivial.

```
notriv(PQ,RS) = cleanup(expel(create(PQ,RS),[PQ,RS])).

expel([],L) = [].
expel([H|T],[PQ,RS]) = expel(T,[PQ,RS]):-
        inside(H,PQ);inside(H,RS).
expel([H|T],L) = [H|expel(T,L)].

create(PQ,RS) =
        [pr(iv1:n(projx(PQ),projx(RS)),
                iv1:u(projy(PQ),projy(RS))),
         pr(iv1:u(projx(PQ),projx(RS)),
                iv1:n(projy(PQ),projy(RS)))
        ].
```

Create an interval from a description of a box.

```
tran(id,Box,(X,Y))  = [(X,Y),(X+L,Y+W)] :-
        Box:length = L,  Box:width  = W.
tran(rot,Box,(X,Y)) = [(X,Y),(X+W,Y+L)] :-
        Box:length = L,  Box:width  = W.

fits([Box,id,(Px,Py)],[(Px,Py),(Qx,Qy)]) :-
        Box:length = L,  Box:width = W,
        L =< Qx - Px,    W =< Qy - Py.
fits([Box,rot,(Px,Py)],[(Px,Py),(Qx,Qy)]) :-
        Box:length = L,  Box:width  = W,
        W =< Qx - Px,    L =< Qy - Py
}.
iv2<<list.
```

D.3.3   Three dimensional interval algebra

```
iv3:{
    fits([Box,id,(Px,Py,Pz)],[(Px,Py,Pz),(Qx,Qy,Qz)]) :-
        Box:length = L,  Box:width = W,
        Box:height = H,  L =< Qx-Px,
        W =< Qy-Py,      H =< Qz-Pz.
    fits([Box,rot,(Px,Py,Pz)],[(Px,Py,Pz),(Qx,Qy,Qz)]) :-
        Box:length = L,  Box:width = W,
        Box:height = H,  W =< Qx-Px,
        L =< Qy-Py,      H =< Qz-Pz.

    trivial([(Ax,Ay,Az),(Bx,By,Bz)]) :- Bx =< Ax.
    trivial([(Ax,Ay,Az),(Bx,By,Bz)]) :- By =< Ay.
    trivial([(Ax,Ay,Az),(Bx,By,Bz)]) :- Bz =< Az.
    trivial([]).
```

```
tran(Box,id,(X,Y,Z))  = [(X,Y,Z),(X+L,Y+W,Z+H)]:-
        Box:length = L, Box:width  = W,
        Box:height = H.
tran(Box,rot,(X,Y,Z)) = [(X,Y,Z),(X+W,Y+L,Z+H)] :-
        Box:length = L, Box:width  = W,
        Box:height = H.
```

Determine the top of a box:

```
top([(Px,Py,Pz),(Qx,Qy,Qz)]) =
              [[(Px,Py),(Qx,Qy)],Qz].
```

and the bottom of a box:

```
btm([(Px,Py,Pz),(Qx,Qy,Qz)]) =
              [[(Px,Py),(Qx,Qy)],Pz]
      }.
iv3<<list.
```

D.4   General library programs

```
list:{
      member(H,[H|T]).
      member(M,[H|T]) :-
            member(M,T).

      append([], L) = L.
      append([H|T], L) = [H|append(T,L)].

      chain([]) = [].
      chain([H|T]) = append(H,chain(T)).

      cleanup([]) = [].
      cleanup([H|T]) = cleanup(T) :-
            self:trivial(H).
      cleanup([H|T]) = [H|cleanup(T)]
      }.
```

Bibliography

[AK91]   H. Aït-Kaci. An overview of life. In J.W. Schmidt and A.A. Stogny, editors, *Next Generation Information System Technology*, pages 42–58. Springer-Verlag, 1991.

[AKN86]   H. Aït-Kaci and R. Nasr. Login: A logic programming language with built-in inheritance. *Journal of Logic Programming*, 3(3):185–215, 1986.

[AKP91]   H. Aït-Kaci and A. Podelski. Towards a meaning of life. Technical report, Paris research Laboratory, Digital Equipment Corporation, 1991.

[AP90]   A. Andreoli and R. Pareschi. Lo and behold! concurrent structured processes. In *Proceedings of OOPLSA/ECOOP'90*, Ottowa, Canada, 1990.

[AP91a]   A. Andreoli and R. Pareschi. Communication as fair distribution of knowledge. In *Proceedings of OOPLSA'91*, 1991.

[AP91b]   A. Andreoli and R. Pareschi. Linear objects: Logical processes with built-in inheritance. *New Generation Computing*, 1991.

[BMS80]   R. M. Burstall, D.B. MacQueen, and D.T. Sannella. Hope: an experimental applicative language. Internal report CSR-62-80, Department of Computer Science, University of Edinburgh, 1980.

[BoS80]   J. Bendl, P. Köves, and P. Szeredi. The MProlog system. In *Proceedings of the International Workshop on Logic Programming*, Debrecen, Hungary, 1980.

[Bra90]   I. Bratko. *Prolog Programming for Artificial Intelligence*. Addison-Wesley, second edition, 1990.

[Bro81]   L. Brodie. *Starting FORTH*. Prentice-Hall International, 1981.

[Byr80]   L. Byrd. Understanding the control flow of prolog programs. In S-A. Tarnlünd, editor, *Logic Programming Workshop*, pages 127–138, 1980.

[CF80]   K.L. Clark and F.G.McCabe. IC-prolog: The language and aspects of its implementation. In *Proceedings of the International Workshop on Logic Programming*, Debrecen, Hungary, 1980.

[Cla78]   K.L. Clark. Negation as failure. In H. Gallaire and J. Minker, editors, *Logic and Databases*, pages 293–322. Plenum press, 1978.

[CM81]   W.F. Clocksin and C.S. Mellish. *Programming in Prolog*. Springer-Verlag, 1981.

[CM84]   K.L. Clark and F.G. McCabe. *micro-Prolog: Programming in Logic*. International series in Computer Science. Prentice-Hall International, 1984.

[CMJS87]   K.L. Clark, F.G. McCabe, N. Johns, and C. Spenser. *The LPA MacProlog^{tm} Reference Manual*. Logic Programming Associates ltd., London, 1987.

[Con88a]   J. S. Conery. Logical objects. In *Proc. Fifth International Conference and Symposium on Logic Programming*, Seattle, 1988.

[Con88b]   J.S. Conery. Hoops – user's manual. Technical Report CIS-TR-88-12, Dept. Computer and Information Science, University of Oregon, Eugene, Oregon, 1988.

[Cor87]   Quintus Corp. *Quintus Prolog Reference Manual, Version 2.0*. Quintus Corporation, California, 1987.

[Dav88]   A. Davison. Polka: a parlog object oriented language. Internal report, Dept. of Computing, Imperial College, London, 1988.

[DD83]   P. Degano and S. Diomidi. A first order semantics of a connective suitable to express concurrency. In *Proc. Workshop on Logic Programming*, Lisboa, 1983.

[Dod90]   A. Dodd. *Prolog: a Logical Approach*. Oxford University Press, 1990.

[FT90]   I. Foster and S. Taylor. *Strand: New Concepts in Parallel Programming*. Prentice-Hall International, 1990.

[Gal86]   H. Gallaire. Merging objects and logic programming: Relational semantics. In *Proceedings of AAAI'86*, 1986.

[GD83]   A. Goldberg and Robson D. *Smalltalk-80: The Language and its Implementation*. Addison-Wesley, 1983.

[GL88]   M. Gelfond and V. Lifshitz. The stable model semantics for logic programming. In R.A. Kowalski and K.A. Bowen, editors, *Proc. Fifth International Conference and Symposium on Logic Programming*, pages 1070–1080, Seattle, 1988. MIT Press.

[GM84]   J.A. Goguen and J. Meseguer. Equality, types and (why not?) generics for logic programming. *Journal of Logic Programming*, 1(2), 1984.

[Gre87]   S. Gregory. *Parallel Logic Programming in Parlog*. Addison-Wesley, 1987.

[Gur90]   C. Gurr. A model theory for class template programming. Master's thesis, Dept. of Computing, Imperial College, London, 1990.

[Hay79]   P.J. Hayes. The logic of frames. In Metzing, editor, *Frame Conceptions and Text Understanding*, pages 46–61. de Gruyter, 1979.

[HM86]   R. Helm and K. Marriott. Declarative graphics. In *Proc. Third International Conference on Logic Programming*, London, 1986.

[Int91]   Adobe Systems International. *Postscript Language Reference Manual*. Addison-Wesley, 1991.

[Jul82]   S. Julian. Graphics in micro-prolog. Master's thesis, Dept. of Computing, Imperial College, London, 1982.

[KMB86]   K. Kahn, M. Miller, and D. Bobrow. Objects in concurrent logic programming languages. In *Proceedings of OOPSLA '86*, 1986.

[Kow79]   R.A. Kowalski. *Logic for Problem Solving*. North-Holland, 1979.

[O'k90]   R. O'keefe. *The Craft of Prolog*. MIT Press, 1990.

[Pap80]   S. Papert. *Mindstorms*. Basic books, 1980.

[Rob65]   J.A. Robinson. A machine oriented logic based on the resolution principle. *Journal of the ACM*, 12:23–41, 1965.

[Sea82]   G. L. Steele and et. al. An overview of common lisp. In *ACM Symposium on Lisp and Functional Programming*, August 1982.

[Sha83]   E. Shapiro. A subset of concurrent prolog and its interpreter. Technical report TR-003, ICOT, Tokyo, 1983.

[SS86]   L. Sterling and E. Shapiro. *The Art of Prolog*. MIT Press, 1986.

[ST83]   E. Shapiro and A. Takeuchi. Objected oriented programming in concurrent prolog. *New Generation Computing*, 1(1), 1983.

[Ued85]   K. Ueda. Guarded horn clauses. Technical Report TR-103, ICOT, Tokyo, 1985.

[vEY87]   M. van Emden and K. Yukawa. Logic programming with equations. *Journal of Logic Programming*, 4(4), December 1987.

[War83]   D.H.D. Warren. An abstract prolog instruction set. Technical note 309, SRI, October 1983.

[War90]   D.H.D. Warren. A private communication, 1990.

[Zan84]   C. Zaniolo. Object oriented programming in prolog. In *Proceedings of the International Symposium on Logic Programming*, Atlantic city, 1984.

Index